D0960149

YOUNG CHINA

YOUNG CHINA

How the Restless Generation Will Change Their Country and the World

Zak Dychtwald

St. Martin's Press
New York

Printed in the United States of America. For information, address
St. Martin's Press, 175 Fifth Avenue, New York, NY 10010.

www.stmartins.com

The Library of Congress Cataloging-in-Publication Data is available upon request.

ISBN 978-1-250-07881-0 (hardcover)
ISBN 978-1-4668-9133-3 (ebook)

First Edition: February 2018

10 9 8 7 6 5 4 3 2 1

FOR MY MOM, DAD, AND SISTER

Contents

1

Organ-Stealing Prostitutes

Myths, Language, and Other Walls Between China and the World

九零后—*jiu ling hòu*, *n.*: The generation China calls post-90s. Sometimes called the Net Generation, Me Generation, or Strawberry Generation for its members' inability to "eat bitter."

When Philip, my Chinese godfather, heard I was planning to take the train to Shenzhen, he wrote me a note.* This was not the first note he'd written me. After we first met, he wrote to say he had marked my birthday on his calendar. Weeks later he wrote to remind me to get a flu shot. Soon he sent another note, this time to suggest that I ought to more seriously consider the merits of bok choy as a source of vitamins to supplement my student diet. He once wrote me a beautiful note that said he would be honored if I met his grandson.

This latest note, however, was a warning about Shenzhen, the Chinese metropolis across the border from Hong Kong. I had told

*Philip's given name is not Philip. Like many from Hong Kong, and increasingly from the mainland, he took an English name. "It is convenient for doing business with foreigners," he told me. One of those foreigners had been my godfather, Jayme. When I planned to study abroad in Hong Kong, Jayme reached out to Philip and asked him to look after me. He took the role of Chinese godfather very seriously.

him I planned to travel to Shenzhen alone later that day. Philip cautioned me against three things. The first two were pickpockets and counterfeit goods, which might complicate my return to Hong Kong from China. The third was this:

> *You must not pick up any hookers from the street. Not only are you running the risk of catching a disease and being robbed, they are also likely to steal your internal organs.*
>
> *Sincerely,*
>
> *Philip, Your Chinese Godfather*

I ended up in Hong Kong by something of a fluke. Columbia University has strict requirements around language proficiency that determine to which countries you may go to study. Hong Kong was a linguistic loophole. Because I had taken a semester of Mandarin during my freshman year, I was eligible to apply to the University of Hong Kong. At the time I'd never been to Asia. Despite my bad experience with Mandarin—I spent more time on that one class than I did on all my others and still got my worst grade in college—I wanted to see the place where everyone told me the future was happening.

But within weeks of arriving I had begun to find Hong Kong disappointingly manageable, something like a showroom for the rest of China. Hong Kong had been a British colony for more than a century before it was legally returned to China in 1997. People spoke English. Many were proud of their Westernization. Before I went, everyone had told me that the future was in China, but all my professors in Hong Kong seemed to be saying that Hong Kong was not China.

Just across the border was Shenzhen, the real China. The city had once been a collection of fishing villages, thirty thousand people living at the mouth of the Pearl River delta. During Mao's rule, the area was deliberately left undeveloped as a buffer zone between Communist China and then-capitalist Hong Kong. During the 1960s, the middle of Mao's rule, Philip's family risked death to slip past the border patrol into Hong Kong's New Territories and make a better life for themselves in the Pearl of the Orient, as Hong Kong was known. Philip was only a boy.

Two years after Mao died in 1976, China opened its doors to the world and its money. My economics professor at the University of Hong Kong put it this way: "Shenzhen's Special Economic Zone became the testing ground for all of China's economic experiments. Most of them worked." Shenzhen's population swelled to twelve million, four hundred times what it had been a few decades earlier. The area was transformed from a southern backwater into the fourth-largest urban economy in China and twenty-third largest in the world, earning the nickname the Overnight City. The joke went that Shenzhen University does not have a history department; the city only looked forward. Although I had great respect for Philip, I was not going to be deterred from seeing China's boom city.

The train from Hong Kong to Shenzhen looked like a typical subway line—plastic seats and metal handrails. The people in suits were doing their daily commute across the border. The man next to me held two big cartons of milk in a bag on his lap. He told me that because mainland milk was poisoned, people would pay top dollar for Hong Kong dairy. The woman sitting across from me motioned to her child to stop staring. I waved, the girl laughed, and an hour passed.

When we arrived, we were separated into lines for foreigners, mainlanders, and Hong Kongers, who still need a visa to get into the mainland. I was stamped through and swept out into Shenzhen Luohu Railway Station, which sees eight million border crossers a year.

As soon as I walked out through the doors of the customhouse, I was slammed by a deluge of noise. Salespeople hawking everything from fruit to suits to consultations on international shipping logistics to factory space by the square meter rushed travelers at the doorway. A handful of dedicated "milk dealers" immediately swallowed the man who had sat next to me; then he rushed out of the pack with a few bills scrunched in his hand. The churn of life was dizzying. I saw signs in English, and tried asking for directions in English, but no one spoke it, unlike in Hong Kong. I tried calling the hostel I had booked, but my phone didn't work in the mainland. I tried to buy a Coke so I could sit and get my bearings, but after what seemed a promising exchange, I received a box of twenty on-the-go tissue packs instead.

The worst part was that I couldn't shake Philip's warnings. I became convinced that the sea of people—the woman with a big wicker basket of oranges, the cab drivers motioning toward their backseats, the middle-aged women beckoning me into their watch stores—were prostitutes in disguise conniving to steal my internal organs.

I sat in the plaza outside the train station for an hour before deciding not to turn back. A classmate had written the address of the hostel in Chinese for me, and I handed the slip of paper to a cab driver. He puzzled at the characters in Traditional Chinese, not the Simplified Chinese used in the mainland. After some consultation with a few other cabbies, he said, "Very good!" and motioned me into his cab. I began to worry when he kept repeating "very good" every time I asked him a question. After half an hour in the cab I had done some calculations: at this speed I would suffer only a broken arm if I jumped out onto the freeway. An arm would heal. Kidneys do not grow back.

Three hours later, I sat at a table in an artists' compound on the edge of town with three students, two guys and a woman, from Shenzhen University. I had arrived in an artists' district safe and sound. The area was hip and modern, a combination of Brooklyn and Seoul. These students had noticed me as I was eating alone in a restaurant and had invited me to join them. They wore bomber jackets, peacoats, and tight jeans. One of the guys was wearing a hat backward and had a tattoo on his wrist. It said FREEDOM. The other guy and the young woman were a couple. They sat close, her hand on his arm, his on her knee.

Communicating was difficult. Before they asked a question in English, they would confer with each other for several minutes. I spoke no meaningful Chinese beyond "I don't want." We didn't get very far—a brief discussion about movies—and mostly just ate in a strangely happy silence. All the while they played host, putting the choicest pieces of food on my plate in place of conversation. They insisted on treating when the meal ended. With the dignity of a diplomat one student managed to tell me, "You're a guest in our country." We went our separate ways with a wave and a smile. That was it. No pickpockets, no swindlers, no prostitutes. I left Shenzhen certain that China was not like the descriptions people had given me, but I also felt ill equipped to understand what the differences were.

During my time at Hong Kong University, six months at the beginning of 2011, I went to Mainland China several times, doing my best to get deeper into China. I went with a robotics team to Shenzhen's computer centers and marveled at the technological fluency of the fourteen-year-olds who were gutting and stripping computers in minutes as they sat at folding tables heaped with motherboards and circuitry. I walked through Internet bars with rows of teenagers and twenty-year-olds *click-click-click-clicking* wordlessly through alternative realities for hours on end. I took tours of factories that manufacture electronic cigarettes as a "quality control specialist" (my friend's cousin sold them in the UK and asked us to put on suits and tour his suppliers) and sat in on a start-up meeting run by twenty-year-olds looking to change the world. What did they talk about when they were alone? How would growing up in a city like Shenzhen mold you? What did these kids—my peers—dream of?

Seeing more of China didn't make me understand it better; it only created more mysteries to solve. It was clear that the China I was experiencing wasn't the China I had been told about. Real China seemed to move behind a wall, and I was seeing only its shadows. The Great Wall, Shanghai's skyline, Suzhou's meandering canals, and even Shenzhen's Luohu station—in all these places I felt like I was looking at a postcard of China, something fascinating but paper thin. As both an empire and a modern culture, one of China's most distinguishing features was its insularity from the world. However inefficient the Great Wall was at repelling enemies, it was an apt metaphor for China's attitude toward the outside: keep out.

After I returned to the United States, I found that China's reputation at home was worse than it was in Hong Kong. When I would ask someone, "What do you know about Chinese people?" I'd hear a smattering of headlines, a description of Chinese people as a Maserati-driving, dog-eating people who live in empty, underpopulated cities but who need to be shoved from behind to fit into crammed subways. They're poor child laborers who also buy more clothes from Kate Spade and Michael Kors than anyone else in the world. The contradictions carried a whiff of Philip's Shenzen warning, but I didn't know how to set the Americans straight. I became determined to go back and dig into China's mysteries.

After I graduated from college in 2012, I left New York for China armed with the address of a hostel and the phone number for a language program. I did not speak the language and I didn't know anyone or have a job. My plan was to try to get through that wall.

二

In 2008, China beamed a new image of itself to the world. It was the first time many people had seen China outside kung fu movies, Chinese restaurants, or *National Geographic* specials. It was China's coming-out party as a modern nation, and it began with 2,008 Chinese drummers lined up on the floor of one of the world's most impressive stadiums, engineered to look like an enormous bird's nest of steel and iron. All were dressed in identical pale yellow Chinese silk ensembles. In front of each was the same ornate iron drum. Suspended cameras panned across the rows of drummers, a sweep of hard, neat lines. In perfect unison, the drummers began to pound their complex rhythm. People moving in such hive-minded coordination was both beautiful and chilling.

This was the first act of the opening ceremony of the Beijing Olympics. Many international reporters and pundits would agree: given the scale, technology, coordination, and complexity of the stage—at one point fifty-eight actors defied gravity as they ran horizontally on a globe several stories high—it was probably the greatest show ever performed in human history. That image of immaculate synchronicity has affected how many people across the globe still think about China: a unified, homogeneous, tightly choreographed glide into the future.

The opening ceremony expressed a Chinese ideal, the blurring of the individual within the whole. Such displays rarely have a protagonist or a hero. Rather, the beauty is in the harmony of all the actors; the hero is the balance of the whole. "This is our new country,"

China was telling the world, "a balanced and unified nation striding in lockstep toward its future."

The reality is different. A century ago the father of modern China and its leader after China's last emperor abdicated in 1911, Sun Yat-sen, described China as a "sheet of loose sand": 一盘散沙 ("Yī pán sǎn shā").* Millennia of rule by emperors had ended. The country had slipped into disorder. Sun Yat-sen led China's rocky transition from ancient empire to modern government. Under his tutelage both Chiang Kai-shek and Mao Zedong would emerge as leaders and then fatefully diverge. Chiang would lead China after Sun but never gain full control. After World War II, Chiang's Nationalists and Mao's Communists would divide the country through a civil war, with the winner set to determine China's future. Against imposing odds and with incredible feats of will, Mao's Communists won. "Chairman Mao," as he would be immortalized, would found today's People's Republic of China in 1949. Both Chinese and foreign historians regard as Chairman Mao's greatest undertaking his attempt to transform Sun's sheet of loose sand into one solid country.

Today China remains fragmented. More than 95 percent of the population lives on only two-fifths of all its land.† China has more

---

*The symbols above the English letters represent a tone, of which there are four. They are easy to read, as the direction of the line over the letter indicates the direction one pitches their voice to accurately pronounce the word. For instance, the first word, Yī, meaning "one" and read in a first tone, is read in a high, flat tone. Pán, in this case translated as "sheet" and read in a second tone, is read by pitching one's voice from low to high. Sǎn, translated as "loose" and read in a third tone, is read by dipping one's pitch from medium to low and back to medium-high. There is no fourth tone in this phrase, so we will use the example of mà, to curse or scold, which is read pitching one's voice from high to low.

†This line dividing China in two was proposed by the geographer Hu Huanyong in 1935 and is best known as the Hu Huanyong Line (also as the Heihe-Tengchong line) and runs from Heihe, Harbin, a city in China's frozen northernmost coastal province

than six hundred billionaires but one of the widest wealth gaps in the world.[1] The east coast cities and the metropolises clustered around the Pearl River delta, with Shenzhen at its head, developed fast, while the center and Western reaches of the country are pushing, and being pulled, to catch up. Different dialects still cause divisions across different regions of China, particularly among older generations.

China has about four hundred million people who were born between 1984 and 2002—the millennials. But in China they're not called millennials: China divides its generations by decades—post-50s (those born in 1950–59), post-60s, and so on.[2]

Those plain vanilla labels give no hint of the vastly different experiences of these generations. The post-50s generation began just a year after China's civil war ended and Mao Zedong founded the People's Republic of China. This made that generation the first born in the modern nation-state of China. The tail end of that generation and the first born into the post-60s generation entered a world of deprivation: From 1958 to 1961, China's Great Leap Forward saw many tens of millions die of starvation. As the 1960s continued, China's push to modernize failed, and Mao plunged China into the Cultural revolution, which venerated the peasant farmer above other social classes and created a cult of personality around the Chairman. It was simultaneously anti-intellectual, anti-modern, and anti-historical; much of China's traditional and historic books and buildings, as well as the best minds of the generation, were laid to waste during the Cultural Revolution.

Here marks a major pivot in modern China's development. The

---

on Russia's southern border, diagonally down and across from Tengchong, Yunnan, China's southwestern province that borders the Tibet Autonomous Region, Vietnam, Laos, and Myanmar (formerly Burma).

first members of the post-80s generation were born in a particularly radical moment for China: In 1978 China threw its doors wide open to invite foreign direct investment and put China's manufacturing boom in motion. At about the same time, China inaugurated its one-child policy, an effort to curtail China's burgeoning population by decreeing that couples could have only one child (the policy eventually included forced abortions and sterilizations).

Then came the post-90s. The student demonstrations in Tiananmen Square in 1989 urged a more democratic government for China and were violently put down. Sensing a moment of national identity crisis, China changed its national education program to reframe Chinese identity for this generation, moving away from Mao and his "accomplishments," emphasizing China's historic might as a country and culture, and defining internal weakness and outside aggression as the reason for China's downfall in modernity. Then, in 1992, Deng Xiaoping, the architect of China's economic boom, planted a tree in Shenzhen as a symbol of the growth he intended to bring to the region.

A decade and a half of growth turned the fishing village into a multimillion-person manufacturing mega city, and the poor, backward country into a modernizing power poised for the world stage. China regarded the Beijing Olympics of 2008 as the country's formal debut as a modern power and culture. By 2011, more than half of China's population lived in cities, and by 2015, more than half of the country's gross domestic production was derived from services, not manufacturing.[3]

The generation-naming system isn't perfect, but it is how China understands itself and why its generations are so different. The young people I describe here were born into a country brimming with ambition and aspiration. Now, the post-90 and post-2000 generations are part of the world's middle class, the first modern Chinese generations less preoccupied with needs and more involved with wants, in particular, "Who do we want to be?" Their generations will define what being Chinese in the modern world means.

三

Like my Chinese godfather, my last roommate in China took an English name. He chose Tom. Tom was born in 1993, three years after I was born. We had very different upbringings. By then the protests and vicious government response at Tiananmen Square had subsided. China was in the midst of a different type of revolution, this time about refrigeration. China's 1.1 billion people had only thirty million refrigerators.[4] Tom was not part of that privileged minority. "We were a normal household, not one of those rich households," Tom's mother told me. Tom was born in a city, but three-quarters of his generation was born in rural China.[5] That same year, the first McDonald's opened in China, in Shenzen, nowhere near Tom's native Sichuan Province. An uncle who had gone to work at a factory in Shenzhen tried eating there and, when he told his family back home about his meal, described the taste of a Big Mac as "confusing."

Tom's family was poor, far poorer than most people in the world: China's average annual income per capita was then about $375, less than in Burkina Faso, Rwanda, and Lesotho; just a touch more than that in India, and a far cry from America's nearly $23,000. The two Asian giants, China and India, one Communist, the other democratic, are often compared within China. During that tree-planting trip to Shenzhen, Deng Xiaoping proclaimed, "Poverty is not socialism. To be rich is glorious."[6] This was a signal to Tom's parents and grandparents that private industry had been decriminalized. Deng's words sounded like a directive, and Tom's family pushed to attain upward mobility. His grandparents and teachers tried hard to learn Mandarin in addition to their local dialect. His older cousin tested among the top five students in the city in English, so she moved to Shanghai to look for a job with a foreign company. She was the talk of the neighborhood.

Views of the outside world were scarce. Home televisions were few. There was no access to the Internet (twenty million American adults had Internet access by 1996).[7] Tom vaguely remembers how, when he was three, everyone gathered in a public hall to watch China win sixteen gold medals at the Atlanta Olympics in 1996. It was the first live broadcast from America he'd ever seen. His parents watched in awe and told him, "Look, son, that is the greatest country on Earth." When Tom was young, he didn't know anyone who had one of the 5.5 million cars in the country. Bicycles of nearly identical make and model, the ubiquitous Flying Pigeon, swarmed city streets. Almost everyone was skinny. Getting visas to travel abroad was nearly impossible. Most embassies, including China's, assumed Chinese families would try to emigrate illegally if they could. Tom's family simply couldn't afford to travel. Once, when Tom was five years old, he waited in line for three hours to eat fried chicken at the first KFC in a neighboring city. It was the first Western food he had ever tasted. The mashed potatoes were a marvelous texture—not quite tofu, not quite rice porridge, but buttery and smooth. It was also the first time he'd ever tasted butter, and it gave him the runs for days.

Tom learned that other countries used to call China "the sick man of Asia." In his history books he read about the Century of Humiliation (1839–1949) and how China, once the strongest, wealthiest empire in the world, grew weak at the hands of its own Qing government (1644–1911). In China's weakened state, Western colonial powers divided China's major cities among themselves, using them as trade ports for tea and silk, crippled the populace with the illegal trade of opium, and made the Chinese second-class citizens in their own land. He read that the small island nation of Japan had occupied China and held it hostage from 1937 to 1945. The Japanese raped Chinese women and tested biological weapons on Chinese peasants. Tom's country was too weak to stop them.[8]

Fast-forward to Tom's high school years. China's GDP per capita had swelled to ten times what it was when he was a child. By then Chinese individuals' wealth was triple that of their counterparts in India, China's old economic rival. Tom's family could afford to eat out all the time—and they did. Now, young Chinese eat three times as much pork as they did when they were small children. Caloric intake had fully doubled since Tom's grandparents were teens, which explains why they're so short—their growth had been stunted by malnutrition—and also why Tom's school now cautioned him and his younger classmates about obesity in gym class.[9] When he was fifteen, Tom cheered as he watched the Beijing Olympics and his country racked up fifty-one gold medals, fifteen more than the United States. His parents couldn't believe it. Tom thought, *Why not?*

A decade later, China was at the center of every global conversation. Tom and his friends saw that when China's economy creaks, the world's groans. As empowering as the global narrative was, national competition kept them preoccupied. Tom was studying for a graduate degree. He was one of 7.5 million students to graduate from college when he did—China now graduates the most college students of any country in the world—and if Tom wanted to have a chance to get a good job, he had to pursue an advanced degree.

In his twenty-odd years of life, Tom has watched his country's economic reality transform from poverty to global power. Chinese travelers constitute the biggest outbound tourism market in the world, and all nations vie for the business of Chinese tourists.[10] When South Africa changed its visa laws to make it difficult for Chinese to enter, the South African tourism community protested. They wanted the business.[11] China sends students abroad in droves, and they are being welcomed by universities with open arms. Tom's friends send him pictures from their classrooms in England. One picture showed a professor's presentation: "China: The Economic Miracle." However, his friends still believe that Westerners regard China with suspicion. China has become the biggest car market in the world and has enough rich people that it is on the brink of becoming the largest *luxury* car market in the world.[12] The Flying Pigeon bicycle is now fashionable—some sell for thousands of dollars. China is poised to become the largest movie market in the world, so Chinese no longer have to put up with films that depict them as coolies with queues or actors in leading roles who speak broken English.[13] Many movies made in Hollywood are suddenly setting scenes in Shanghai or hiring Chinese actors. The way Tom and his generation view themselves, and are viewed by the world, is evolving.

Older Chinese, who still view themselves and their country as inferior to the United States and many Western powers, find it simply inconceivable that China is a member of the Group of Twenty, the international forum of government leaders and central bankers from the twenty biggest economies. Now, the world is focused on the great power relationship between the United States and China, a notion that is simply not believable to older Chinese. But to Tom, China's inclusion is simply logical. In 2014, Alibaba, China's tech and e-commerce giant, reaped the richest initial public offering (IPO) in the history of the New York Stock Exchange. By then China's GDP per capita was twenty times more than when Tom was a child and six times more than India's.

Young Chinese see their country as the underdog of the modern era, a narrative heavily reinforced by China's education system. From many people's perspective, it is one of the greatest comeback stories in the history of storytelling, the great, true story of the fighter that everyone said couldn't make it—too weak, too overpopulated, too old, too slow, too outdated, too sickly, too far behind. They were bullied, beat up, sabotaged. And now, against the odds and opposition, China has risen to power.

四

Every Chinese student learns this saying early in life: "Diligence is the path up the mountain of knowledge; hard work is the boat on the endless sea of learning."*

The line is also apt for those trying to approach China, its people, and its language. To hear someone speak Chinese is to recognize their diligence, how far they have trudged up the mountain of knowledge. Outsiders can learn about a country's economics and politics in translation. They cannot know a person and a people without also knowing their language.

Tom's generation grew up studying English for about ten years—China has three hundred million English speakers, whereas the United States has only one million Chinese speakers. He and his generation grew up watching Western movies and TV shows, reading Western books, paying attention to Western celebrities, and cheering the West's sports stars. His favorite movie is *The Matrix*, and he can quote Barney from the TV show *How I Met Your Mother*. He doesn't

---

*书山有路勤为径, 学海无涯苦作舟: *Shū shān yǒu lù qín wèi jìng, xué hǎi wú yá kǔ zuò zhōu.*

have access to Facebook, but more people in China use the Chinese social app WeChat than there are people in the European Union. Despite the great firewall, the Chinese Internet regulations that censor the content Chinese may see, Tom believes he still has a much better view of the world than the world has of China.

Language lies at the core of that discrepancy. The world's lack of understanding of China is in large part the result of its decision to build literal and figurative walls around the country and its culture. When China began to trade with other nations, it was illegal for Chinese citizens to teach foreigners their language. To do so was punishable by death.*

The DNA of Chinese culture is baked into the language. In the 1910s and 1920s, a faction within China who wanted to do away with the pillars of Chinese culture, specifically Confucianism, which they saw as hindering China's ascension into modernity, advocated for the abolishment of the Chinese language. Qian Xuantong, a professor of literature at what was then National Peking University, advised a contemporary in 1918: "If you want to abolish Confucianism, you must first abolish the Chinese [written] language."[14] Because they could not disentangle the language and the culture, Qian and other academics advocated elimination of the language. Some advocated the adoption of Esperanto. They failed. Today China's national language is Mandarin, which the FBI classifies as one of the five most difficult languages for native English speakers to learn.

When I moved to China in 2012, my first goal was to learn the language. I am far from a linguist. I had unsuccessfully attempted

---

*In part this law was designed to stop religious missionaries from proselytizing the Chinese.

to learn Latin and French at different points in my life, so I spent time researching the best ways to "acquire," as I learned the pros term it, a language. When I got to China, anything I had to do, I did in Chinese, from changing the language settings of my phone and computer systems to awkward, unsuccessful dates. I downloaded Anki, a spaced repetition system of flashcards,* then Pleco, an invaluable phone app that I still use daily, and got to work making flashcards of complete sentences.

I progressed in phases. One day my landlord, a thirty-year-old woman, applauded my progress and told me, "You speak so cute!" That afternoon I was in a coffee shop and asked the server, a university student, about her day. Her response? "Wow! Your Chinese is so cute!" A few days later a Chinese coworker patted me on the back after I had used the word for *lifetime* instead of the word for *cup*. She said, "Your Chinese is really coming along! You speak so cute!"

The last time someone had described me as cute, I had not yet hit puberty. I mentioned this to my neighbor. He laughed and told me, "Oh, it is because you talk like a baby."

Studying then took on more urgency as I worked to reduce the distance between my Chinese personality and my American one. My neighbor's comment also reminded me that when my Chinese friends spoke English with me, they, too, were having difficulty representing their true selves.

---

*A Spaced Repetition System (SRS) is a tool that learns with you to present study material before you forget it. Based on past performance, the SRS will manage the timing and frequency of chosen material. For instance, I have correctly identified the flashcard for the word *I* in Chinese often enough that my SRS knows I don't need to see it anytime soon. The phrase for *nuclear deterrence*, on the other hand, will show up much more often, as I have yet to master it. When managing thousands of inputs, an SRS decides what you need to study so you just need to sit and do it.

My victories came in tiny increments. At the beginning my goal was only to distinguish exactly where my landlord's sentences stopped and started. Then I wanted to be able to explain the measurements of my bed to a saleswoman so I could buy sheets of the correct size. A month later my goal was to describe the rent I was willing to pay for an apartment and where I wanted to live: inexpensive, and near Suzhou's famous canals. Then I started to travel, and that's when I learned from a young Chinese man, Guo, and his friends that China's walls had not only kept people out but also kept people in.

Guo and I met on an overnight train headed south. He was nineteen and headed back to his university after vacationing in Suzhou. China's sleeper cars have cubbies of six beds. Guo and his friends had the three bunks opposite my row. They stared at me with curiosity. No other foreigners were in our train car. Finally, Guo asked in halting English, "Can you speak Chinese?"

China's matrix of railroads spreads across the country, more than forty-six thousand miles of steel track. Of those, more than twelve thousand miles are suitable for bullet trains, which means China has more high-speed rail than the rest of the world combined.[15] You can get almost anywhere in the country by train, and during that first year I did. I had realized that I could learn the language anywhere, so I would work for a month or two teaching English at a night school or tutoring prospective Chinese study-abroad students for the SATs, then take a break from my assignments to travel the vast country for weeks until my money ran low. Then I'd come back and start the cycle again. That first year I spent more than two hundred hours on buses and trains.

As the days flew by, I would talk mostly with other young people. We were drawn to one another. It was like peering through a hole in China's wall and finding someone on the other side staring back.

Like the train rumbling through the night, my conversation with Guo bumped along in fits and starts. People walking to the hot water spigot at the end of the car to boil instant noodles or refill tea thermoses lingered and listened. Parents and children poked their heads out of their bunks to see what the commotion was all about. Little Li, the fifteen-year-old high school student who had the bunk below mine, said in Chinese, "They think it is funny to hear a foreigner speak our language."

Everyone had questions about America. Guo asked, "Does everyone eat just bread and hamburgers?" A dozen pairs of eyes zeroed in on my reaction.

My first thought was a firm no: *American food is extremely complex! We are a melting pot of cultures, and our diverse cuisine reflects that.*

After mulling it over, I replied, "I mean, sort of." It was difficult to deny entirely, but it also was impossible to respond in full with my broken Chinese. "Pizza, too," I added.

Turning to one another, they laughed and nodded. Just as they'd suspected.

"In California do you see lots of movie stars?"

"No," I replied, "there are no movie stars where I am from."

Guo's friend on the top bunk jumped in. "Actually, yes, there are. Most movie stars live in *Hollywood*, which is in California." He said Hollywood in English for added flare.

I explained that I am from Northern California, not Southern California. "It takes six hours to drive from my home to Hollywood," I managed to say. They looked disappointed.

The person in the middle bunk quickly brightened and asked, "Do you live close to Hotel California?"

The crowd waited in silence as I stalled. How to explain that the

Eagles' 1976 pop hit is not about a hotel at all but the spiritual emptiness of the glitz and glam of LA?

"Maybe? I'm not sure. I don't know that hotel from the song. Maybe it doesn't exist."

Guo looked skeptical. "Hotel California" had become a massive karaoke hit in China. How could I not know where the hotel is located?

"Does every home have a *shǒuqiāng*?" The question came from someone standing behind Guo. All eyes widened. The crowd leaned in expectantly. I swallowed hard.

"Sorry, what?"

Little Li laughed and rolled his eyes.

"Shǒuqiāng," Guo repeated, encouraging me with a nod. Then he took my hand and, spreading out my fingers, started to trace the first character on my palm: 手, *shǒu*. The first character I recognized. It means "hand." I held up my hand and Guo nodded enthusiastically. He continued to trace. The next character was more complex, 枪, *qiāng*. I had no clue.

A child sitting on his mother's lap held up his little fist, index finger extended. "Pew, pew, pew!" he said, as his hand recoiled with each sound.

Shǒuqiāng means "handgun." Only hunters are allowed to have guns in China. Until recently police could not carry guns. The idea that just anyone could have a gun was too far-fetched for my friend to imagine, but they had seen our action movies. To Chinese news outlets, stories about American gun violence are as perverse and exotic as stories about Chinese dog-eating festivals are to Western news outlets.

"We see it in the news. People kill each other all the time!" Guo said, shaking his head. "You Americans are really crazy." The crowd shook their heads in agreement and slowly dispersed to their bunks.

Nearly all Chinese learn about the United States through media, which everyone consumes in bulk. And so the vast majority of people in China perceive Americans as burger-eating fat folks with guns and groovy tunes.

五

Chinese tones are particularly difficult for Westerners to learn. The concept of pitching your voice to change the fundamental meaning of a word—not from a statement to a question but from *horse* to *mother*—is unknown in the romance languages. A well-known Chinese poem, "The Lion-Eating Poet in the Stone Den," by Yuen Ren Chao (1892–1982), illustrates the difficulty. Here is an excerpt:

Shishi shishi Shi Shi, shi shi, shi shi shi shi.
Shi shishi shi shi shi shi.
Shi shi, shi shi shi shi shi.
Shi shi, shi Shi Shi shi shi.
Shi shi shi shi shi, shi shi shi, shi shi shi shi shishi.

This masterpiece is aptly titled "Shi Shi shi shi shi." The entire poem consists of ninety-two characters, each and every one of which is pronounced *shi*. By using different tones to say "shi," the indistinguishable *Shi Shi shi shi shi* becomes *Shī Shì shí shī shǐ*, which can then be understood as 施氏食狮史, "The Lion-Eating Poet in the Stone Den." The challenge for Westerners studying spoken Mandarin really boils down to making a lion-eating poet emerge from a chain of *shi*s.

Mistakes with tones can make Mandarin indecipherable. A friend of mine from Costa Rica, Jon, was living in China and once walked into a convenience store to buy a gauze face mask. It was a bad-air day in the freezing city of Harbin, and the temperature—thirty degrees below freezing—only made the air worse. Jon's Chinese was, by his own admission, bad. He thought he was asking the storeowner for a mask but did so in toneless Chinese. The storeowner's face grew pale and his eyes widened as he searched Jonathan's face for some hidden meaning. My friend nodded his head eagerly and pointed to his mouth, repeating the request.

That was enough. The shop owner rushed from behind the counter and shooed Jonathan out of his store, slamming the door behind him. The shop owner's reaction was understandable. Instead of asking for a face mask, Jonathan had just asked for a specific sexual favor.

Spoken Chinese is difficult, but the written language is even more complex. The Asia Society estimates that full Chinese literacy requires knowledge of three to four thousand characters. Native literacy requires familiarity with more than ten thousand characters.[16] Those distinct symbols can then be arranged and rearranged to form thousands of words.

If you understand the twenty-six symbols that represent one or several sounds in English, you can pronounce just about any word in the English language. With Chinese, if you don't recognize one character, reading it aloud from the page is impossible. Chinese is a logographic language; every symbol or character represents a word or has an intrinsic meaning. The character 戴, pronounced *dài*, my last name in Chinese, is not just a sound. *Dài* means something on its own—"to respect."

In the United States people often ask whether I speak Mandarin or Cantonese. China actually has five major groupings of dialects, two of which are Mandarin and Cantonese. From 1849 until the late twentieth century, almost every Chinese emigrating from China to the United States was likely to speak Cantonese, the language of the Guangdong region, formerly known as Canton. Many immigrants even came from Shenzhen. They lived close to Hong Kong's Victorian Harbor and in an area of the country devastated by floods and famine in the 1840s. The natural disasters prompted the first emigrants to leave to participate in the Gold Rush in the United States and made peasants who remained in that area of China sympathetic to the Taiping Rebellion, which began in 1850. By the time the rebellion ended fourteen years later, southeastern China was in ruins and twenty million people had died. Survivors left if they could. Thus a disproportionate number of people of Chinese descent living abroad speak Cantonese. In reality, there are thirteen Mandarin speakers for every Cantonese speaker, and most Cantonese speakers are now made to speak both.[17]

China's post-90s generation is the first to be predominantly fluent in Mandarin, in large part thanks to TV, Internet, and learning in school. Still, only 70 percent of the entire population speaks Mandarin, leaving four hundred million people, mostly older, able to communicate only with people from their own region.

In 1956, mainland China switched from traditional Chinese characters to a simplified system. But Hong Kong, Taiwan, and Macau still use traditional characters. If a Hong Kong restaurant's menu is in traditional characters, some of my Chinese friends cannot read all of it.

While it's impossible to understand China if you don't speak Chinese, knowing the language does not mean you automatically understand China.

My first real Chinese friend was Huan Huan. We had similar interests, hobbies, and curiosities, and we enjoyed good banter in Chinese. Until I met him, most of my Chinese friendships had formed around our differences. The young Chinese I had met during my first year in China were interested in me as a foreigner. I was interested in them as Chinese. Huan Huan was different. He was the first friend I made after my Chinese language skills caught up with my personality, and he invited me to visit him at his family's home village for Chinese New Year.

As I waited for the bus that would carry me to Huan Huan's village—a twelve-hour trip—I juggled gifts of whiskey, tea, and candied meats from Chengdu. The Chinese custom is to bring local delicacies as a gift. But because modern life has scattered Chinese to different cities and regions, they bring back the specialties of their new home to share with family and neighbors. As a foreigner, two bottles of Irish whiskey qualified as my local delicacy. That night Huan Huan and his family held a large dinner for neighbors and friends at their house. At the table were Huan Huan's parents, uncles, and his "little brother"—really just a cousin, because, like many Chinese of his generation, Huan Huan was an only child. I worked at being a model guest, paying especially close attention to my *pleases* and *thank yous*.

At some point during the meal, I realized Huan Huan was looking increasingly agitated. After I thanked his mother for more rice, Huan Huan finally called me outside for a private chat.

"Are you uncomfortable in there?"

"No, very comfortable."

"Is the food to your liking? Is everyone being respectful?"

"Yes, of course. The food is all excellent." It was delicious.

"Then, goddamnit," he said, "you've got to stop saying thank you. Our guests are taking it the wrong way. I told them we were brothers. They think I've pulled in a random foreigner off the street to flaunt my life in a big city."

Manners don't translate well from Chinese to English and vice versa. Chinese does not have a word for *please*. The closest to *please* is *qǐng*. The word suggests more of an invitation or a request than an expression of cordialness. "Welcome, Mr. Dychtwald, qǐng follow me to the boardroom."

Like *please*, *thank you* can be unintentionally off-putting. China's is a culture of treated meals, of buying things for other people, and of having things bought for you. The buying is an expression of familiarity and affection. "Among friends, there is no need for thank you," Huan Huan would reprimand me as he paid for our roadside barbecue and beers. "You thank strangers for kindnesses; they are expected of friends."

My Chinese friends are quick to point out that in Chinese etiquette, actions speak louder than words. To compliment Huan Huan's mother's food, I ate more of it. Everyone noticed. She glowed, wordlessly. If you really want to thank someone for their generosity, repay that person in kind. Huan Huan taught me the silent language of the give and take of relationships in China.

七

My time in China formed like a wall of the Grand Canyon, layer stacked upon layer of individual experiences that added color and texture to the whole. I can most easily think about those layers through the bits of language I was learning at the time.

The foundation, or bottom layer, was the discussion of American eating habits and guns on the overnight train. Above that was a layer about drinking etiquette—whom to toast first, how to toast properly. One layer higher was why you say *please* and *thank you* to strangers, not to friends. A few layers up were the experiences of learning about the Chinese concept of friendship and the importance of sibling-like relationships to a generation of only children. Shimmering between the dusty layers of everyday life was the pursuit of freedom, evidenced by the tattoos on the wrists, backs, and legs of people across the country. Tempering that freedom was responsibility and tradition—I watched a just-married Chinese couple kneel on stage before their parents to be acknowledged as new members of the family. In a country with no recent history of religion, this was the only formal sealing of the matrimonial bond. Above that layer was death, a layer that I can't remember or even use the vocabulary I learned—*hǔohùa* (cremation)—without thinking of my friend Wei Wei, who was made to watch her grandfather's body enter the furnace at a government-mandated cremation center. That layer was gray like the soot on the pants of Wei Wei's little sister that came from burning offerings to their grandfather's spirit throughout the night. The next layer was a Buddhist scholar's explanation of the difference between everyday Chinese life and Buddhism while we watched a sky burial—a corpse left on a mountaintop to be picked clean by vultures. Unlike China's current materialistic life of addition—new phones, new cars, new houses—Buddhism is about the process of subtraction, he said. Streaking across the different layers was a vein of quartz that represents an understanding of where modern Confucianism is breaking down and where it continues to bind China together.

The night before I was to fly back to the States from Chengdu, which had become a home for me in China, I stayed up drinking *baijiu* (a sorghum alcohol, typically one hundred proof or more) with Tom. At this point almost all my friends were Chinese, as were my current and previous roommates, people I considered my brothers and sisters, people to whom I would reach out or who would reach out to me at important moments. The reward for the hard work of learning the language was rich friendships with people like Tom.

That night he and I spoke a mixture of Mandarin and Sichuanese dialect as the booze settled in. We talked about the difficulty of trying to span cultures, of presenting China to the world, of the nearly impossible challenge of trying to speak for another culture that has a voice but whose message needs to be translated for a global audience.

Tom said, "In China, we have a tradition of 旁观者清" ("*páng guān zhě qīng*"). The Chinese idiom means "the observer sees clearly."

"China does a terrible job of presenting ourselves to the world. With the image of China in Europe, America, and the West, we just look like brainwashed young people, *1984*-style governance, hair in queues . . ." His voice trailed off.

"Look, man," he continued, placing his glass on the table. "As long as you don't make all of us out to be organ-stealing prostitutes, we're making progress."

2

Bella and the Books

China's Competitive Study Culture Forges a Determined Heart

"The university here is lazy," Bella sighed as she waited at the front of a pack of students scattered around the entrance to the library. Lights along the campus drive illuminated the dark morning. Bella wore half the clothes in her closet, five thick layers, to ward off the chill. Her breath drifted through the sky. Other students milled about as they sipped the rice porridge that street vendors had ladled, piping hot, into flimsy plastic cups. Others ate egg wraps, cooked on the bottom of an upturned pot placed over hot coals. Bella munched on one of the two vegetable buns she picked up every morning on the way to the library. Pressing its warmth against her bare hands, she said, half asleep, "Our *high school library* opened earlier than this. Don't they want us to succeed here?"

Bella, who was twenty-three, came from Zhejiang Province on China's eastern coast, just south of Shanghai. "Thin like a willow and just as common"—Bella's way of describing herself—she blended seamlessly into the crowd of Chinese college students that frigid morning. She had a warm, bright smile and exuded a kindness that could be mistaken for meekness. She had devoted the entire year after her graduation from college to preparing for a test to gain admission to graduate school. The results of the test would define her future. She wanted to become a translator, and a good score on her admissions test was her only ticket.

At 7:45 a.m. someone finally opened the library doors. Bella raced to secure her usual seat with the same five students who joined her daily at a table for six in a library filled with hundreds.

Each month Bella would spend more than 320 hours in the Suzhou University library, over eighty hours a week. By that point in Suzhou's bitter winter, Bella had sat in the same room at the same desk with the same people for five months. Translation books stacked around a small square on a long, rectangular wooden table marked Bella's territory. Similar book barriers divided the table into six neat spaces, all occupied by students who, like Bella, spent more than ten hours a day in their book-made cubbyholes. The table was one of fifteen in the study room, and the study room was one of twelve in one of Suzhou University's many libraries.

I once asked Bella what the young man who had set up shop next to her for the last several months was studying.

"I'm not sure," she said, shrugging her shoulders.

I pointed at the desk. Five economics books marked the border between Bella's study space and this student's. She giggled. "Economics."

"Where is he from?"

"Ummmm . . ." Another shrug.

"How old is he?" I asked.

"I think around my age? Maybe a little older."

"What is his name?" I ventured.

"I don't know. We have never spoken."

Bella suppressed a smile, furrowed her brow, and put her hands on her hips in mock severity, then told me, "We're here to study, remember?"

Bella would live a full year in this library, laboring every day toward her dream of getting into one of the best translation programs in the country and the opportunity to become a professional translator. The odds? Bella rattled them off from memory: Be one of fourteen students to gain a place from a field of six thousand applicants. Two-tenths of one percent.

二

It wasn't so long ago that no one in China received much of a classroom education. In 1975, only about 11 percent of Chinese had graduated from high school. Mandatory education stopped after junior high, and in any case the Cultural Revolution had made a mockery of the classroom. Bella's parents were members of that uneducated generation. China's modern economy was built on people like Bella's parents and grandparents: uneducated laborers with a solid work ethic. Those generations were so hungry to work that they became known for continually asking their managers for overtime in some of the world's most menial factory positions. These same parents were determined to see their children get a better education.

In 1999, the Chinese central government and the Ministry of Education announced a lofty college enrollment expansion reform that would increase enrollment by half a million students, nearly double what it was the year earlier. Over the next fifteen years, the annual number of Chinese graduating from higher education ballooned sevenfold. In 2014 Bella was one of 7.26 million Chinese to walk out of university with a new degree.[1]

Bella was a member of the largest college graduating class in Chinese history, but that meant hers was the worst year to graduate in terms of job opportunities and the economy. She could not find a job, or at least not one suitable for a young woman with a college education. "The competition," Bella said, when I asked her what was the hardest part about finding a job in China. "There are so many people like me—a college degree from an okay university, good test scores, so-called motivated team player—that makes it impossible to differentiate ourselves." In his memoir *Decision Points*, former US president George W. Bush recalls asking then-Chinese president Hu Jintao, "What keeps you up at night?" The Chinese president responded without hesitating: "Creating 25 million jobs a year."[2]

But not just any jobs. Transitioning from one million college graduates to more than seven million in just fifteen years set a demanding pace for job creation, particularly the higher-end jobs appropriate for college graduates.

China has not yet built the economy that Bella and her generation of white-collar workers will run; it has not made the transition from a manufacturing giant to a service-sector dynamo. China has the talent but does not yet have the jobs. In the meantime, students submit waves of graduate school applications as they try to differentiate themselves from their peers. Bella was a drop of water in the swell.

While studying for her graduate school admissions test, Bella slept on a bottom bunk at Suzhou University in a small dorm room that looked out on the side of a concrete bridge spanning one of Suzhou's famous canals. She shared the room with five other young women. It had no bathroom, and only a shared sink in the hall. Fifty or so young women shared a few toilet stalls. If Bella wanted to shower, she washed in a building ten minutes away in a large, communal shower hall. When it snowed in winter, she washed her hair in a plastic tub with water she boiled in an electric tea kettle. Because the dorm had no heat, she wore much of her wardrobe to bed. Many Westerners might call her lifestyle monkish. But most students in China live the same way.

Like most in her generation, Bella was an only child, born ten years after China's family planning program, the now-infamous one-child policy, took effect in 1979. She has translated articles about her generation from Chinese to English. Once she handed me a piece of paper riddled with notes. On top was the title 《小皇帝》 ("*Xiǎo huángdì*"), "Little Emperors." She pointed to the middle of the page and asked in Chinese, "Does this term make any sense? I think I'm translating this correctly." The words were "behavioral ticking time bomb." This phrase has cropped up in Chinese publications for dozens of years. It was originally translated into Chinese from a 1988 article in *The Times* of London, "China's Brat Pack: Generation of Only-Children," and became part of the collective consciousness of China, both as a warning and a bit of a challenge. These reminders of how the West views China are peppered throughout media and even classroom textbooks. As a country that commemorates its Century of Humiliation—the period between the First Opium War and the end of Japanese occupation (1839–1949)—and its time being referred to as "The Sick Man of Asia," China likes to remind itself of its doubters.

I nodded yes, her translation made sense. Bella motioned to all the students with their heads bent over their desk and whispered, "Boom!" Mr. Economics lifted his head and looked over the book barrier, adjusting his glasses higher on the bridge of his nose. Bella dived below her book barricade and giggled.

三

Bella's family is part of China's burgeoning middle class. Her father had formed a collective of anglers to sell their catch at the local market in their coastal village. After experiencing minor success, he had started a hair salon, a restaurant, and an arcade. All eventually went under. Despite their failure, the family had made far more money than Bella's father and grandfather had made by casting nets. Today her father owns and runs several small local restaurants. "My dad may not be the best businessman," she told me, "but he can fill a table with delicious seafood in no time flat."

Bella was very much the center of her family's attention. She fondly recalled leaving primary school and spying her grandfather in the crowd of eager grandparents waiting outside the school gates. During winter all would be wearing the same navy-blue jacket of thick cotton, a Maoist fashion relic. Practicality was deeply ingrained in that generation. Her grandfather would excitedly hoist seven-year-old Bella onto the back of his bike, and the pair would ride to the local convenience store to get an ice cream. Cones secured, they would then plunk down on a park bench and slurp away in grinning silence.

"I realized only later that Grandpa liked taking me to get ice cream so much because he wanted to eat it too," Bella mused. Bella's grandfather was born in 1940. Much of Europe was already engaged in World War II. Japan had brutally occupied parts of China since 1931. When Bella's grandfather was five, the Japanese left and Mao's

Communists went to war with Chiang Kai-shek's Nationalist Party. Chiang fled to Taiwan in 1949, when Bella's grandfather was nine. He survived famine when he was eighteen and kept his head down during his late twenties and early thirties to avoid trouble during the Cultural Revolution, when he had had his own kids.

Bella's household had some sort of meat, fish, or other seafood every single night for dinner while she was growing up, an achievement that made her grandfather tremendously proud. By Western standards she grew up modestly, but hers was the first Chinese generation that did not largely grow up without such necessities as protein.

As soon as she started primary school, study became a way of life. Six-year-old Bella would arrive at school at 6:45 a.m. and stay until 4:30 p.m.—nine hours a day, every day. After school Bella would go home and study at the kitchen table while her mom and grandma made dinner, invariably rice, vegetables, and fresh seafood.

By high school Bella was arriving at 5:30 in the morning and not leaving again until after nine at night. That included Saturdays. By her third year of high school she and her classmates were staying at school until about midnight. Including Sundays.

High school was split between normal classes and "self-study." As early as primary school, Bella was placed in a group of academically talented students. Bella's year had three classes for good students and seven classes for the other students. A group of sixteen-year-olds sitting silently, studying in a classroom after school, seemed unlikely to me.

"Would you guys actually study? Or would you talk?"

"Study."

"Silently?"

"Silently. Yes, self-study. If you had a question you could ask the teacher. Of course, you would also have class. Self-study was only at nights and in the early morning. Even the worst students would study on the weekends in their second and third year of high school."

Bella was quite young when a teacher told her to come to school more often. I asked her why.

"Because I'm clever," Bella blurted out, and her hands immediately shot up to cover her mouth.

四

No building at Suzhou University, including the library, had heat. Few buildings in southern China are equipped with heat, despite the freezing temperatures. Insulation in most buildings was abysmal—without heat, what is the point?—and the library kept its windows open to air out the stuffy study rooms.

"We are in the South," was the typical response. "There is no need." Suzhou is actually just about smack dab in the middle of China's coastline, but historically, politically, and culturally, it is a "southern city" and therefore is considered to be hot. It is nearly as far north as you can go in China and not find buildings with central heating.

Although Suzhou sees snow only once or twice a season, the winter cold could seep into your bones. Most students studying at the library brought a water heater, a thick plastic sack of water covered in felt or faux fur that plugged into the wall and sold for the equivalent of about five dollars at most corner stores. My favorite belonged to Mr. Economics: a water heater with Steve Jobs's face on the front. Bella took breaks from writing to warm her hands on a light blue water heater with the Disney character Tinker Bell in the top right corner.

The test designed to find the "best candidate" for a university or graduate program is incredibly thorough although only minimally focused on Bella's proposed course of study. On Bella's patch of desk, test preparation materials were stacked up higher than her slim shoulders. The titles gave little indication of the discipline for which she would actually be tested. On the table was a summary of Confucius's *Analects*, Jane Austen's *Pride and Prejudice*, an English grammar book, an abridged modern Chinese history handout, and a primer of "need-to-know" Maoist and Marxist thought. The way she leafed through them made it clear that she was as familiar with them as with a family photo album.

Bella's test, like nearly all graduate entrance exams, would have four parts. Two parts would be about her prospective postgraduate degree. A third part would test her knowledge of English. That meant every student testing for any graduate degree had to pass basic English. Maritime engineers who planned to spend their lives lodged in the bowels of a ship needed to understand the correct usage of participles in English. Minority dance ethnographers, people whose careers would take them to areas of China where people didn't even speak Mandarin, had to be able to conjugate English verbs backward and forward. Failing to test well in English often doomed qualified candidates to second-rate schools in third-tier cities.

The fourth section, on politics and history, was especially long, although many test takers considered it the easiest. It included concepts they'd been memorizing since primary school. It focused on Chinese history and modern philosophy. Although Bella was testing to become a translator, she still had to have a firm grasp of the political philosophies of Marx, Mao, and Deng. Together, Marxism-Leninism, Mao Zedong Thought, and Deng Xiaoping Theory were known as the Three Represents, an awkward translation from Xinhua, the Party news organ. The Three Represents refers to the three schools of thought that best represent the core of the Chinese Communist Party. High school students seeking admission to college, candidates for grad school, and applicants for membership in the Communist Party had to pass tests on the Three Represents to get where they wanted to go.

The history portion could be a bit trickier. A big chunk includes foreign policies and actions in regard to China. One had to know the politically correct answer. For instance, students anticipate having to write about the territorial conflict between Japan and China involving the Diaoyu Islands (as China refers to them), or the Senkaku Islands (as Japan calls them). China claims historical rights to the Japanese-occupied string of small islands in the East China Sea. The topic might show up on the test in the form of this question: "How did Japan's aggressive politics violate China's territorial rights in recent history?"

Bella was quick, creative, and driven. All of her high school and college teachers recommended her for grad school with the highest praise. With an accountant's precision she stretched her meager savings from a summer job, and supplements from her parents, to extend her studying time.

But, for admission, a file of recommendations was worthless. Leadership qualities, extracurricular activities, community service—these didn't matter at all. Instead, a Chinese student's future rests on an intense three-day test. Have a bad three days and your future is blown.

五

No one knew the frustration of the college testing system better than Ou Lei, a student from a city two hours outside Chengdu, the capital of Sichuan Province. The first time a friend brought Ou Lei to my apartment, I thought he had brought his uncle. Ou Lei's face, although not wrinkled, looked somehow weathered. He had an old man's belly. He was dressed like the Communist Party cadre they film for CCTV news pieces, bland men in generic polo shirts tucked into generic slacks, their faces expressionless, their heads nodding approvingly as they survey a pile of gravel that will become a hotel or a highway or a Starbucks.

Everything about Ou Lei was proudly middle-aged, which is why I thought he was lying when he told me he was only twenty-one. Ou Lei's manners were impeccable. He spoke like a lawyer: concise, professional, and deliberate. A modest, nearly imperceptible laugh seemed to be the greatest indulgence he allowed himself. His hair was parted down the middle. Even to an outsider, he appeared to be a well-groomed Party member. His presence made me painfully aware that I had not swept my apartment in a week.

Ou Lei explained that he would be matriculating at a university in the fall, which is late for someone his age. In high school Ou Lei had been known as an exceptional student. His teachers had told his parents he should test for admission to Peking University or Tsinghua University, the two most prestigious in China.

In China people do not say they've been admitted to college; they can only "test in." Admissions rates are not measured by how many students per hundred applicants are admitted but by how many students per ten thousand are admitted. For example, if you are a resident of Beijing, these two universities collectively will accept just eighty-two out of every ten thousand applying from your city—an admissions rate of 0.82 percent.

While the admissions process in China is comparatively transparent, geography makes a big difference. Beijingers have it easiest by far. If you are from Guangdong Province, home to the megacities Guangzhou and Shenzhen, Beijing and Tsinghua will collectively accept only two out of ten thousand students. China is made up of twenty-two provinces, four municipalities, five autonomous regions, two special administrative regions, and the disputed Taiwan Province. Each has a different admissions quota, and often those admission quotas reflect developmental goals. Bella's home province of Zhejiang fares comparatively well, getting spots for twelve students from every ten thousand applicants in 2015. Ou Lei's home province of Sichuan gets only five. For students in most provinces the combined odds of getting into either of the top universities is about 0.08:100.

Ou Lei had every advantage in the book. Both of his parents worked in government; his father was a high local official. Ou Lei went to a good boarding school. When he was fifteen, he rented an apartment off campus so he could better focus on studying.

After we had communicated for some time over WeChat, the social mega-app used by nearly everyone with a phone in China, I took a bus north of Chengdu to Ou Lei's hometown, where he was doing some work for his father. Within Sichuan Province this city of a few hundred thousand was well known for its generous portions of delicious grilled meat, confirming once again that Sichuaneses' webs of association are created in their stomachs.

We sat down at a street stall a few minutes from Ou Lei's old elementary school. An hour later we had a graveyard of thirty bare skewers, several greasy and garlicky plates of grilled leeks, and big empty bottles of beer. Ou Lei had many questions about my college trajectory, particularly how I had fared on the American college entrance exams, the SAT and ACT. He asked extremely specific questions: What topics were we tested on? What time of day did we take the test? What were the conditions of the testing facility? How many times were students allowed to take the test?

Finally, he said, "I took the *gāokǎo*, the Chinese college entrance exam, five times."

I choked on a chunk of pork. Ou Lei smacked my back, chuckling his lawyer's chuckle, his lips hardly moving. The Chinese college entrance exam can be taken only once a year, no matter what. To take it a second time means waiting until the next year rolls around. Ou Lei was implying that he had spent the last five years of his life preparing for, taking, and failing to earn adequate marks on China's college entrance exam to gain admission to a college that would, in his and his family's estimation, match his ability.

"Yes, five times," he confirmed once I'd regained my composure. "My first failure took place when I was only sixteen as a sophomore in high school. Typically, a young scholar is in their senior year when they take the test. My teachers saw great promise in me, and I was an avid studier."

Ou Lei pulled out a picture. The small, square photo showed a bright-eyed kid with lean features.

"This is me when I was sixteen."

The kid in the picture bore little resemblance to the man in front of me. He was handsome and lean with an air of ease in his teenage face.

"Each time I took the test, I performed under what I, my teachers, and my parents perceived to be my optimum potential. After repeated failures the doctors defined my inability to perform according to expectation as being stress induced. My other medical conditions," he said, motioning to his belly, "were also determined to be stress induced."

Ou Lei and his family finally decided it was better for him to settle for a good, not great, university in Shanghai, where he could build on his father's relationships. On school breaks he would return home to help at his father's office. Even though he began taking the gāokǎo at age sixteen, Ou Lei would not finish his undergraduate degree until he was twenty-five.

"I find it frustrating to be unable to validate my intelligence. I will rely on a 后门, *hòumén*, a back door, when it comes time to take a job."

Ou Lei was referring to using connections, likely family connections, to secure a job. His generation has become loudly defiant of the type of glad-handing and nepotism that seemed to define who got ahead in China's developing economy in generations past. "I am not proud of it, but I would be foolish not to seize this opportunity," he told me.

六

Bella and I sat in the linoleum hall outside her study room, separated from it by thick glass. From here we could see Mr. Economics. Today, I noticed, his shirt looked clean and pressed, his hair coiffed. He had begun to eye me suspiciously every time I came into the library,

I asked Bella if she liked studying. Her giggles rattled off the library's metal chairs. She shook her head no. I asked her why she was doing all this if that was the case.

"I do not know what it is like in your home, but here there are doors to your dreams. China has many people. Those doors are very crowded. Being the very best on one test is the only way for people without connections to enter through those doors," she told me. "No one in libraries likes studying. But we all love our dreams."

Bella grabbed my Chinese notebook and wrote two characters:

"决心," *juéxīn*. I recognized both but had never seen them expressed together. Bella explained, "This character, 决, *jué*, means 'decided' or 'determined,'" using my pen to point to the character on the left. The character on the right I already knew. It is one of the first characters a student of the Chinese language learns.

"Heart."

Bella nodded. The two characters—determined and heart—combined to mean determination, to express resolve. Bella nodded emphatically, the trace of a smile lingering on her face. She went back into the study room. Mr. Economics lifted his head to watch her. Both soon fell back into the rhythm of study.

七

Winter slowly turned to spring, and Bella's morning walk to the library was no longer the zipped-up shuffle through the stark campus. A carpet of fresh grass had grown, and all of Suzhou University's cherry blossom trees were in bloom, a sea of pillow-white petals floating overhead.

For nearly a full year Mr. Economics and Bella had shared the same meter of desk space. One day, with only weeks left before the test, he finally worked up the courage to talk to her, asking, "I'm sorry, could I borrow a pencil?" Flustered, Bella said sorry, she didn't have any, and kept on working. With that, a flame, guarded in secret for a year, was snuffed out.

After a year of preparation Bella took the test that would allow her to enter the graduate school training program to become a professional translator. Bella was required to test within her local pool. Because she was not a resident of Jiangsu Province, where Suzhou is located, she had taken a six-hour bus ride back to her hometown of

Ningbo in Zhejiang Province. A week later she returned to Suzhou to collect her things. We talked over lunch.

She told me she had tried her very best on the test. Yet after months of eighty-hour weeks in the library, waking up and going home in the dark, sacrificing sleep, comfort, friendship, and fun, Bella's score was short by three points. She was in the top 2 percent of testers, but not in the top 0.2 percent.

Bella would not be going to graduate school this year.

She had options, though. She could go to an inferior school in central China or take the test again next year, though I doubted she would do either. Toward the end of the studying process, Bella seemed to be sick of academia.

"Being a translator was never as important as being happy or feeling fulfilled," she told me. "And for that ideal, my heart remains determined."

3

Uneasy Lies the Head That Wears the Crown

China's Little Emperors and Their Heavy Expectations

Jiangguo's big eyes beamed out from beneath well-styled hair, combed over and sealed in place. A blue argyle sweater with gray and orange accents hung easily from his shoulders. His brown corduroy pants looked newly pressed. Jiangguo looked prepared to discuss his résumé for the position of regional manager at the Samsung semiconductor factory up the street.

Jiangguo was five years old. While he waited for class to begin, his thumb remained mostly in his mouth. The heels of his Velcro-close shoes lit up every time he shifted his weight. He stood in a row with four other children in the center of the high-tech classroom. Their gazes were trained on my right hand, where Cici, my puppet and co-teacher, rested.

I sighed. It was difficult to shake the feeling that in front of me were the little emperors I had heard so much about before I came to China. China's one-child policy meant that all of a multigenerational family's attention and resources were heaped on just one kid. The result was expected to be a generation that had been spoiled rotten, the so-called little emperors.

The uncomfortable implication was that if these were China's little emperors, I was their court jester. After all, I was dressed in a highlighter-orange jumpsuit, with my right arm elbow-deep in a green turtle hand puppet. I taught weekends at a training school for wealthy preschool and kindergarten students. The national media, government, and parents alike have attacked China's education system for producing good testers but not good thinkers, creators, or team players. My school offered a solution. It aimed to plant the seeds of English through immersion learning while its young students became comfortable with technology. It emphasized group play and team building. Students who grow up as only children often need practice playing with others their age, especially in China where the emphasis on rote learning is high and the number of children with siblings is low.

I looked at the turtle puppet. He looked at the crowd. Together we pronounced the word *microscope* with exaggerated slowness. His wide-set, googly eyes bounced and bobbled as he surfed over the heads of Jiangguo and his classmates, asking them in English, "What amazing technology are we going to learn about today?" The two young Chinese teaching assistants translated in singsong voices.

"Repeat after me," I said. "Microscope." The teaching assistants coaxed the five young students to repeat the word *microscope* with them.

To my surprise, a murmur of "microscope" bubbled up from the back of the class. I looked at Jiangguo and his classmates. None of them had so much as opened their mouths.

The class door at the back of the room shut abruptly, and Jiangguo's grandmother looked at me guiltily from behind the glass partition. At the back of class an entourage of thirty adults, five or six for each of the students, stood watch over the class, separated from us by the big glass partition, a setup that bore a striking resemblance to a zoo. They shifted noisily. Becky, one of the TAs (they all went by their chosen English names at work), turned and politely reminded the crowd to please let the students answer for themselves. Sherry, the school manager, moved around them with her electric smile and tailored dress, trying to convince the parents to buy larger packages of classes. Many complied. With only one child to spend on, why not?

Jiangguo's family was easy to pick out. As Jiangguo munched on his thumb, his mother, father, paternal grandmother, paternal grandfather, maternal grandmother, and an uncle watched anxiously. His grandparents could be seen pointing at him and commenting on his progress, his interaction with other kids, or the way he held a seashell. His mother stood in back, arms folded across her chest, beaming at her son and scribbling on a writing pad she kept with her at all times. His father's hair was combed back exactly like Jiangguo's. I suspected the same person had styled both. All his relatives stood throughout the hour-long class, watching intensely as little Jiangguo twiddled a microscope, fiddled with a computer program, played with a robot, or just stood quietly in the middle of the room.

Through the classroom window we could see the world's largest LED screen reigning over the most developed part of the city, the gleaming new glass and steel of Suzhou Industrial Park. The district, like many of China's city centers, had not existed a decade or two earlier. I looked back at this group of little emperors: a class of five students with a three-person teaching team and an entourage of more than thirty adults pressed against the glass in back. I sighed again.

During a break, Sherry asked what was wrong. I told her I felt like a performer for these little emperors.

Without missing a beat, Sherry nodded toward the back of the class. "The original little emperors are in the back of the room," she said, flashing her electric smile. And then, with a no-nonsense look, she told me, "Now get back to class."

Stunned, I stood for a moment in a corner of the classroom before doing the math. The Western media had dubbed only children "the little emperors" in the early 1990s. Today, the demographic created by the one-child policy—four grandparents and two parents who focus all their attention on one child—is referred to as the "4:2:1 problem." I was so used to taking the "little emperor" concept for granted that it had not occurred to me the original one-child generation had already grown up.

China has been tracking the developmental pitfalls experienced by generations of only children for decades, long before we in the West started paying attention. In 1987, when China's first only children were turning seven, China released a propaganda film called *China's Little Emperors*—a "how-not-to" film about raising the first generation of only children. It plays like a Chinese child-rearing version of *Reefer Madness* (which claimed the effects of "marijuana cigarettes" were the loss of sanity and committing aggravated assault with an axe). Overindulgence and excessive pressure, the Chinese movie claimed, would lead to societal ruin. The overriding fear was that when these hundreds of millions of spoiled only children grew up, they would unleash their awfulness on the country.

Many Westerners have asked me, "What kinds of contributors can these little emperors be to society given their excess-oriented foundation?" Hedge fund managers want to know, "What are those little emperors looking to *buy*, exactly?" Even foreigners who have worked in China for years will often grumble, "Those spoiled little emperors are a pain in my . . ." as a kid steps on their shoes at Pizza Hut.

Sherry was right. The first group of these only children had already grown up. They are my friends, classmates, tutors, teachers, bosses, managers (Sherry included), and, technically, clients. As I looked out the window at the new Suzhou Industrial Park, it was tough not to think that if the stereotype of little emperors has not changed in thirty years, it is nearly the only thing in all of China to have remained the same.

二

The front gates of Suzhou University open up to the part of the city called Suzhou Industrial Park, a mix of new residential apartment buildings and factory headquarters. The city district is the manifestation of Deng Xiaoping's admiration for Singapore. The Southeast Asian "tiger economy" had achieved large economic success under the leadership of the late Prime Minister Lee Kuan Yew. Lee's government achieved its economic success without emulating the democratic style of governance in the West, and so became a model for Chinese political minds to study. Deng was impressed with their social order and city planning, and in 1994 Prime Minister Lee and the Chinese vice premier signed an experimental agreement to develop Suzhou Industrial Park together.

The layout of the city district has a sprawling feel compared with other parts of Suzhou—it is spacious and carefully planned, and the roads are as broad as highways. Along the park's wide lanes the logos of Microsoft, IBM, Oracle, L'Oréal, and Samsung beckon from the sides of new industrial warehouses.

On the other side of Suzhou University, across a small river and following paths meandering between trees and red brick school buildings, the back gates of campus opened up to old Suzhou, the Suzhou that earned the moniker "heaven on earth" centuries ago. The university's back gate opens onto a narrow alley lined with cheap student eats. Come nightfall, college students streamed out the back gate and into Suzhou's milky bluish-black twilight, splitting off into "fly dives," bare-bones eateries known for good food and minimal décor.

Some broke off and formed a line at the Egg Wrap Grandmaster's stall, the most famous savory crepe wrap stall in Suzhou. Each wrap cost the equivalent of sixty-five cents and could feed two. Often the line was twenty students long, grouped in clusters of two or three. Students looked on in silence as the grandmaster, with an expert flick of his wrist, methodically dropped the mixture in a thin circle on the griddle, cracked an egg on top, and sprinkled it with chopped scallions and spices. A hundred paces from the grandmaster's stall, the alley converged on an eight-hundred-year-old canal. At dawn and dusk an old man punted a small boat up and down the waterway, ducking beneath the arched bridges and the willow branches. He used a net attached to a long bamboo pole to fish trash out of the canal. Not half a mile away in the other direction, Samsung's robust semiconductor factory clicked and whirred. At the end of each day, I would make the trip by electric bike from my job at Suzhou Industrial Park, through the university, and out the back gates to eat at Trade Winds.*

At the time, Trade Winds was the most modern restaurant on the alley. Opened by a graduate of Suzhou University, it featured a long

---

*Several years ago, many cities around China outlawed motorbikes, both as a way to clean up city air and incentivize green industries. Now, the streets are packed with electric mopeds that people charge every night in their apartment complexes.

countertop that encircled the griddle and gas ranges, which made talking easy. The owner claimed he modeled it after the late-night tavern on *Midnight Canteen*, a Japanese TV show that was a mixture of melodrama and food worship; the show had a major cult following in China. Trade Winds's walls were covered with Polaroid pictures of young people. If you hung out there, each face from the Polaroid wall would eventually squeeze through the sliding door and hunker down at the bar for a bowl of the signature red-cooked pork noodles. The place had a homey feel, and many students treated it as such, eating and chatting there after class. It was a community.

Xiao Lu was a central part of that community. A particularly sharp bioengineering student, Xiao Lu was a customer-turned-employee who worked at Trade Winds when he wasn't in class. He washed dishes and talked with the customers after the lunchtime rush. All the while his biochemistry books were open at eye level on the top shelf over the sink. He often read while he worked. Once, when just the two of us were in the restaurant, he told me that his happiest memories were from Trade Winds. Soon, though, he would graduate, and the pressure of finding a job was beginning to eat at his nerves. I would watch him at the countertop, meticulously filling out countless applications for chemical engineering positions, while the rest of the students talked during their break from class.

Mostly they talked about school and dating like any group of twentysomethings. But they didn't shy away from contentious topics—job discrimination, sexism, Taiwan, Tibet, and the recent relaxing and subsequent cancellation of the one-child policy—at some point they talked about everything. Months after the Sandy Hook school shooting in the States, we talked about gun laws and, inevitably, Tiananmen Square. In 2014, a small number of China's police in Shanghai were, for the first time ever, allowed to carry guns while on patrol, rekindling debates about gun laws and the most famous and violent government crackdown in recent Chinese history. One popular argument was that the Tiananmen Square Incident (or Tiananmen Square Massacre, depending on whose history you're reading) spiraled out of control not only because of politics but also because of China's tight gun laws. I listened as an engineering student explained that because China's police did not carry guns, the military had to step in to stop the students from physically storming the capitol. "In America they'd say they were committing an act of terror against the capitol," he claimed. Some disagreed. Others nodded. Most just listened.

One day I walked hurriedly into Trade Winds after work and slammed the door behind me. Xiao Lu raised his eyebrows and looked up from his books. A few regulars sitting at the bar greeted me. "What's up?" Xiao Lu asked.

Work had been frustrating. As I peeled off my orange jumpsuit with the school's logo on the front, I explained to the Trade Winds regulars how excessive it all seemed: one foreign teacher (me), two TAs, the head of the school, my green turtle puppet Cici, and a mass of family members all teaming up to teach these five-year-olds how to say a few words in English.

My frustration soon degenerated into criticism of my students. "This is why China's only children have such a bad reputation abroad," I ranted. "Jiangguo and the rest of my class are all little emperors!"

My words landed with a thud. People sitting next to me stared quietly into their bowls of noodles.

Wei Yu, a twenty-year-old economics student, broke the silence. She looked at me sternly and said, "A little outdated with this kind of 'little emperor' talk, aren't we?"

Gesturing with a pair of chopsticks, Zhang Jing, who was finishing his master's in mathematics, added, "This is like saying, 'You know how American youth love their hopscotch and nickel arcades!' "

Xiao Lu had been quiet behind the counter as he worked on the stack of bowls and chopsticks in the sink. He finished wiping off the metal base of the large rice cooker and put it down on the counter.

"That term, 'little emperor,' is total bullshit."

I was taken aback. Xiao Lu doesn't swear.

"Why?" I asked.

Xiao Lu took a deep breath and threw the dish towel over his shoulder. "As a foreigner, you cannot begin to understand the tremendous amount of pressure put on your little students," Xiao Lu said. "Think about what you're seeing next time you're in class: six people standing around watching a five-year-old learn English. Do you think that kid wants to be there? Wants to be studying English on his Saturday instead of playing in the park? Wants all that focused attention? No chance."

The students around the countertop stared at Xiao Lu. He had rarely put that many sentences together in a day, let alone a minute or two.

"But it is the only way a family thinks their kid can get ahead today," he continued, "so his parents and grandparents watch him, groom him, tutor him meticulously to make sure he will be able to get good grades, get into college, get a job, marry young, buy an apartment, and ultimately help support his parents and grandparents. We get more attention, more food, more resources. In exchange we give up our youth."

Taking the dish towel off his shoulder, he turned around, flipped the faucet on, and turned the page of his biochemistry book with the back of his hand.

"In summary: two characters," Xiao Lu said, turning around once more and holding up two fingers in the air, "压力, *yālì*."

Pressure.

三

On the following weekend, back in the classroom, Jiangguo had won me over. He was shy but curious, enthusiastic but well mannered. He played well with the other children and engaged with the lesson material. In spite of my grumpiness the week before, I couldn't help but like him. On the day we were doing our "Ocean Explorers" unit, the other teachers were hiding seashells around the classroom. As I peered at them from behind the whiteboard, I observed two kneeling TAs as they helped little Jiangguo to enlarge the fragments of a seashell under the microscope. In the background his entourage of family observers nodded approvingly.

The effects of China's one-child policy look different all across the country. On the east coast, in the ethnically Han-dominated, wealthier major cities like Suzhou, the government strictly enforced the one-child policy. But it had a host of loopholes, especially for China's ethnic minorities and many rural families, so poorer inland provinces were often less affected by the policy. As a result, many poorer, less-educated families were able to have more children. An estimated 150 million families have only one child. Only about a third of all households in China were strictly subjected to the one-child policy, but on the east coast and in most cities in China, that statistic feels impossibly conservative.[1] The Communist Party ultimately abandoned the policy in part because people with less education and rural families were, in effect, repopulating China. In other words, the Party believed its one-child policy was having a negative effect on the "quality"—the government's term—of the population.

Jiangguo stood in the center of the classroom as he learned to program a robotic bumblebee the size of a toy car. Depending on which arrow he pressed on the yellow bee's back and how many times he pressed it, the bee would whir to life and move in a certain direction. Programmed correctly, the bee could navigate mazes we laid out on the floor for the children.

The equipment at the training school was state of the art. Each child was provided with an iPad, all the robotic bumblebees and electronic sets of Legos were top shelf, and our "Pre-K Computer Programmers!" games, as well as the computers they used, were first-rate. Also, foreign teachers, aided by one or two local assistants, taught most classes. The school spared no expense. The teacher-student ratio was often 1:2. It was a privileged group, but far from rare in China.

When the class was dismissed, Jiangguo ran out of the buzzing yellow classroom, through the large glass doors, and into the arms of his grandmother. Soon he had plopped down on her lap to be fed a freshly peeled apple. While I spoke with his mother about his progress, Jiangguo snatched the iPhone out of her hand and navigated to the folder labeled "Kids' Games," and began playing an English learning game in which he selected fruit to feed animals at the zoo.

His mother gestured with a notepad covered in scribbles that caught my attention. From what I could make out from beneath her hand, she had covered the page with notes in both English and Chinese. I caught a glimpse of the word *seashell*. Slowly, I was able to make out all the words we had learned in the last few weeks of class: *microscope, science, seashell, jellyfish, shark, dolphin, amoeba*. Jiangguo's mother had printed them neatly in her notebook, which was now ready to present to Jiangguo like a teacher's whiteboard, with Chinese pronunciation guides next to the words.*

---

*Using Chinese characters to imitate the sounds of English words is still quite common among older Chinese who can't read pinyin, the romanization of the Chinese script that young Chinese now learn alongside or before Chinese characters to stan-

His mother, who spoke excellent English, worked for an international company in Shanghai.

"These notes aren't for you, are they?" I said, pointing at the full pad. She blushed, but did not withdraw the notebook. Instead, she showed me the pages and asked if she had made any mistakes. "It all looks perfect," I replied. She flashed a proud smile at her husband. English levels, especially among middle-aged and older Chinese, are a reflection of worldliness. Her husband and I could communicate only in Chinese.

"These notes are for Jiangguo. They will be his homework tonight."

I looked at her, confused. "I didn't assign any homework."

She laughed. It was the type of laugh that signals the end of a conversation. She turned back to her husband, and I left to do the rounds speaking with the other parents.

Suddenly, broken sobs came tumbling out of a corner of the main waiting room of the school. I recognized the timbre of Jiangguo's little voice. The room full of families turned to look. Just as quickly, they turned away to politely avert their gaze.

There Jiangguo stood, his chest expanding and contracting visibly with the sobs. His six relatives hovered over him. His grandfather and his paternal grandmother held his arm and patted his back, talking over each other as they tried to soothe him. His maternal grandmother and mother were the only ones who seemed unmoved. They continued to hold a sheet of paper in front of him, repeating something I couldn't make out as I walked toward them.

"Mmmmmm. Mmmmmmm. Miiiiiic. Miiiiic. Miiiiic-roooooo. . . ."

---

dardize pronunciation. Older Chinese people say "ha-lou" instead of hello because that is how it is transliterated in Chinese: *hālóu*.

Looking down, I could see the word MICROSCOPE printed in big block letters on the piece of paper. The Chinese translation, 显微镜, *xiǎn wēi jìng* ("lens to make the very small visible"), was written in tidy Chinese script beneath it. It was the first sheet of paper in a stack of twenty.

His mother watched my expression change before stating matter-of-factly, "Jiangguo will have to take the *gāokǎo* [the college entrance exam] only thirteen years from now. He needs to start getting ready. We want to give him a competitive edge."

四

If demography is destiny, as the common saying goes, then for the last six decades China has been tampering with its own fate.

China's one-child policy created a baby bust, an artificial plunge in the average birthrate, through forced and unforced abortions and required family-planning measures. What gets far less attention is that this baby bust came on the heels of, and really in reaction to, the biggest baby boom in human history.

In a thirty-year span—1949–79, the three decades before the one-child policy began—China's population increased by 440 million people. When Mao and the Communists first took over China, they regarded a large population as a strength. Mao banned the import of contraceptives and condemned birth control. At its peak, the average fertility rate in China was nearly seven children per woman.

China's baby boom was also a story of plummeting child mortality rates, a factor that drove the boom at least as much as the banning of birth control. Chairman Mao's rule brought turmoil but also greatly improved the health of the average Chinese family. When Mao took over the country, 30 percent of children were dying before the age of five. Thirty years later, shortly after his death, child mortality had plunged to about 6 percent.[2] Today it is about 1 percent.[3]

In a speech delivered at the Supreme State Conference in 1957, eight years after he and his Communist Party formed the People's Republic of China, Mao stated to those responsible for charting China's future: "China's greatest advantage is our large population; China's greatest weakness is also our large population." China had roughly 20 percent of the world's population but less than 10 percent of its arable land and about 7 percent of its potable water. By the late 1960s, ten years before the one-child policy officially began, Mao feared his population had grown too large. He created the Later, Longer, Fewer program and began forced abortions. The fertility rate plummeted to fewer than three children per woman. By the time the one-child policy began in 1979, three years after Mao's death, the world's largest baby bust was already well under way.

The leading edge of China's giant boomer generation is now in its late sixties. From the front of the classroom I could see China's modern history on full display in the creases etched around the mouths of Jiangguo's grandparents and the bend of their sturdy backs. Although most people did not die prematurely during the Mao era, they merely subsisted. China's baby boomers are almost uniformly shorter than their children by a full head. They endured famine, malnutrition, and hard physical labor as children. Their skin is worn. Their hands are used and rough. When they smile at Jiangguo, the skin around their eyes is a sea of wrinkles. Despite the comparative wealth of their children, Chinese boomers still often dressed in simple Mao-style cotton trousers and jackets.

The hard upbringing of China's boomers played a big role in molding the stereotype of the little emperor. In China a grandparent plays a crucial role in raising children. China is one of the few industrializing countries in the world where 隔代教育, *gédài jiàoyú* ("skip-generation child rearing"), is commonplace. The first generation raises the third generation—grandparents raise their grandchildren or, more commonly now, their only grandchild—thereby freeing both parents to work. Skip-generation child rearing creates a more involved corps of elders, which multiple experts on aging I've spoken with, both Chinese and otherwise, suggest could play a role in keeping China's massive boomer generation healthier and more active than their aging counterparts around the world. Betty, my TA at the school, echoed the thinking of most proponents of skip-generation child rearing: "It gives grandparents a sense of significance. We don't put our grandparents out of sight. They remain an active and much-needed part of society. Sure, there is a bunch of annoying bits [for the child] of having your parents and your grandparents be such a large part of your life. But there are a lot of positives as well."

A grandparent-led childhood is part of why excess, and greater wealth, is so central to the experience of China's only children. A study published in the *International Journal of Behavioral Nutrition and Physical Activity* found that a child raised by grandparents in China is twice as likely to be overweight or obese as a child raised by their parents.[4] Of course. A population that survived hunger during the Great Leap Forward would have no comprehension of the concept of overeating.

China is traditionally more of a "show, don't tell" culture when it comes to the expression of love. Here, food is the most basic unit of love and the most intuitive way for Chinese grandparents to quietly express their devotion. They heap it on. Partially as a result, 23 percent of Chinese boys and 14 percent of girls younger than twenty are now obese or overweight, higher percentages than those found in the populations of Japan and South Korea, the East Asian powerhouses that developed before China did.[5]

五

When the one-child policy was first decreed, vast numbers of people were thrown into a panic. Some even protested, despite the risk of government retribution. In 1985, six years after the policy began, protesting citizens in the southern inland province of Guangxi carried a big red banner with white characters that read:

> 计划生育好, 政府来养老。
>
> *(FAMILY PLANNING IS FINE; GOVERNMENT, COME CARE FOR THE OLD.)*

The pushback against the one-child policy was not "our body, our rights." Instead the country wondered, "Who will care for our old?"

Chinese children are, by tradition, a retirement plan. China operates on a system often summarized by the six-hundred-year-old phrase "养儿防老, 积谷防饥," pronounced *yǎng ér fáng lǎo, jī gǔ fáng jī*. It means, "As one stores up grain against lean years, one also rears children against old age."

Retirement is also partly why so many more boys than girls survived infancy in only-child households.* Tradition dictated that a son

---

*According to the United Nations, before implementation of the one-child policy, sixty males and fifty-three females died before their first birthday per one thousand live births of each gender in China. By the 1990s the figures were twenty-six males and thirty-three girls died per thousand live births before the age of one. In the 2000s, twenty-one boys and twenty-eight girls died per thousand live births. The reasons for these deaths included accidents and illnesses. But "it would be a 'fair inference' to

would stay in his family and a daughter would join the family she married into. *Dream of the Red Chamber* (1792), considered one of the four greatest novels in Chinese literature, describes a married daughter as being "like spilled water" because she no longer nourishes the family tree. That's why Chinese children have different words for their maternal and paternal grandparents. They call their paternal grandparents Grandma and Grandpa. But they traditionally call their maternal grandmother 外婆, or *wàipó*—"Outside Grandmother." Traditionally, only your father's parents are considered part of your direct family.

China has embedded the idea of caring for elders within the larger notion of what it means to be a good person. Inscribed in the bedrock of modern interpretations of Confucianism is this saying: "Of all behavior, filial piety comes first" (Bù xiào yǒu sān, wú hòu wéi dà). It inextricably ties the moral concept of "good person" to "good son or daughter."

But it was easier to be a good person in the past. Historically, in China, most people did not age and retire. They died. When Jiangguo's grandparents were born in 1950, the average life expectancy at birth was between thirty-five and forty years old. Alongside the baby boom and the incredible drop in infant mortality, China in the last century has undergone one of history's greatest longevity revolutions: by 1980, China's life expectancy rose to over sixty years old, and today it is over seventy-five.[6]

---

suggest that infanticide has had a role in this, says Jonathan Cave, an economist at Warwick University . . . Actual infanticide . . . is rare, though . . . some families, faced with limited resources, may have chosen to prioritize boys in terms of healthcare and nurturing. Couples in rural areas were permitted to have a second child if the first was a girl—this was partly an effort to reduce neglect and infanticide, says Cave." See Justin Parkinson, "Five Numbers That Sum Up China's One-Child Policy," *BBC News Magazine*, October 29, 2015, http://www.bbc.com/news/magazine-34666440.

So, historically, the life cycle was simple: you'd turn eighteen, have children, raise them, they'd turn eighteen, and then two years later you'd be dead. Grandparenthood was usually a relatively quick experience. Caring for the old was also straightforward because you had help: a Chinese family had a lot of children and few, if any, elderly. The Confucian society was based on China's demographic structure, which was historically shaped like a pyramid. At the bottom was a broad base of young people; at the top was a narrowing segment of the elderly. Built around the family, Chinese society was stable and self-supporting.

Not anymore. China's population is getting older. The number of Chinese citizens older than sixty-five will increase from 100 million in 2005 to 329 million by 2050. The boomer generation was able to pull China out of poverty and fuel China's manufacturing boom partly because they were so numerous. In 1980 the median age in China was twenty-two. Now the median age is about thirty-five years. The Pew Research Center projects that the median age will be forty-six by 2050.[7] As the age of China's working class changes, the type of work they are able to do also changes. Jiangguo's generation is too few in number to sustain an economy dependent on manufacturing. If they want to be able to support aging Chinese, they will have to earn more and work better jobs.

Jiangguo's education is both an extremely local issue and a national priority. Jiangguo's family pressured him to perform well in school for their and his well-being, and the future of his country will rely heavily on his intelligence and ability to innovate. Jiangguo's generation will have to shoulder the tremendous economic burden of caring for their aging country. Long life is a blessing, but it comes at a sizable financial and cultural cost.

So Jiangguo spends his Saturdays learning English words for a test he will take thirteen years from now. His success represents the difference between China's transforming itself into a new era of continued growth and stalling under the weight of its aging demography. For China's so-called little emperors, uneasy lies the head that wears the crown.

六

The applications Xiao Lu filled out during dishwashing lulls at Trade Winds paid off. He was offered a position as a chemical engineer at L'Oréal. Naturally, we celebrated over a meal. We took the bullet train to Shanghai, which had cut a three-hour drive down to a twenty-three-minute glide, for some refined dining. We watched Suzhou blur into Shanghai in a matter of minutes. Partly because of its proximity to Shanghai, Suzhou had been transformed from a "heaven on earth" to just another suburb of China's megalopolis of twenty-four million people. Industrialization brought wealth, but Suzhou has lost much of its ancient beauty and charm. Yet in a sense Suzhou remained a heaven on earth to a Chinese family: Jobs there paid well and the air quality was not too bad. It was known nationally as a great place to raise a family.

Xiao Lu's new job had come through at exactly the right time for him. A week earlier someone had posted a notice on the back gate of Suzhou University; the notice consisted of only the character 拆, *chāi*, a simple word that has become emblematic of China's persistent development. It means "to tear down." The same notice was pasted on the doors of all the establishments along the narrow food alley, including Trade Winds. *The Financial Times* estimates that 40 percent of Chinese local government revenues come from land sales; Guan Qingyou, director of Tsinghua University Center for China Studies—

Energy and Climate Project, believes that number to be as high as 74 percent.[8] Soon, 拆 would be spray-painted in red on many of the old restaurants and apartment buildings along the student alley, including my small concrete apartment building. The street was one of the few areas in Suzhou that had kept its local, quiet charm, but now it would be razed to develop a tourism district.

Despite the rapidity of development in Suzhou, emerging from any subway station in Shanghai feels like stepping out into Las Vegas. With all the flashing lights, people, cars, and noises, it's a city that feels ready to burst. Xiao Lu and I reeled for a minute before transferring to the subway line that would take us to the restaurant.

A family of five squeezed behind us into the subway car. Xiao was surprised to see more than one child and speculated that they were Miao Chinese, perhaps able to have more children as part of the exemption to the one-child policy for ethnic minorities. For most, having a second child without paying the fine for doing so would make it impossible to get a local *hùkǒu*, an identification card that verifies you are a local resident and allows you to attend school. Without the hùkǒu, which is often described as an internal passport, second children were essentially considered illegal migrants in their own cities.

The fine for having a second child in China once was many thousands of dollars, depending on which province you were from. The fine increased with income and was almost always double a family's yearly wages. The highest fine was paid by the filmmaker and choreographer of the Beijing Olympics' opening ceremony, Zhang Yimou, who was reported to have paid $1.2 million for his third child.

The one-child policy was relaxed in 2013 and then abolished entirely in 2015 in an attempt to regenerate China's workforce. Xiao

Lu and I had discussed the changes. Now couples who are both only children are allowed to have a second child. The problem is, most families are choosing not to.

Xiao Lu looked at the family of five. "When I was growing up, my neighbors had two children. They just paid the fine," he said. "For my neighbors the fine wasn't so bad, really. My neighbors were better off than most and had savings. They decided they'd rather have the kids than a large bank account."

Young Chinese couples today seem to have little desire to have a second child. Before the one-child policy was done away with, thirteen provinces had fertility rates significantly below the allowances, and the fertility rate has changed the most in those urban and coastal areas where the policy was most strict.[9] Cities like Shanghai and Beijing now have fertility rates of about 0.7, which means women are having only one child or none at all. Demographers joke that urbanization is the best form of birth control, and China's fertility statistics show that in an increasingly expensive and competitive China, families were choosing to have fewer children, even when the one-child policy was still in effect.

"When I was young, I was able to attend the extracurricular clubs and courses, which cost money. When I had trouble in a class, we were able to afford a tutor," Xiao Lu told me. "When I was in high school, our house had a computer and Internet. I took gāokǎo study courses online. I never had to look after anyone younger than myself. I was given the tools to help me succeed in life.

"Now I live in Suzhou. I just got a highly desirable job, and those other kids with siblings are all still stuck in our hometown with few future opportunities. You know why?"

Xiao Lu did not wait for me to answer: "Because my family was able to invest all of their resources in me."

From Xiao Lu's perspective as a single child, the decision for many to not have a second child is an issue of competitiveness. Why have a second child if you'd only be putting both at a disadvantage?

When representative samples of a thousand schoolchildren from four Chinese provinces were examined for a comparison of the success rates of only children and firstborn and later-born children, the study found that only children significantly outperformed multi-child households on academic tests. Entitlement, self-centeredness, depression, anxiety—none of these long-predicted side effects were found to be present at significantly higher rates in only children. The study concluded, "Taken together, these results suggest that the one-child policy in China is not producing a generation of little emperors." Rather, the only side effects seemed to be superior testing ability and an extra inch or two around the waist. The study found that single children in two provinces were more obese.[10]

Xiao Lu watched the children play together in the subway car and shook his head.

"I was able to be competitive enough to get into this university only because I am an only child. It is the first step to being competitive in life, to being able to attract a wife, look after my parents in old age, and support my child."

"Just one child?" I asked.

Xiao Lu grinned, "It will depend on what I can afford. But, yes. I think it's for the best."

4

How to Eat Your Parents

China's Housing and Marriage Markets Collide

Li described himself as average. At twenty-six he was of average height, had average looks, and held a slightly above-average job at a bank. His suit was tailored slim, industry standard. The black-framed glasses he wore were generic; up to 90 percent of young Chinese suffer from near-sightedness.*[1] His thick black hair was cut close along the sides and a bit longer on top, the haircut you'd get if you walked into any barbershop anywhere in China and said, "I'd like a haircut." When he talked about money, kids, politics, or relationships, his expression remained blank, befitting his dispassionate role as a bank teller. In China his job commands a certain amount of respect. His parents beam when they tell their friends. "Don't be

---

*Researchers have established a link between education styles and nearsightedness. Whereas China used to report around 20 percent of its population suffered from myopia, that number has soared to 90 percent for teenagers and young adults. Korea, who boasts another memorization-centric Confucian education system, reports 96 percent of students suffer from nearsightedness compared to a third or less in England, the United States, and Germany.

impressed," Li said every time anyone seemed on the verge of complimenting his position. "I'm not the guy planning investments."

By most measures, Li was successful. He came from a lower-class family and had recently entered China's new middle class. It was a transition the vast majority of people were pushing, and being pushed by the government, to make. Li was at the top of his graduating class in high school, which, he pointed out, might have meant something if he had been from a first-tier city like Beijing or Shanghai or Guangzhou or the newly minted first-tier city Chengdu. But because his hometown is a fifth-tier city and he was now living in a fourth-tier city, being first in his high school class didn't mean much. Still, he hadn't cracked under the weight of the fearsome gāokǎo and had gone to a good college. Although he had harbored hopes to study abroad, his English, by his own admission, was never good enough. "And my parents couldn't afford it anyway." His income was around 9,000 renminbi (RMB) a month, or US$1,400, and a fair notch above the national average. His work and wage earned the respect of everyone who asked. In China everyone asked.

Yet, despite all these obvious successes, Li was a parent eater.

"You're a what?" I asked, sure I'd misheard.

"A parent eater," he said patiently, shrugging his shoulders ever so slightly in his padded suit. "I eat my parents."

二

When I first read about parent eaters, 啃老族, *kěn lǎo zú*, I thought the expression was a joke. China's demographic predicament is grave, and I thought this was the often-boisterous Chinese Internet responding with a solution: If we have too many old people, why not simply eat them?

Chinese netizens are well known for their knack for linguistic contortions. For a stretch in the early 2010s, online forum goers had taken aim at their country's rampant chicken-fart problem. The Chicken Fart Crisis, as it came to be known, happened at a time when the double-digit growth of China's gross domestic product was driving up housing and food prices far faster than wages. The result was the average Chinese person *felt* significantly poorer, despite a consistent wage.

People flocked to online forums to air their complaints about the rising GDP. Before long, *GDP* became a red flag for China's censors who were attempting to limit public discourse on contentious topics. How do you write about GDP without using the term? The Chinese language is ripe for punning, and when discussing hot-button social issues Chinese netizens have become especially adept at finding words that sound the same (have the same phonetic base) but are pronounced with different tones.* They do this to evade the word-searching government censors.

So people began writing about chicken farts. In Chinese "chicken farts" is written out as 鸡的屁, *jī de pì*, a close homophone to GDP. "The rapid rise in chicken farts in China's major cities is ruining the quality of life!" people wrote angrily.

If chicken farts could plague the country, why not parent eaters? While I was living in Chengdu, I took a private lesson twice a week

---

*Even the slang for censorship has found a homophone to avoid the censors. Censors claim they are "maintaining public harmony" by removing items from the Internet, so when netizens found something had been censored, they would complain about comments or articles that had been harmonized. Soon the censors caught on. Netizens then substituted the term *river crab* for *harmony* because the terms are homophonic in Mandarin but have different tones: the difference between *héxié*—harmony—and *héxiè*—river crab—when spoken is a failing fourth tone in the second syllable. Now Chinese say sensitive articles are often "river crabbed."

with Tina, my lighthearted, joke-loving teacher of Chinese. I sent her an article about parent eaters with a laughing emoticon. The next day when I went into class, Tina had a printout of the article on her desk. It was covered in red ink, bold arrows, and hard, decisive characters. Tina shot me a cold look and pointed at the article. "What is funny here?" she asked.

It turned out the parent eater phenomenon in China was no joke. A parent eater is a young adult who continues to rely on his parents for financial support past the age deemed socially acceptable. In his well-distributed essay, the Chinese sociologist Chen Hui explained that China's parent eaters are young adults who have reached employment age but lack financial stability and so undergo what he terms "delayed social weaning."[2]

What Chen describes is a symptom of the changing way of life in China, friction between a traditional way of thinking and the realities of a rapidly shifting country.

Few shifts were as tectonic in scale as the exodus from farmland to city center. Starting in the late 1980s, a population roughly the size of that of the entire European Union moved from China's countryside to its city centers.

The government's push to urbanize was designed, in part, to stimulate consumption, and it worked. Food, water, heating, clothing, experiences—the trappings of city life—all are expenses that can be minimal in the more self-sufficient countryside. In the city the very definition of *need* was changing. What makes life in the city good? An iPhone? An apartment? A car? For the government, more consumption means hitting GDP growth targets. For people, especially young people, it means a tremendous new pressure to buy, to have, and to own.

"Parent eating began in the West," Tina informed me. "It is

probably another example of the negatives of more interaction with Western culture, like fast food, pornography, materialism . . ."—and then, as we often did, we argued for the rest of my lesson period.

Tina is correct that the phenomenon of adult children who rely on their parents is a global one, but she is wrong about the causes. In the West the biggest reason behind our own parent-eater problem was the global recession, followed by technology, which killed even white-collar jobs such as office support, and high levels of student debt. In the United Kingdom, the number of people aged sixteen to twenty-four who are not in education, employment, or training (and known by the acronym NEET) was high even before the recession and continues to be higher than the unemployment rate for the labor force in general. In the United States, "boomerang kids" continue to return home to live with their parents after graduating from college. A 2014 *New York Times* article claimed that one in five Americans in their twenties and early thirties was living with parents, while 60 percent of young adults received parental financial support.[3] The same was true in Germany, which has *Nesthockers*; Italy, which has *bamboccioni*, meaning big babies; France, which has *la generation kangourou*; and even Taiwan, which has *nítè zú*, a transliteration of NEET.[4] Tina was right in that parent eating is now prevalent in the West, but China has been doing it for centuries—and was less affected by, and recovered faster from, the Great Recession.[5]

Traditionally China had always had a bit of parent eating in its family system. China's pioneering sociologist Fei Xiaotong described the Confucian system of intergenerational relationships as 反哺模式, *fǎnbǔ móshì*, a "return and feed" model.[6] The first generation takes care of the second generation, and then, later in life, the second generation is expected to return and take care of the first generation.

In layman's terms, the Chinese system was one of "I eat you, you eat me later." Parent eating was a tradeoff, not just tolerated but also expected. In China families rarely split until new families were created; a young man and a young woman would rarely leave their family home until they married and started their own family together. Their new home would be part of the severance package. In many Western countries a twenty-five-year-old still living at home risks being called a slacker. In China a twenty-five-year-old man still living at home is called a bachelor.

The return-and-feed model was never built to support kids for so long in an environment so costly as China's modern cities. Couples used to have children soon after they married, and parents' lives were short. A child's reliance on parents would end when the child married at eighteen and moved next door, where costs of living were reasonable. When parents subsequently had to lean on their children—the back half of the return-and-feed model—their dependence would not last long because parents would, on average, die before turning forty. A culture within which living was inexpensive, life expectancy was short, and people married young mitigated the stress on both the parents and the children.

Today young men and women need to go to college to get jobs, so the average age of marriage nationally has been pushed back to twenty-seven for men and twenty-five for women. In cities that number is much higher, breaking thirty for women in Shanghai in 2013.[7]

The result is that young people feel squeezed by tradition and necessity. Li told me, "We are told we need to get college degrees to succeed. Then, while we get college and lean on our parents for support, we're labeled parent eaters. We can't win." The "delayed social weaning" is, in part, the necessity to earn a degree and save more for marriage.

The psychological stress from dependency on their parents is sizable. Sixty-two percent of China's post-90s generation say their closest relationship in the world is with their parents.[8] The massive migration to cities in China means that young people often live away from their parents for the first time in Chinese history. The National Bureau of Statistics estimated there were roughly 300 million people working outside their hometowns for at least six months in 2014. Li is one of them. The distance, though, does not mean parents and children are not as close, or that adult children want to be worse sons and daughters to their parents. "How am I supposed to feel?" Li asks, "A grown man needing to ask his parents for help."

And while Chinese young people are having an existential crisis, their parents are going broke by footing the bill for their child's urban existence in China.

The whole parent-eating phenomenon has sparked intense interest in how different cultures raise their children. The most common question I was asked was, "Is it true that American families cut their child off financially after the age of eighteen?"

Tina and Li shared one characteristic that distinguishes China's parent eaters from others around the world: both were gainfully employed at well-paid jobs.

I began to subtly broach the topic with a number of my twenty- to thirty-year-old friends who had jobs: How much, if at all, are your parents helping to support you financially? Jing Jing, a yoga teacher at a ritzy studio in Chongqing, received significant financial support from her parents every month. Yang worked for the government, and he was living in an apartment his parents had bought for him. Xiao Ye ran a hostel, but her parents still wired money into her account every month. Dozens of friends and acquaintances and masses of bloggers and commenters airing their grievances online all confessed to being some version of a parent eater.

And these were not just recent college graduates. Most surprising was the number of young people in their late twenties and early thirties; all were making above-average wages, and a fair number were married apartment owners with kids of their own, yet they still depended heavily on financial support from their parents.

三

When I walked into Li's apartment with him, the TV was on. His wife was watching *A Beijing Love Story* while tidying up. Their apartment was new. The flat screen TV was large—Li liked to watch European soccer leagues in high definition. They had an electric mahjong table that we'd play on later that night with his friends. At the end of a game, a round plate rises from the center of the table, revealing a space into which we'd push the 144 tiles from our last game, and a new set, organized in neat rows, would push out from the inner workings of the table in front of all four players. The two bedrooms were well furnished, and the couple had a stationary bike to the left of the TV. "Work has gotten Li a little belly," his wife kidded. Clearly, they were doing well.

Li motioned to me that it was time to go eat. We walked down from his fifth-story apartment into the fourth-tier city of Bijie, in Guizhou Province. When I told a friend from Chengdu where I was headed, she responded, "I didn't know China had fourth-tier cities." It does, and, although it is relatively unknown outside the province, the mountainous, misty city of Bijie was packed with 6.5 million residents. With a population nearly twice the size of Berlin, Bijie's population has doubled twice since 2000. Yet Bijie is only the fifty-fourth-largest city in China. The Chinese government's separate efforts to develop western China and encourage urbanization sent people to Bijie and the surrounding areas to look for jobs and a life away from the countryside. Between 2011 and 2013, China used more cement than the United States had used during the twentieth century.[9] Every inch of Bijie seemed to be covered with a film of yellow-gray dust from the perpetual construction.

"How much are apartments in your hometown?" Li asked me.

I shrugged and said I didn't know.

He stopped on the sidewalk, leaning backward to counterbalance the incline of Bijie's hilly roads.

"How do you not know?"

"I just don't know," I told him. Li raised his eyebrows.

I asked Li what apartment prices are like in Bijie. Li finally began to walk toward the restaurant again.

"Thirty-four hundred renminbi per square meter," he replied without hesitation. That's about US $47 per square foot.

"That seems expensive for a fourth-tier city," I said.

Li shrugged. "Not bad. Suzhou is nearly six times that at nineteen thousand per square meter [US $260 per square foot]. Didn't you used to live there?" Prices in Suzhou were skyrocketing as transportation to Shanghai became faster and faster.

"What about Beijing?" I asked.

"Forty-seven thousand five hundred RMB per square meter," Li told me. (That's roughly US$654 per square foot. Housing in San Francisco averages about US$900 per square foot; Berlin, about US$425 per square foot.)

"Shanghai?"

"Forty-three thousand RMB per square meter," or about US$598 per square foot.

"Tianjin? Dalian? Sanya?"

"Nineteen thousand; ten thousand; seventeen thousand six hundred RMB," Li replied. "I checked this morning."

I took out my phone and checked one of the many housing apps. All of Li's price quotes were accurate within 200 RMB.

Ask anyone in their twenties what current housing prices are in China's major cities, and they will recite them with scientific accuracy and a touch of religious awe. A handful of friends have related to me nightmares they'd had about housing costs. When Suzhou's housing prices rose by 44 percent in 2016, friends who had planned to live there mutinied; they picked up their things and left for neighboring cities that were less expensive. Other friends who had already bought a place to live in Suzhou celebrated their smart investment.

Parent eating today is a strange mutation, an adaptation by young people to finance their costly urban lives. Liebig's law of the minimum states that growth is limited by the necessity present in the least amount. Apartments are not exactly scarce in China. Despite the ongoing migration to many Chinese cities, China has thirteen million empty homes. China's developers have been creating more supply than there is demand in many places. Cities that remain largely unpopulated are often called ghost towns. In part, they exist because urbanization is a relatively safe bet. Between 1990 and 2015, China's urban population grew from 26 percent of the population to 56 percent, a difference of around 450 million people, or the entire US population plus two United Kingdoms.[10] The government plans to have 70 percent of its population living in cities by 2030, another 250 million city dwellers.[11] Bijie's dusty buildings and quadrupled population fresh from the countryside testify to that. Developers seem to wager that the apartments will fill up over time.

Still, apartments are China's scarce necessity because they are priced as if they are incredibly few. According to the International Monetary Fund's price-to-wage ratio for housing, seven of the ten most expensive cities in the world for residential property are in China. As *Forbes* has reported, an apartment in a coastal second-tier city like Xiamen can cost US$300,000, whereas the average annual wage is about US$12,000.[12]

Why do Chinese continue to buy? Because, for young men especially, owning an apartment is viewed as the essential first step toward being eligible for marriage.

四

Li breathed deeply, appreciating the night. The mountain air in Bijie was cool and damp. When the wind stirred, it blew the pollution from factories out of the city. On the side of a bus, where you often find an ad, the government proclaimed this slogan in confident yellow type: STRIVE TOWARD THE ESTABLISHMENT OF A COMPREHENSIVE MIDDLE CLASS! Li flicked his cigarette to the curb, and we stepped into the restaurant he had chosen.

Northern Guizhou Province has excellent food, a mix of Sichuanese spices and techniques from the various minority cultures of China's third-poorest province. Guizhou is a land filled with the lush green mountain ranges and winding rivers of classical Chinese painting, but what makes the province so beautiful also isolated it culturally and economically from the rest of China for centuries. Roads were difficult to build through mountains and across rivers, so pockets of minority cultures developed naturally in isolation from the main thread of Han culture in other parts of China. Limited access also meant inhibited economic potential. Without a link to the outside, Guizhou could not take part in China's export-led economy.

Li seemed emotionally frayed. He had recently returned from a week of celebrating Chinese New Year in his hometown. He'd had to face the mythic question-asking task force known as 七姑八姨, *qīgū bāyí*, or the "seven aunts and eight uncles."* Each year young Chinese avidly read the online strategies published for facing the thorough inquiries by their seven aunts and eight in-laws into their love life, finances, living conditions, exercise regime, the number of times they eat out each week, the consistency of their mealtimes, the average time at which they awaken each morning, their methodology for cleaning vegetables bought at local markets, and so on. On the pretext of being concerned family members, this high council of relatives asks unending questions and can issue harsh judgments.

"Going home, everyone asks the same three questions. 'Are you married? How much money do you make? Do you own an apartment?' And I mean everyone," Li had said on the walk to the restaurant. He described the process of going home the way people talk about body searches at the airport—invasive, uncomfortable, and, he felt, unwarranted. "My aunt took my wife aside and asked about the number of times we had sex per week now that we were married. She recommended every other day to optimize our chance of pregnancy."

Li beckoned to the server, who gasped audibly at seeing me and Li seated together. "I've never seen a *living* foreigner before," she said, using perhaps the most unsettling but locally common way of saying

*This phrase directly translates to "seven paternal aunts and eight maternal aunts."

she'd seen Westerners only on TV. "He's from Xinjiang," Li said. She nodded that she understood. It was not the first time I had passed for a Uighur, the Muslim minority from Xinjiang Province, north of Tibet.

After politely asking what I'd like to eat, Li ordered too much food. Chinese etiquette demanded that he order half again as much as we could eat. Leftover food at the end of a meal is a sign of security and abundance, recognized in part as a reaction to social trauma during the hard years of the Cultural Revolution. Among business people and government officials, this excess had become such a problem in China that the government runs national ad campaigns to discourage the practice. Li, though, would not be deterred.

The server came by with six tall bottles of beer, and Li gratefully cracked one open. Unlike uneaten food, untouched bottles of beer at the end of the meal can be returned.

Li filled two small glasses, carefully pouring mine first. We toasted to family.

"What did you think of my apartment?" he asked, setting the beer down on the lacquered wooden table. I told him I liked it.

"Thank you," he said, then laughed, an edge of sourness in his otherwise flat voice. "I will make sure to tell my parents. They bought it for me."

Li took a big swig and mostly stayed quiet, watching a little girl at the table next to us play with an iPhone.

Four beers remained when our food arrived. A whole fish in a sizzling metal pan thunked down on the table. Stir-fried green beans and wood mushrooms, twice-cooked pork, and sweet-and-sour soup hit the table, with more on the way. When the table was completely full, the server stacked the new dishes on the intersections of the other dishes, creating a three-dimensional Chinese food tower. A boy at the table next to us commented on how much food we had. His father looked at Xiao Li, looked at me, and then called to the server to order more for his family.

We dug in. I asked Li if he was worried that his wife had married him *because* of the apartment.

He looked at me blankly before shaking his head. "You're missing the point. My wife loves me," Li said. "I love her. We fell in love and then began dating in college. This isn't the era of arranged marriages anymore.

"But—and this is a big but—her parents' approval of me was an enormous factor in the decision," Li continued. His normally dispassionate features were tinged with a pinkish-red glow from the alcohol. "They demanded that I have an apartment. 'How is this person going to provide for you if he can't guarantee a roof over your and your children's heads?' they said."

A committed host, he pincered a choice piece of pork and put it into my bowl. "And my parents, also of that generation, understand that logic all too well. They said, 'No one will marry our son if he can't even guarantee a roof over our grandchild's head!' "

"So what ends up happening?" I asked. He put his chopsticks down and formed his hands into a bridge, as if counseling someone at the bank. Leaning in, he spoke in an urgent whisper, "My parents got their savings together. My grandparents got some too. We got three generations together, took out most of our savings, and spent it on that one apartment upstairs."

Li sounded pained when he talked about the money his family has spent on him. He heaped more fish-sauce eggplant into my bowl. "There was nothing else to do. My wife's family wouldn't let me marry her without one."

五

Few people have a better understanding of the tangible social pressures of marriage in China than Xu Rong Su, a matchmaker at the marriage market in Shanghai's People's Park. China's new online matchmaking industry racks up hundreds of millions of dollars annually, but Xu's operation was old-school low tech. She sat at a foldout table in a row of other matchmakers with a thick binder in front of her. The binder was full of laminated sheets of paper, the sort of setup kids use to store their favorite baseball cards. The binder, though, was full of people.

Each page was a different advertisement in identical format. The upper left-hand corner featured a big picture; all the necessary statistics took up the rest of the page: age, height, profession, income, and property.

Zhu Geliang
Age: 26
Height: 180 cm
Profession: Bank Manager
Income: 9,000/month
Apartment: Owns

Behind Xu, the park had wrapped hundreds of yards of clothesline around trees and lampposts. Each line was crammed with more laminated ads numbering in the many hundreds, maybe thousands. "My job is to curate these ads. If you want to wade through these thousands of ads, be my guest. If you want to find your wife this month, sit down."

For women, Xu says, the first two stats, age and height, plus the picture in the corner, matter the most, particularly age. The last two, income and property, especially the latter, are most important for men.

Xu explained the basis for the simple universal statistics set out in each ad. To her, especially in a city like Shanghai, some stats stood out more than others. "Owning an apartment is the most basic prerequisite for finding a good match in this day and age. If you don't own an apartment, you're making my job much more difficult. How can you provide security in these tumultuous times without an apartment?"

Like so much involving Chinese relationships and marriage, it came back to 安全感, *ānquángǎn*, the sense of safety or security. My friend Mei, a twenty-two-year-old student at Wuhan University whom I met at Outside Island, a hostel in Chengdu, was about to marry her college boyfriend. Her parents wouldn't agree to it until he bought an apartment. Mei told me, "In China things change so fast and *plans can't keep up with the changes.** In a night your business could evaporate. In half a decade your whole sector can be rendered obsolete. Owning an apartment gives you a feeling of security, something that can't get stripped from you at a moment's notice."† They had considered eloping first—they loved each other—but

---

*If China were to have a sitcom about its last four decades of development, the main character's catchphrase would almost undoubtedly be 计划赶不上变化, or *plans can't keep up with the changes*. It is a commonly used phrase to describe an apartment being torn down, a radical change in technology, a pivot from the government, and all of the good and bad changes that make steadfast long-term planning in China a near impossibility without making enormous room for variability.

†Apartments in China only provide the illusion of ownership. China often exercises eminent domain, seizing land and repurposing it for public projects. Few mass land seizures have been better documented than those associated with the Three Gorges Dam project, which displaced about 1.3 million people. Some people are remunerated poorly, others handsomely. Even displacement can be cast as fortune intervening in China. Some families receive so much money for their property that their sons or daughters are called *chāi èr dài*, "generation demolition money," a play on the famously advantaged *fù èr dài*, "second-generation wealthy," and *guān èr dài*, "second-generation public officials."

doing so would tear her family apart. Finally, her husband's family bought a small apartment in a third-tier city outside Wuhan.

Sohu, one of China's biggest media platforms, ran an article titled "Why Are Chinese Obsessed with Buying Apartments?" The piece likens the ability to buy an apartment to being a good hunter in a tribe: the good hunter harvests resources for his family. The article continues, "In China's collective unconscious there is a serious phobia of 'shortage,' passed on generationally. In recent memory, the vast majority of people remember lacking the most basic of food and clothes." The article, published in 2016, went so far as to say that apartments have the symbolic value of a nurturing womb.[13]

A friend of mine from the University of Hong Kong who was working in Shanghai had agreed to let me try to find him a match at the Shanghai marriage market. He was thirty, had graduated from a top European university, and worked at an international bank. As soon as I listed his stats—financial analyst, nearly six feet tall, high-income apartment owner—people's eyes lit up. I left with a pocketful of phone numbers and flyers, and for weeks I continued to get inquiries about my friend's availability.

While I was chatting with all the parents who were passing out flyers for their sons and daughters or sitting in front of a billboard with their child's relevant statistics, it became clear that women's families were being asked to shoulder some of the financial load of a new apartment in expensive cities like Shanghai.

Just outside the Shanghai marriage market, I met Old Shu, who was packing away the flyers he had made to give to other parents who were seeking a spouse for their child. He handed me one of the sheets. His daughter was twenty-nine, had studied abroad, and had a job in finance. Old Shu believed she was a catch. He asked to hear about my friend. When he heard my friend is in finance, he said,

"See, common interests!" When he heard about my friend's age, however, his face dropped. "Your friend could not be interested in my daughter."

Old Shu had been coming to the marriage market for two and a half years. He had stopped telling his daughter about his efforts, but occasionally introduced her to one of the other people's sons and told his daughter the young man was a friend of a friend.

I asked Old Shu why he thought his daughter had not paired off yet. "If you ask her, it is because she hasn't found the one," he said. "But I see the way people look at me when they ask if she has an apartment. If we aren't willing to put up half [the purchase price] for an apartment, we won't even be considered."

Her age was the other limiting factor. The expectation that men will have an apartment before marriage and marry before age thirty is crushing for many young men. Similarly, the expectation that women will graduate from college but marry and get pregnant before they're twenty-seven feels completely unfair to young women. Clearly Chinese society is sending mixed messages. China's young people are caught between cultural expectation and modern reality.

"My daughter is exceptional. She's a good person. But all we do here is talk about money, apartments, and wages. It's like haggling over meat at the market," Shu said. "It's dehumanizing."

六

The automotive factory, a state-owned enterprise that employed the father of my teacher, Tina, had issued her parents their first apartment. But the Communist Party stopped allocating apartments through work units in 1998.

After 1998 the Party allowed citizens to start owning real

estate . . . sort of. In China you buy the apartment, not the land underneath it. Contracts for residential real estate expire after seventy years. In effect, the apartment you've bought is only a long-term rental.

This was how the government gave birth to the private real estate sector in China. Real estate also serves the practical purpose of establishing the buyer as a resident of that city; it gives them that city's *hùkǒu*, or internal passport. The hùkǒu system has been in place in China for millennia in one form or another, effectively controlling migration within the country by limiting government services, most notably education, to residents of a specific location. A worker from Li's home province would have a huge amount of trouble sending his kids to school in Suzhou without a hùkǒu. Buying an apartment is the easiest fix. In Beijing people can buy apartment spaces called "study spots" that are just big enough to establish residency so a child can attend local schools.

According to Qin Shuo, author and the editor in chief of *China Business News*, the Chinese economy has been hijacked by the real estate sector, which relies to an unhealthy degree on high housing prices and continued urbanization.

"For many, the extremely high housing prices lie at the intersection of the success or failure of countless average Chinese's 'China Dream,' " Qin writes. "The melancholy is difficult to describe."[14]

When Li's family bought the apartment, they did so on the basis of a picture in a magazine and a concrete skeleton. The location was right—"Bijie is expanding in the direction of my apartment, so it ought to gain steadily in value"—and the price fit their budget. They paid in full, and Li moved in as soon as the apartment was completed. It took another week after he moved in for the building to turn on the water. Li's family bought his apartment outright with cash; 80

percent of Chinese buy their homes without a mortgage, compared with half of American homebuyers. Chinese don't like to rent; 90 percent of Chinese own the home they live in.[15] (Ninety percent probably does not include in the vast number of migrant workers who go largely uncounted in Chinese cities.)

Li's parents had been stashing money away for years, diligently saving about a third of their income in preparation for their son's marriage. "My parents like the idea of investing in land," Li explained. "They don't trust banks. They hand in the money and they get a receipt, a number on a piece of paper. An apartment they can feel. An apartment can't disappear overnight."

Despite both the push for consumption from the government and the inevitable increase in consumerism after Chinese began moving to cities, they are still among the best savers in the world. They have a gross savings rate equivalent to half of China's GDP.[16]

七

Parent eaters are the result of the friction between this security-oriented cultural imperative and reality; an apartment is essential for marriage, but the cost of an apartment can cripple a family financially. Like two tectonic plates, tradition and modern reality grind against each other in a socially evolving China. Li and the other members of his generation are stuck in the fault line between the two shifting masses.

It all comes back to expectations, Li believes. "A Chinese man's life trajectory boils down to this: 'Buy an apartment, buy a car, have kids, then die.'" He took another swig of beer. It was a line I'd once read on the Internet. It had been floating around Internet chat rooms and office water coolers for several years. One article titled "Buying

Marriage Apartment: Helplessly Becoming a Parent Eater," reflects the basic predicament: buying an apartment to be seen as an eligible bachelor means relying on your parents to do so. The phrase carries a weariness from the constant constriction of social expectation.

"It sounds dark, doesn't it? But it's true. The first three [apartment, car, kids] you're supposed to get before you turn thirty," Li said. "Then you just sort of wait for the last one."

Perhaps the most stressful aspect of the apartment-car-kids-death formula is its dogged pace. The whole "grow-up-and-settle-down" process was meant to happen before you turned thirty, and even that has been relaxed from the more traditional age of twenty-seven.

When it came to expectations, Li was on track. "I've got an apartment that my parents bought for me," he assured me. "I bought a car a month ago." He lifted his hand and pulled down two fingers as he listed each item, check and check. He lifted a third finger and put it halfway down. "I'm married, so I'm halfway to a kid. And after an apartment and a car, kids seem pretty damn easy."

Li pauses. "But I watch TV, and I can't help but feel behind. It never feels like we have enough."

The disconnect between the lives lived on TV and those in reality was everywhere. And Western TV shows are not the worst—Chinese TV shows are. They show these perfect Beijing lives: attractive couples, nice cars, and impossibly expensive apartments. I told Li about an article I'd read that explains how Monica, Phoebe, and Rachel from the TV show *Friends*, Li's favorite American TV show, could never have afforded their amazing apartment in the West Village of Manhattan.

Li motioned toward the window of the restaurant. "This is an issue of scale," he said. "We're still a developing country. My wife was just looking at the chic lifestyle from *A Beijing Love Story*. Does Bijie look anything like Beijing?" Being in the process of modernization means places in China are separated not only by distance but also by time. "We live ten or fifteen years behind them in wages," Li said. "But that is the lifestyle we're shown on TV."*

"Why doesn't the government just control the price of housing?" I asked Li.

"The housing market is too important to the government for money making," Li explained. "The industries supporting infrastructure and housing development help keep China's economy growing, plus the land sales bring in money for the government. That's not changing."

"At this point we know it is dumb," Li said. "When the Chinese real-estate market was pretty much guaranteed to improve dramatically over time, it was a solid investment." Predictions of bursting real estate bubbles had reached all corners of China. Still, many believe that the government's reliance on the stability of the housing market to bring in tax money means the bubble will never burst, although it could inflate and deflate.

"Do you think I wanted my family to shell out all that money for an apartment? To break the bank for an apartment that could actually *lose* value over the next ten years? No. That's why I didn't ask for it. But my parents wouldn't hear of it. The only reason it doesn't feel completely insane to me is because my friends all live in apartments their parents bought for them, and they're married to women who wouldn't have seriously considered them without an apartment. Call

---

*Li also pointed out that *Friends*'s Monica inherited the rent-controlled apartment from her grandmother. Li noted, "Our government does not have this 'rent-controlled' idea, OK?"

it a 'China specialty,' if you will, something that we only have here in China. We have a housing market propped up on marriage."

Li looked at my face and laughed. "Finish your rice," he said, patting me on the back. He then used an old saying I'd heard Chinese grandparents repeat to their young grandsons: "Every grain of unfinished rice will one day be a pimple on your wife's face." With that the check came, and we were pleased to retreat from the unsavory topic into the pleasantries of bickering over who should pay.

He treated on this occasion, as I had already learned was the correct thing to do. I was younger than he and a guest in his city. At twenty-four and twenty-six years old, respectively, observing rigid social formalities such as who treated whom might seem silly, but we did it nonetheless. When the check came, I reached for my wallet, ceremoniously. He pushed my arm down, ceremoniously. Several other tables of guests looked on approvingly, supportive of Li's persistence in the matter and seemingly amused by mine. We argued a bit, some light physical jockeying for show, and we settled by agreeing that, when he comes to America, I will treat him. He and I both knew he probably won't ever come to the United States, but it was the right thing to say. Etiquette was observed. The guest-host relationship remained intact, and both he and I left the table quite pleased with the interaction, and full.

5

Sex for Fun

The Quiet Revolution

When Xiao Guo and his girlfriend, Mei, walked into Outside Island Hostel in Chengdu, they were greeted by a fifteen-foot projection of two people having sex. It stopped them dead in their tracks, suitcases at their sides. Outside Island was a youth hostel built in a four-room apartment on the top floor of a thirty-four-story residential building just inside Chengdu's third ring road. Xiao Guo and Mei had read about it on a travel forum. On the projector screen in the hostel's living room, which covered the entire back wall, a Chinese man was panting, his shirtless chest heaving with the effort of exertion. Fifteen young travelers were engrossed. Some sat on the edge of a bright red couch, others on green sheets laid over the tile floor, and a few stood leaning against the green walls at the back of the room. All hailed from different parts of China, including Tibet and Taiwan. Zizi, a rambunctious longtime tenant of the hostel, sat on a carpet with a few other guys smoking cigarettes; a guitar leaned on his leg. On the wall beneath the projector screen, someone had drawn a Buddhist nun with her skirt hitched up, tongue out, and fingers in the air as if she was at a Van Halen concert. On screen the man was propped atop a curvy woman in a bra in the backseat of a Mini Cooper. The room was quiet except for the up-down-up-down *squeak-squeak-squeak* as the Mini Cooper rocked back and forth.

The people in the room were oblivious to Xiao Guo and Mei, who remained frozen in the doorway. Video sex was new in China, and rarely did people watch it in mixed company on a fifteen-foot screen. No gaze strayed an inch from the screen. The look on the faces of the two young women from Shanghai who had checked in the day before said, "I wish this would end."

Suddenly the heavy steel door behind Xiao Guo and Mei slammed shut and the spell broke. Fifteen travelers swung their heads to look at Xiao Guo and Mei. Thirty eyes widened, fifteen faces blanched, then burned red. Long seconds passed. Xiao Guo pulled Mei and their luggage closer to him, as if preparing to be attacked.

Just as Xiao Guo looked ready to grab Mei and make a break for it, someone yelled, "It's not what it looks like!" and the tension burst into peals of laughter, the hostelers rolling around on the couch, falling off chairs, and waving their arms as if in denial. Ye, the twenty-four-year-old owner of the hostel, rushed to explain to Xiao Guo and Mei that the man having sex on screen was the Chinese sketch comedian Da Peng. Xiao Guo and Mei exhaled with their whole bodies, finally recognizing the famous actor.

On screen Da Peng groaned, tensed up, and . . . to the scream of his girlfriend, vomited all over the backseat of the car. "Sorry, I get carsick," he stammered. The joke earned only scattered chuckles.

Xiao Guo and Mei were on their first romantic getaway as a couple. They were from Xi'an, an ancient capital of China at the eastern end of the old Silk Road. They dutifully asked if I'd been there and seen the Terracotta Army. The other hostelers decided that Xiao Guo and Mei, both of whom are tall and slight, had 夫妻相, *fū fù xiàng*, an auspicious husband-and-wife quality in the way they looked together. They fit in easily with the young crowd and best with one another.

Without much preamble, when Mei had gone to their room to organize her things, Xiao Guo told me this was the first time he and Mei would share a room. By then I'd gotten used to people confiding in me about sex. I was the first and only foreigner to stay at Outside Island, and often the first foreigner anyone had ever spoken with outside of a classroom. Because I was a Westerner, they assumed I'd been around the block. Sex was not a taboo so much as an unknown, something that they'd been told was bad for them when they were kids, only to learn later in life that all the adults had been doing it the whole time. Sex on TV and in movies was becoming more commonplace. Though sex was seldom depicted as explicitly as Da Peng's romp in the Mini Cooper, sex was implied, suggested, and a regular part of dialogue in screenplays and TV shows, to say nothing of the endless amounts of sexual conversation and content on the Internet. The proliferation of sex in Chinese media seemed natural. Sex sells, and the world wants to sell to China.

I asked if this was also his first time sharing a room with any girlfriend. "Mei is also my first-ever girlfriend," he said.

The couple had talked about it, Xiao Guo told me. That night they would try sex.

二

China is in the midst of a sexual revolution. Lest your mind wander to orgies and wild sex romps, the sexologist Li Yinhe marvelously clarified what is happening: "China is in the midst of an *extremely quiet* sexual revolution."

Li Yinhe was talking about sex in China at a time when an extramarital sexual relationship still was punishable by death. She is the Chinese Dr. Ruth, and one of the most groundbreaking popular academics alive in China today. My friends did not think I was cool until I posted a picture with the famous sexologist. "Dude . . . do you know who that is?!"

"Most Chinese are still not promiscuous," Li Yinhe told me, as she sipped chrysanthemum tea in a Beijing teahouse. "They still emphasize monogamy. But people now are getting comfortable with the idea of sex for sex's sake."

China's quiet sexual revolution is not about sleeping with everyone; it is about sleeping with someone and doing it now instead of later. In 1989, the year of Tiananmen Square, only 15 percent of Chinese engaged in premarital sex. By 2009 that figure had jumped to 70 percent. Several professors and the real experts, those young people who put together large singles dating events, assured me that the number was closer to 85 percent in cities. This radical shift has indeed occurred under the radar. The mild Li Yinhe said with a nonchalant shrug, "It's true. The majority of people in China are now having sex for fun."

Outside Island Hostel had three private rooms and three rooms with six bunk beds each. Along with a small handful of others, I was a long-term resident, spending six months with a nightly rotating cast of characters. I was the first and last foreigner to stay there, as it eventually shut down. Ye, the boss, normally let me sleep in one of the single rooms, but if three couples arrived, I had to sleep in a balsawood bunk. So my night's sleep became linked to these handholding, mild-mannered couples, and I became particularly sensitive to their comings and goings.

The hostel was on the top floor of a thirty-four-floor apartment building in a fourteen-building complex that took up a whole city block. About five thousand people lived within that single square block. The hostel, one of thousands of youth hostels scattered across the country, was an outpost for college students and recent graduates.

It also became a getaway for couples. Chinese college dorms sleep three to six people per room. Recent college grads often lived with their parents or shared cramped apartments. Space is a luxury in China, and traveling gives young people time to breathe. Traveling also often gave young couples their first opportunity to be alone behind closed doors.

Looking back, it's hard to believe the number of young couples like Xiao Guo and Mei from all over the country who came and went while I was living at Outside Island. They'd arrive from nearby Mianyang and Deyang, college towns with tens of thousands of students each. Others would come from Beijing or farther north. Some came all the way from Taiwan.

After being around so many Chinese couples, I started to notice real differences in the way they and young Western couples hold space. Chinese couples exude softer, calmer, more secure attitudes than typical Western couples. Couples like Xiao Guo and Mei, for example, were often touchy, usually in one or another phase of physical contact. When he returned to the couch after fishing for something in their room, Xiao Guo would instinctively reach for Mei's lower back or waist, not to pull her closer but to confirm his presence. She would lean toward him ever so slightly, and they'd be together. It was almost like two gears gliding past each other until—*click*—they'd lock in place.

Their physical relationship reminded me more of the cues between a husband and wife than young lovers, a different type of subdued passion, an air of mutual reliance. In college each lived in a single-sex dorm with three roommates. At the hostel couples would often leave the group before everyone else, go back to their room, and we wouldn't see them until the next morning. Then there they'd be, leaning in close on the red couch, poring over their phones as they plotted their route for the day.

Xiao Guo told me he and Mei had met in college. They both studied engineering. He was a year older, and a friend within their major had introduced them. He got her WeChat account and the two had begun texting, timidly at first, then all the time. They met once to study together. When they had studied for a long time, they realized they were both hungry, so they went for a meal together. Then they started studying together every day. Two months later, here they were at Outside Island, and Xiao Guo couldn't stop beaming.

Before dinner that night, I asked Mei about the first time she met Xiao Guo. "It was cute how nervous he was with me that first time we went to study. We studied for five hours before he suggested we go get some food. You could hear my stomach growling from across the room, and he still didn't pick up the cues," she said, smiling as she recalled their first sort-of date.

"Were you nervous at all?" I asked.

"Not as nervous as Xiao Guo," she said. "I've been in a relationship before." The two students from Shanghai raised their eyebrows.

Virginity used to be a prerequisite for marriage in China. Authors like Yu Hua write about static sexual ideals in a rapidly changing China. In his novel *Brothers*, for instance, a dozen judges of a beauty contest expect the women to parade in bikinis and insist that they sleep with the judges if they want to win the cash prize. The person who makes a killing at the beauty contest is the man selling fake hymens. All the women buy several of them as they get in bed with all the judges. And yet the judges espouse their search for someone with true, traditional virtue.

For women, virginity was equated with virtue. Traditional Confucian society regarded women more as reproductive accoutrements than sexual beings. "Orgasm equality" was far outside Confucius's *Spring and Summer Annals*. One of the simplest and most commonly referenced distillations of traditional thoughts on sleeping around comes from the most famous Confucian during the Qing Dynasty, Wang Yongbin (1792–1869). In *Fireside Chats* he wrote, "Of a thousand virtues, filial piety is foremost. Of a thousand vices, licentiousness is the most grave."[1] As a feminist podcast host who calls herself Debbie describes the Confucian outlook, "It was like ancient slut-shaming. All women were expected to be virgins, or they were unmarriageable." Dating was out of the question.

Modern China, especially under Mao, was not much better. While young Americans danced naked and made love in the mud at the Woodstock festival in 1969, China often treated sex outside wedlock as a crime against the Chinese Communist Party. Casual dating did not exist five decades ago in China. As Richard Burger, author of *Behind the Red Door*, explained in an interview, "[Chairman Mao] considered any discussion of sex outside the home to be a form of Western spiritual pollution and he insisted on total faithfulness and monogamy."[2]

Premarital sex was not only criminalized but also heavily moralized. For *Sexuality and Love of Chinese Women*, published in 1996, Li Yinhe interviewed many women about how they experienced sex and sexuality during and after the Cultural Revolution. At the time the book was considered taboo. One woman told her, "We got our marriage license in September in 1976. Our wedding was in October. It was only after both were completed that I dared to have any contact [with my husband]." A middle-aged single woman explained, "Before I was thirty-seven years old, I was always very traditional. I thought before marriage, you couldn't have any of this type of activity. I was afraid if I wasn't a virgin when I get married, no man would ever treasure me."[3]

Today those expectations for women in cities are all but nonexistent. Research suggests that women—smart women, to be exact—are actually ruling the dating world. National statistics published in 2015 show that female doctoral students have more relationships than any other group the researchers interviewed, averaging nearly seven romances per woman.[4] (However, the researchers did not specify the nature of these romances.)

In the past I had met guys who billed themselves as traditional and said they were seeking a woman who was "pure" (they actually used that word). I asked Xiao Guo if he ever gave any consideration to Mei's former boyfriend. Xiao Guo just shrugged. "Why would I care? It is the twenty-first century. I think she's beautiful. She's smart and she's interesting. We like the same music and we share similar ideas about our futures. I feel like I can rely on her. What more could I ask for?"

三

Bringing about a sexual revolution requires both a will and a way, and, oddly enough, it was the Chinese government that unwittingly provided the tools for China's sexual awakening. The one-child policy and the introduction of widespread access to birth control effectively cleaved sex from reproduction. The government made contraception readily available to every Chinese citizen. The one-child policy made it possible, for the first time in Chinese history, for Chinese couples to have sex without worrying about pregnancy. China had the kindling for revolution, but, after years of telling citizens that sex for fun was a criminal act, it lacked the spark.

China wasn't always so stodgy, according to my friend's father, Old Zhang. I met Old Zhang when I visited his home as a guest of his son, Little Zhang. The elder Zhang enjoyed sweater vests and watching the NBA. One day, while Little Zhang slept off lunch, Old Zhang and I sat on the couch watching TV together. The house did not have heating. The temperature outside was below freezing. Old Zhang and I sat with our feet under a table whose central pillar doubled as a space heater. We began to watch a documentary entitled *China Within the Mosaic.*

"We have discovered stone sex toys here in China dating back as far as thirty-five hundred years ago," the elderly TV host began. Old Zhang sat straight up on the couch. A blocky stone penis glided across the screen. Old Zhang began fumbling for the remote lodged between couch cushions. The host continued, then began to compare histories of sexuality in all cultures. Remote finally in hand, Old Zhang hesitated, chewing on his lower lip as if weighing his options. His curiosity, it seemed, had been piqued. "You foreigners are pretty open about these things. It is the twenty-first century, right?" he asked me. We settled in.

Ancient Rome, the host explained, had an extremely indulgent sexual culture. The Japanese were rougher, wilder, probably in reaction to their stiflingly formal public lives. Old Zhang nodded. Ancient India mythologized sex, coupling intercourse with religion.

"And here in China, our ancestors' sexual culture emphasized gentleness, modesty, courteousness, restraint, and magnanimousness," the host asserted. Old Zhang nodded again, approvingly.

Old Zhang went on to lecture me about sex and Confucius, the most intellectual birds-and-bees conversation I've ever had. "Gentleness, modesty, courteousness, restraint, and magnanimousness" are ideal qualities expressed not just for sex but for life in the *Spring and Autumn Annals*, the court chronicles of the Zhou Dynasty (722–481 BC). Zigong, a disciple of Confucius, used the phrase to describe the way his teacher would respond to everyone he met. During sexual intercourse Chinese are meant to embody those qualities that Confucius displayed during his life, Old Zhang and *China in the Mosaic* seemed to be saying.

Chinese have never had a dominant religion, much less one that espouses the concept of original sin. Rather than being dictated by religion, attitudes about sexuality changed from dynasty to dynasty.

Both Taoism and Buddhism, specifically Vajrayana, better known as Tantric Buddhism, had found homes in China more than a thousand years ago. Taoism, which is both a religion and a philosophy, emphasizes the nurturing of the body and regards sex as an indispensable means through which to achieve maximum health and longevity. Men are seen as full of the yang essence, representing light and heat. Women have the yin essence, representing coolness and dark. Sex, in Taoism, is known as a "merging of energies," a way to pursue the sacred balance of the opposites in life.

Confucianism repositioned sex as a pragmatic practice for creating a family. Burger writes, "Confucius believed that sex, like eating, was a necessary human function, the main purpose of which was to produce children."[5] Sex is not linked with shame. It requires a man and a woman because that is the only combination that results in a child. It requires monogamy because a traditional family unit, the core of a Confucian society, is necessary to raise a child.

四

At Outside Island, every morning the building's elevators would be packed with elementary, middle, and high school students in their uniforms on their way to school. One student in particular, a sixteen-year-old sophomore at a local high school, always took the time to practice a few lines of English if she ran into me on the elevator. She had introduced herself as Little Fish, the literal translation of her Chinese name.

"Hello!" she'd say. "The weather is very sunny today!" she'd say. Or, "Have you eaten yet?"

One day I shared an elevator with Little Fish and her mother. They were fighting.

"Your teacher told us you have a boyfriend! Who said you can have a boyfriend? Do you want to ruin your chances at college? Dating not for the sake of marriage is hooliganism!" her mother said, then ended the discussion with, "No boyfriends till you test!" Little Fish stood with her head down while the elevator moved. Behind Little Fish was an advertisement for a local plastic surgery practice. It featured a woman in lingerie, her enhanced chest spilling out over the bra. BIGGER . . . IT'S JUST NOT THE SAME, the ad declared. Little Fish's mom looked past her daughter, as if seeing the ad for the first time, looked at me, shook her head, and then, arriving at their floor, stormed off. Little Fish plodded sullenly in her wake.

In declaring "dating not for the sake of marriage is hooliganism," Little Fish's mother undoubtedly thought she was quoting Mao—

it's one of the most repeated aphorisms the chairman never said. It's a trope of growing up, a line that almost everyone's teachers, parents, grandparents, or aunts and uncles have used to bring a teen up short at some point; because it expresses sentiments with which Mao would have agreed, it is often misattributed to him—and it is so common that it is now a universal punch line for young people. Dating, unless it is expressly for testing marriage potential, is moral hooliganism.

The next morning when I saw Little Fish in the elevator, I said hello. She only nodded and kept her eyes on the floor. "Have you eaten yet?" I asked. She nodded again. It was another week before she asked me about the weather.

A high school relationship, or dating, is often known by another name in China: *gāokǎo* killer. It is said to destroy a young student's ability to focus on nothing but preparing to take the college entrance exam. Parents and relatives often try to forbid relationships completely, with teachers sometimes getting in on the act.

They're fighting a losing battle. Recent statistics from Peking University claim that average young Chinese born after 1995 have their first romance at age twelve. Little Fish was already late to the dating game.

Attitudes about sex are just one of many aspects of Chinese culture that has undergone significant change in recent decades. From the thirty-fourth floor of Outside Island, we could track the progress of a hulking metallic apartment complex that would house ten thousand people being erected a block away. The contractors had broken ground only three months earlier. Now the building's concrete skeleton was complete, and cranes were working around the clock. Between the construction site and Outside Island was a plot of farmland, curving rows of gray cabbage and a few shacks with tarps over the roofs. That is just how China is. Some things change fast, other things change slowly, and all share the same space. Little Fish's mother believed young people shouldn't date; Little Fish believed that romance was normal. Little Fish's mother had not grown up looking at breast enhancement ads in her apartment complex because these apartment complexes had not existed.

Xiao Guo's arrival at Outside Island as a virgin was not unusual. Teens often sneak their first dates, first handholding, and first kisses while in high school, but they wait for their college years for their first intimate experiences. The major American movie trope of losing your virginity on prom night does not exist for most twenty-year-olds in China because almost everyone remains a virgin, and no one has a prom.

Generation gaps come into focus around issues of sex. According to the statistics, China's post-80s generation generally had their first sexual encounter at twenty-two. China's post-90s generation was more likely to lose their virginity at twenty. With sexual outlooks changing in China, I met more twenty-eight-year-old virgins than twenty-two-year-old ones. I know because, over the course of a friendship, they've told me. It was nothing to be embarrassed about.

The average age of first sexual encounter continues to decrease. People born after 1995 are, according to the statistics and to many parents' horror, having their first sexual encounter when they're seventeen, just one year older than Little Fish.

五

"Check this out," Zizi, the guitar-playing hostel resident, told me. What sounded like Japanese emerged from his Xiaomi phone speaker with a whine. I knew it could be only one of two things: animé or porn.

Porn is illegal in China, although it proliferates. People, often Uighur women carrying bundled-up babies to deflect suspicion, according to the stories, used to sell porn on DVDs in alleyways and under bridges. Peculiarly, most of my Chinese friends describe how porn used to be largely the domain of China's ethnic Muslims, alongside offers of dried fruit, lamb kebabs, and currency exchange. "Want discs?" the women would whisper to passersby. When foreign content was more tightly controlled, pornography was one of the handful of windows into the outside world.

Now China watches more online porn than any other country in the world, representing perhaps as much as a third of all Internet porn traffic.[6] The industries surrounding sex are generally on the rise in China too. In 2015, thirty million Chinese bought sex toys online instead of walking into one of China's twenty thousand sex shops. China makes 70 percent of the world's sex toys, and sales of sex products are up 50 percent at the online retailer Taobao.[7]

Because making porn has always been illegal in China, Zizi and his friends had never really seen two Chinese people having sex unless they filmed themselves. Part of what had made Da Peng's comedic soft-core sex scene in the car so unsettling was that he and the other character were speaking Mandarin while having sex on screen. If someone in China wanted to be able to identify with someone on screen, to see someone having sex who looked like them, they watched Japanese porn. Most young Chinese guys and some women grew up watching on a computer—and now on phone screens—as two (or three or four or four and a squid . . . Japanese porn runs the gamut) graphically get down to business.

The video on his phone Zizi meant to show the group was, in fact, porn. Everyone groaned, but Zizi persisted. "No, no, no. Check this out. It is not what you expect."

The couple on screen was in what appeared to be in a fitting room. They were engaging in what appeared to be sex. Ye, the hostel owner, cast an accusing look at Zizi. It appeared to be exactly what everyone expected.

After a few seconds of blurry amateur production, the group watching the video froze.

In crystal clear Beijing-standard Mandarin, a background voice said on the video, "Dear customers, welcome to the Uniqlo store at Sanlitun. There are no fitting rooms on the first floor. Please proceed to the second and third floor if you need to try clothes on."

In the living room of Outside Island, everyone watching the video on Zizi's cell phone stared at each other for a few moments, processing what they'd just heard. "Call me 'husband,'" the guy in the video mumbled, followed by a few obscured, furtive thrusts. "Say we'll always be together."

The group couldn't contain their laughter.

"Oh. My. God."

"No way."

"This can't be real!"

But it was. The "Uniqlo Incident," as it came to be known all over China, lit up the Chinese web like a pinball machine. Everyone saw it. The sex itself was nothing special—a young couple getting it on in a Uniqlo changing room and filming it with a phone. For me, it immediately brought to mind Old Zhang and the description given in *China in the Mosaic*: "Gentleness, modesty, courteousness, restraint, and magnanimousness," though perhaps it was light on the restraint.

The video went viral almost instantly and thus ensued the whack-a-mole experience that is censorship on the Chinese web, especially now that WeChat is built around private conversations compared to WeiBo's public blogging platform. The government takes something down; a copy pops up somewhere else. The government deletes the copy, and another one boings to the surface. *Smack, boing, smack, boing*—until one party or the other runs out of energy. Plus, now that social media is primarily mobile, Chinese netizens know to just save it to their phone.

The Uniqlo sex tape and the Internet commotion that followed felt like a collective sigh of relief and sparked a fairly open national conversation about sex. That the video clearly featured two Chinese people made it relatable. That it seemed consensual, good-natured, and a touch adventurous made it easy to talk about. Sex scandals in China too often consist of little more than leaked pictures of government officials posing with prostitutes. This was just two people having a consensual romp, what Chinese netizens call a 野战, *yězhàn*, an "operation in the field." It gave people a reason to talk about sex, and the nation's twentysomethings ran with it.

Sex education in China is notoriously nonexistent, and families don't discuss sex. "Chinese culture is particularly ill-suited to talk about sex in public, let alone to children," Li Yinhe told me. For the post-90s generation, most sex-education classes were held once or twice in high school. They were essentially a course in basic anatomy. Then, at the end of the lesson, the boys would be asked to leave and the girls would be told about periods and pregnancy. Most would have already gone through puberty. A few women had told me they knew people who had had abortions. What I found most shocking was that at least half the people I talked to over the years never had any sex education in school. Not one class. And parents avoided the subject. Even the sexologist Li Yinhe said that she had not yet had a conversation about safe sex with her son, and he was then sixteen.

Chinese sex on screen had crossed the line, the Communist Party decided. The Uniqlo sexcapaders were found, arrested, fined, and released. The Da Peng Mini Cooper episode eventually was censored by being stripped from all its host sites.

六

Mei sat with her hand on Xiao Guo's knee. The two scanned through Baidu's NuoMi app, which translates to Sticky Rice, for local deals at good Sichuanese restaurants. The app works like Groupon and lists hundreds of signature dishes at discounted prices that restaurants offer to attract customers. You can pay online within the app, walk in, have your phone scanned, and eat, all without breaking out your wallet. Mei was scouting for tomorrow night's meal, as tonight we'd all be cooking a big communal dinner.

The two women from Shanghai and a few guys from Fujian were busy in the kitchen. Others were milling about, playing cards or watching movies. Someone had put on *How I Met Your Mother*, the sometimes banned, sometimes not, American TV show that had become a major hit in China, often supplanting the old favorite *Friends*, as English-language background noise for studying.

Zizi was busy working his phone to secure a date. A week earlier, he had met a young woman on Tantan, a Chinese dating app akin to Tinder. They'd been talking around the clock, and he had invited her over for the dinner that night. She had agreed. "One more for dinner," Zizi called into the kitchen.

One of the women from Shanghai poked her head out of the kitchen and yelled, "Dating not for the sake of marriage is hooliganism!" She got a few laughs. Zizi went into his room to put on a button-down shirt.

Tantan and other Chinese dating apps had met some resistance from the government. Conversations that included words the Party deemed inappropriate would elicit a warning popup on your screen that said such content is not allowed. Phrases like "one-night stand," "hookup buddy," and even the euphemism for erotic massage, which translates literally as "big precious sword," all produce warning messages. Even onomatopoeia for sex, 啪啪啪, *pa pa pa*, runs afoul of the app's basic filter.

In all fairness to the censors, the purpose of their work was not only to curb casual arousal. The filter was partly designed to interfere with sex workers' new favorite tools for meeting johns. A quick sign-on to Tantan, or especially Momo, another Chinese dating app, made clear that some people were using it for the business of giving others pleasure. Prostitution was illegal but policed only lightly. Kaiser Kuo, cohost of the *Sinica* podcast, once remarked that the government at one time kept prostitution legal in part to facilitate the transfer of wealth from the rich to the poor in China, and to help close the wealth gap. While discussing prostitution in China, a Party official told me, "Sexual dissatisfaction is a large cause of trouble. If people are working so hard and not having some form of leisure, some form of pleasure, they will be upset." He then pointed out that almost all recent shootings in the United States had been perpetrated by lonely young men. Within twenty years China is expected to have thirty million more men than women of marriageable age.[8] As Richard Burger points out on his appearance on the *Sinica* podcast, "They [government officials] believe that a sexually satisfied population is a more productive population, less likely to complain."[9]

Outside Island and the sixty or so other hostels I stayed at all over the country—I stayed at Chinese-oriented hostels when I traveled in Asia outside China—brought into relief one major difference between Chinese and Western travelers: few random hookups occur in Chinese hostels. In Western hostels sex is pervasive. While traveling throughout Southeast Asia and Europe, I've seen many Western hostelers with their hearts set on a travel romance. It has been my bad luck to have been present while these hookups occurred loudly in the next room or, during one really bad night in Thailand, in the bunk bed above me. China is simply not that casual, at least not yet.

Less machismo surrounds sexual culture in China than in the West. Rarely have I met the Chinese equivalent of the fraternity brother who maintains a list of the women he's bedded. Instead, guys more often talk about sex with a certain amount of respectful awe—mixed with a persistent curiosity and a bit of innocence.

The exception, my friends remind me, seems to be Chinese study-abroad students. Mao's concerns about Western spiritual pollution seemed to play out in the sexual sphere: young people returning to China from an American college frequently seem to have had a crash course in fraternity parties and casual sex. This, of course, is anecdotal, but it is a persistent theme.

As China modernizes, people often ask me whether that means China is becoming Westernized and, if so, to what degree. Most of what young Chinese men know about American sexual mores they learned from two types of movies, Hollywood films and porn. However little English a young Chinese person spoke, they could almost always say, "Put your hands up!" and "Oh, baby, ya, baby, come on, baby."

Westerners also have a bad reputation for a sort of sexual colonialism—they visit China and other places in Asia just to have sex. As a guest on a Chinese-language podcast, I once was asked by the college-age female host, "Is it true what they say, that foreigners leave their own country with no girlfriend and come to China and get two?"

七

After our big communal meal, we all went up to the roof with guitars and beers to watch the sunset. Xiao Guo sat with his arm around Mei and both sipped on Tsingtao, smiling widely and singing along as Zizi played the guitar. His Tantan date, a twenty-year-old from the nearby art school, fit in easily with the group. The light receded behind Chengdu's skyscrapers. Filtered through the fog, smog, and haze, the gray buildings were awash in a pastel yellow, then orange, red, and finally a fuzzy nighttime blue.

Xiao Guo and Mei retired early. The few guys broke into toothy grins, sharing looks and nodding their approval. Zizi picked up a guitar and began strumming Miserable Faith's most famous love song, an acoustic ode to the singer's wife. Zizi's date looked on with fawning eyes. The four other young women were now red in the face, either from the beers or the now overt sexuality, and soon slipped downstairs to their bunks. That night all the guys stayed up late smoking cigarettes and talking longingly about girlfriends they'd had or hoped to have one day.

Zizi's Tantan date spent the night. I ended up sleeping on one of the balsa-wood bunk beds.

Xiao Guo reported the next morning that his night with Mei had been a success, although his inexperience had made him nervous. That was all. He seemed remarkably calm for a twenty-two-year-old who had just had sex for the first time. He did not communicate his experience as a conquest. He didn't brag. He did say that he hoped things would work out with Mei and that they would return so we could all have a reunion at Outside Island the next year.

I asked if they would get married.

"One step at a time," he replied.

6

A Leftover Woman

How Marriage Expectations and Government Priorities Bind

A month before Chinese New Year, I returned home to my apartment in Suzhou, Jiangsu Province, to find that my roommate, Wendy, still had not moved out—although I had asked her to do so before I left for Chengdu. She lived in the smaller bedroom of our first-floor apartment in a 1990s-style cement complex; Wendy's room had once belonged to my landlord's daughter, who went by the English name of Smile. Smile and her father, Uncle Peng, as he had me call him, had gotten into a fight with Wendy while I was gone. Uncle Peng would not say what the disagreement was about. Smile later told me her parents were not comfortable with the idea that an unmarried man and an unmarried woman were sharing an apartment. They thought Wendy was trying to take advantage of me, "a foreigner who didn't know better." They wanted her gone. But Wendy—who worked as an English tutor for those preparing for the *gāokǎo*—appeared even more firmly dug in than she had been before I left. In my absence, her belongings had crept steadily beyond the confines of her room, edging toward my door across the narrow hall. Calligraphy ink filled one of our two rice bowls, notebooks lay scattered on the square dining room table, and a wet pile of jackets sat on one of our three dining room stools. The apartment was, without exaggeration, freezing cold. Residences in cities south of the Yangtze River usually do not have central heating. The temperatures in Suzhou do dip below freezing, but rain rarely turned to snow because of the high humidity. Wendy kept the windows open, and the tile walls of an already dank room had become clammy to the touch.

Although I was disappointed that Wendy hadn't honored our agreement to part ways as roommates, I can't say I was surprised. With Chinese New Year approaching, my roommate had bigger problems than my trifling request to vacate the premises: Wendy had to see her parents.

She was thirty-one and unmarried, which put her in one of the most heavily criticized and often lamented social classes in China: she was a 剩女, or *shèng nǚ*, "leftover woman."

For Wendy, going home meant facing the firing squad of questions she'd been subjected to during every Spring Festival for the last seven years: "Do you have any children?" No. "Are you married?" No. "Ah, how old are you?" There followed the disappointed silence reserved for one who has reneged on a tacit cultural agreement sealed at birth.

Wendy's name was, of course, not Wendy. She had chosen the name herself. Wendy was born to a family in rural Jiangsu, China, in 1983, seven years after the Cultural Revolution and four years after China's reform and opening-up policies switched on the gas burners under China's economy. Wendy's parents had been grappling with their second language, standard Mandarin. They had never called their daughter Wendy. Still, she introduced herself as Wendy to almost everyone in Suzhou, Chinese and foreign alike.

China's rapid modernization since the mid-1980s has left the Chinese people in simultaneous possession of the old world and the new, the third world and the first, tea-drinking traditionalism and tech-wielding modernism. The country's palpable achievements are easy to track: the four-hour commute to Shanghai from Suzhou when she was younger is now twenty-one minutes on the high-speed railway; young people are fluent in Mandarin, the national language, whereas older generations struggle with Mandarin as a second language and so continue to be far more regional in their mind-set. At the same time remnants of old China persist in the attitudes, postures, and traditions of the nation: a woman should be married by age twenty-seven.

Wendy grew up in a rapidly modernizing country and therefore is a product of the twenty-first century—she speaks conversational English and decent French, Hugh Grant is her ideal man, and she lived with an American friend who happened to be male, an indecent arrangement by most parents' standards. She also held on to some traditional anachronisms—she refused modern medicine, wouldn't use indoor space heaters during winter (the warm air dries out the throat and the skin), and went on and on about how, were she to have a baby, she wouldn't shower for at least a month because her body would be too weak and she'd get sick, probably die, and leave her baby defenseless.*

---

*"Sitting the month," *zùo yuèzi*, refers to the restorative month-long period after childbirth when women are meant to regain their strength. During that month new mothers are supposed to stay at home or in one of the thousands of hospitals in China specifically designed for postnatal care. The controlled cleanliness of the environment is meant to protect women in what is described as their weakened state after birth. Cold

These examples are simple: this is old and that is new. But distinguishing which was which often was more difficult.

Such was the case when Wendy first described herself as a leftover woman. Was this modern slang or ancient idiom? Wendy repeated the word in Chinese, 剩女, *shèng nǚ*, and wrote it down for me in one of the notebooks she carried at all times. *Nǚ* means "woman" and is a radical taught on the first day of an introductory course in Chinese character writing. *Shèng* was tougher. I'd seen it before next to 菜, *cài*, the word for a dish of food, and together they literally mean the food leftover after a meal. But *shèng* could easily mean more than one thing, so I was stuck.

This was a familiar predicament for mid-level Mandarin students. Each character means something by itself—often it has multiple, unrelated definitions—and then can combine with a second, third, or a string of characters to gain a full meaning. Sometimes these combinations are practical: the words for *old* and *home* combine to mean hometown. Other times they are poetic in their practicality, as if an ancient Chinese poet had come back to life and done his best to describe modernity's awesome advances: trains are "fire cars" and movies are, eerily, "electric shadows." Other times the combinations were far more cryptic. I assumed *shèng nǚ* was a case of multiple or hidden meanings.

So I asked Wendy directly. Few things are more horrifying than learning you have addressed a question about a perceived social in-

---

fruit and cold drinks are forbidden. All types of "cold" things, from weather to water to food, are limited or forbidden. Whereas women once were restricted to limited bathing, with the advent of indoor heat and showers they are now supposed to shower, with the water at 104 degrees Fahrenheit. The traditional concept is more than two thousand years old, having originated during the Western Han Dynasty (206 BC–9 AD) and remains widely popular within Chinese medicine.

adequacy to someone who is affected by said perceived social inadequacy. For instance, it would be truly unfortunate if a young Chinese person learning English in the United States politely asked someone who weighs a hundred pounds more than their ideal body weight to please define the term *morbidly obese*. I was doing just that.

Shèng nǚ, Wendy explained, does in fact mean leftover woman. According to Wendy, it refers to a woman who has not married by the age of thirty. Everyone else I've asked since then, as well as the official literature promulgated by the All-China Women's Federation, the state-run organization meant to stand up for women's interests, marks the expiration date at twenty-seven, an inconsistency I did not bring to Wendy's attention. The idea behind leftover women is that a Chinese woman who is older than twenty-seven and not married has something wrong with her, that she is flawed, that she is and remains socially "inedible."

"Like bad food," Wendy asserted factually, her face an expressionless mask in our cold apartment. She was sitting at her desk facing an open window. Outside, a cold winter rain was coming down in sheets. An old laptop was open on her desk, and the lonely brightness of a British romantic comedy paused on the screen threw shadows on Wendy's round face. Her suitcase dominated the space between her bed and desk, so she could not swivel her chair. The door to Wendy's room barely cleared the edge of her single bed, which was pushed tightly against the wall. The walls were bare and cracked. If Wendy had not been so opposed to the use of heat, the room would have been cozy, albeit a bit cramped. Instead, it was quite literally freezing. Dressed in a hat, mittens, boots, and a puffy winter coat, Wendy would sit at her desk watching foreign movies and listening to the sound of the rain. As she explained, Wendy absently played with an abacus our landlord had left behind. Her face bore the blank look she always wore when she explained new pieces of language or tried to teach me to cook a local dish.

The tradition behind the concept of leftover women was one of the most doggedly persistent I encountered in China. The Chinese often joke about how they make small talk—a couple of pro forma questions—"Where are you from?" "What do you do?"—and then, without missing a beat, "How much do you make?" "Do you have a boyfriend?" "Are you married?" "Do you have a child?" At first I thought people were asking me the second set of questions in the hope of setting me up on a date with a friend—a delusion that, as an American, I was a hot-ticket item in China. We'd exchange numbers and I'd wait for a match, but it turned out they were just curious to see if I was married and, if I was, whether I had a Chinese wife. These basic questions seemed to provide enough data to satisfy most people's social-measuring mechanisms. Once you provided the answers, you could almost hear the gears whirring, the motor thrumming, and then—*thud*—you had been successfully categorized, labeled, and stored.

Chinese ask these questions daily and often. Strangers ask them the first time you meet, and then friends and family constantly ask them again to see which stats may have changed. A change necessitates a recataloging, so the gears grind, and the motor churns back to life. The process is unabashedly judgmental and, with people like Wendy, brutally unforgiving as the machine yet again spits out a verdict. With a malicious look of pity, the questioner stamps you as Leftover and files you under Inadequate, which is stacked right next to Failure.

I'd been around a handful of times when strangers had leveled these questions at Wendy. Wendy never bucked or fired back roughly. She would shake her head no with a bland smile, her mouth moving but her eyes still staring a few feet past the person to whom she was talking. The look was unreadable. It had the toughness of something hardened over time.

Since my return, however, Wendy had seemed irregularly distraught. It became clear she wanted to talk. I had read about a strategy used by local managers of Chinese factories during the 1990s when workers had grievances. It was called "talking into exhaustion." The idea is that you let the distraught person vent, say everything they want to say for as long as they want to say it, and the process will quell the person's grievances.

Wendy began talking at midnight. By 3:30 a.m., when Wendy was showing no signs of exhaustion or catharsis, I asked if we could break for sleep.

Here is what Wendy told me: She both strongly resented her parents and felt an even stronger commitment to them. Her parents had not berated her so much as pestered her about her life. By their measure, Wendy told me, she had failed them: no grandchildren, no son-in-law, and no prospect she would be able to support them in the future.

They had raised Wendy the same way many Chinese parents had raised their children. On the one hand, Wendy's was the generation of little emperors. She received food, clothes, and especially attention in exaggerated amounts. She was, on the surface, spoiled, the gleeful recipient of her entire family's focus.

On the other hand, all that attention had a sharp edge. When Wendy was a child, no one applauded her efforts unless they produced desired outcomes. Her mother would outright call her stupid each time she did poorly on a test, a berating I witnessed regularly with other students and was told about by many Chinese friends. Westerners would regard Wendy's mother as lacking empathy and understanding.

"Tiger mothers," hard driving and results driven, like Wendy's, were prevalent in China. The West has come to applaud the results achieved by tiger mothers. But no one asks what happens to the cubs who can't cut it, who do not become concert cellists or medical students. Pushed just as hard, the kids who do not achieve positive results face the rawest rejection a child could face from their parents: "We're not mad, we're disappointed."

That same high level of parental involvement persists throughout the lives of young Chinese adults. When they are young, test scores are of paramount importance, so parents will heavily emphasize study. Once the children, especially the women, hit their midtwenties, that energetic, involved parenting is channeled toward marriage.

And so, as Spring Festival rolled around, Wendy would again confront her culturally awkward status as a single woman as she filed onto a "fire car" to fulfill another long-standing tradition: returning to her "old home." There she would spend time with her parents and all the people she grew up with ("Still not married? Really?").

"Older Chinese women have always faced the leftover woman stigma. It is a tale as old as time," Wendy said. Done with her explanation, she turned back to her movie.

二

Wendy was wrong. Although the idea that women should marry young is consistent with traditional China, labeling someone as a leftover woman is a recent innovation. And it seems to have been an invention of the Communist Party itself. Leta Hong Fincher pioneered research surrounding the leftover woman phenomenon while completing her Ph.D. in Sociology at Tsinghua University, in particular the term's ties to government. Beginning in 2007, the All-China

Women's Federation defined the term *leftover woman* as referring to a single woman older than twenty-seven, according to the state-run Xinhua News Agency, the official mouthpiece of China's Communist Party. "Since then the Chinese state media have promoted the term through articles, surveys, cartoons, and editorials stigmatizing educated women who are still single. These state organs refer to a crisis in growing numbers of educated women who "cannot find a husband," Fincher Writes in her book *Leftover Women*.[1] Today, the term *leftover woman* has become mainstream. Wendy's parents know it. Wendy is used to it. Smile and her parents, my landlords, who barely speak Mandarin, knew it too.

The campaign shaming women into marrying young at first seems inconsistent with the Communist Party's traditional attitude toward men and women. In 1949 Mao declared, "Women hold up half the sky." It was a somewhat radical statement at the time, as some women still underwent foot binding, an excruciating process of tightly wrapping the feet of young girls to stunt their growth to make them more attractive to men. A woman with bound feet could do little work of any kind. To have a wife with bound feet was a luxury. It announced the household could afford servants.

Mao's decision to be more inclusive of women was pragmatic. He needed women to work if his newly formed People's Republic of China was to be successful. To "Surpass England and Catch Up to America," the drumbeat slogan driving China's Great Leap Forward, an attempt to push China into modernity overnight, the chairman would need the full strength of his population. Mao exhorted all the nation's comrades to work as one toward a common goal. In Chinese, *comrade*—同志, *tóngzhì*—means "of the same ambition." Mao was a man of great ambition. He enabled both halves of his mighty population to achieve his ambition for his country. It is no wonder, then, that the Chinese Communist Party's preferred term of address, *Comrade*, is gender neutral.

Today in some ways China has a more level playing field in the business world for men and women than most other developed countries. China is already home to two-thirds of the world's self-made female billionaires. Of China's fifty wealthiest women overall, thirty-six are said to have earned their fortunes themselves.[2] In the realm of self-made money, Chinese women are in a league of their own, globally. More women in China work in government than women in the United States; 24 percent in China and 19 percent in the United States, according to World Bank data.[3] However, in China notably few women hold senior positions in the Communist Party. With the exception of the 10th Party Congress in 1973 and the 11th Party Congress in 1977, women have never made up more than 10 percent of the total membership of the Central Committee of the Communist Party, and no woman has ever been a part of the Politburo Standing Committee, the most powerful decision-making body in the Party.[4]

China's efforts at gender parity are far from perfect, but there is a sense that capable women are able to rise, if not in government, then certainly in the private sector. But with the leftover women campaign, the Party seemed to be reneging on the gender equality Mao seemed to have attempted to establish.

In its attitude toward women, the Chinese Communist Party is pragmatic, not progressive. Mao needed women to work so that the country's economy would function. His priority was growth. Today the Party has a different set of problems. Economics is just one factor in creating a happy populace. While growth remains a major area of focus, the Party is focused on a different priority: stability.

One of the biggest threats to China's future stability is tens of millions of single men. During a lecture I attended Fincher explained, "The irony of this campaign to denigrate single women is that China's one-child policy, preference for sons, and widespread abortion of female fetuses have caused a surplus of *men* due to the severe sex-ratio imbalance, which the State Council called 'a threat to social stability.' "[5]

As of 2015, China's population had thirty-four million more men than women, according to China's National Bureau of Statistics.[6] Because Chinese parents want only the best for sons-in-law—they should be tall, rich, and handsome—the rejected men are also likely to be undereducated, poor, and not-so-great looking. In the minds of government officials, this population of unmarried men is a potentially destabilizing force. Few threats to social stability are greater than tens of millions of angry, uneducated, and sexually frustrated men who feel like they're being cheated of participating in what their society bills as the central activity of a good life: creating a family.

Part of the Party's solution to its "leftover men" problem is to make sure all eligible women partner up. Just as the Chinese government intercedes in the economy to buffer it against market forces, the Party is attempting to influence the singles market by convincing women they're less valuable than they actually are. Wang Xing Xing, a twenty-three-year-old economics student at Sichuan University, told me, "Products gain value through scarcity, right? On the marriage market in China, women ought to be way more valuable than men because of our messed-up demographics. That doesn't really seem to be the case, though, because, with women, there is this idea that their value depreciates over time while men's value increases. Men's jobs improve, they become more stable, less emotional. If we live in a society that values looks and children, then a woman's age is the greatest threat to her value on the market."

Just as the Party exercises central control of the Chinese economy by artificially manipulating market factors to try to create a favorable economic outcome, so too is it influencing the national marriage market. A healthy stock market makes for a stable society. The Party takes the stance that a healthy marriage market does too. As Fincher discusses in her research, the Party advances a message that stigmatizes aging women who aren't marrying by calling them society's leftovers.

The Party singles out women who are putting off marriage to focus on their career, high-powered women who don't see the point in marriage for marriage's sake. China's state media pinpointed the problem by accusing the women of clinging to the "three highs": high education, high professional standing, and high income. As Xinhua has said repeatedly for nearly a decade:

> [Leftover women] pursue perfection in excess. The problem is many of these women are too clear headed; they can't tolerate weaknesses in their partner, especially since more and more women seek the "three highs" in their own lives. Their standards for their career and partners are so high, by the time they want to marry, they discover that almost all the men who are equal in their education and age are already married.
>
> For the group of white-collar women who don't find a partner, loneliness is a common occurrence. As these unmarried women age, the feeling of loneliness gets worse and worse.[7]

By targeting women with the "three highs," the Party also doubled down on its effort to improve the so-called quality of the population. The one-child policy had made exceptions for ethnic minorities, who often lived in the less-developed West, and some people who lived outside the cities. The result was that the people who had the most children were often the least educated and worst paid. The women with the highest levels of education, salaries, and social standing were not having children, putting them through the best schools, and giving them the best opportunities. By advancing the stigma of the leftover woman the Party hoped to shame these high-achieving, well-resourced women into motherhood.

A twenty-eight-year-old named Lulu was a prime example of a woman who was pursuing the three highs. Lulu and I met at the WeChat Business Expo. Her large pop-up shop, if the massive exhibit can be called that, included more than twenty tables and a broad stage with a catwalk. It was front and center and by far the biggest at the expo. More than fifty representatives of her brand buzzed around the installation talking to potential customers. At the center of the runway stage that cut through the middle of Lulu's stall, a thirty-foot screen projected an infomercial of Lulu explaining her company's facial moisturizer. The real Lulu sat at a long rectangular table with a group of fifteen of her all-star sales team fanned out around her, smiling and greeting potential customers.

WeChat Business is an entirely new business sector in China. Its sudden popularity has changed the way the Chinese regard entrepreneurship. Essentially, Lulu and her team do direct sales through their phones. They use their WeChat "Friend Circle," selling first to their network of friends, like Amway or Cutco sales personnel, and then progressively expand their clientele. Unlike their Western counterparts, the members of Lulu's team can do all their business from the comfort of home. Whereas trying to do direct sales through their Facebook account would get most Westerners blocked by most of their contacts, in China people are far more receptive. If the deals and products are good, no one flinches, and WeChat Business has won a reputation for enabling young men and women to become successful entrepreneurs armed with only their phone, their friend circle, and mailing slips. At the expo, Lulu's team was looking for both customers and more agents to sell their products. And each time a recruit made a sale, the recruiter got a cut.

After I had talked to Lulu for a while at her exhibit, she invited me to join one of her sales meetings after the event. Naturally, it was over a large dinner. Some people chatted while others at the table enjoyed the dishes stacked high on the big lazy Susan in the middle of the table. Lulu was independently wealthy. Although she was born into a wealthy family in China's Liaoning Province, she had, through her own entrepreneurial spirit, built herself a small fortune before she was thirty. She got her start on a cooking show on CCTV. When WeChat Business began, Lulu took advantage of her modest fame and extensive network to begin selling. She was twenty-two when she started ordering beauty products wholesale and selling them through her ever-growing network of customers. Her monthly shipping bill alone can run up to 10,000 RMB (US$1,450) a month. Each package costs on average 5 RMB (US$0.73) to ship. So even though she acts more as a boss than a salesperson, she still ships two thousand packages a month. "I used to have to fill out those package slips myself," she told me.

In part, she was driven by her desire to have the financial means to take care of her parents. She doesn't exactly need to look after her parents, but it is what a good child ought to do. Lulu is a single child. Whereas caring for parents normally falls to a son, Lulu has taken on the responsibility herself. "My parents only have me as a child. I have to be both their son and daughter. If they get sick, who will care for them?" she said.

And a husband? "Women are entering into the business world because men are less and less reliable," Lulu told me. "Every day in the news is another story about people cheating on their spouses, about 小三, *xiǎo sān*." *Xiǎo sān* translates to English as "little third" and typically refers to a woman involved with a man already in a relationship. "In this day and age, you can rely on only yourself."

The young women at the table, all agents and managers who work for Lulu, nodded emphatically. Lulu was at the top of an organization hundreds of women strong. Yet almost all these women were married. "Raise your hand if you have a husband," Lulu said.

Seven of the nine women did so.

"Keep your hand raised if you have a child."

One woman put her hand down. The women laughed. The belly of the woman who had lowered her hand bulged beneath the table. Her first baby was due in three months.

"Keep your hand raised if you make more than your husband."

Five of the seven women did so.

Turning to me, Lulu raised her well-plucked eyebrows. "See?"

Most of Lulu's agents held up more than half of their family's sky. They had subscribed to the idea of marriage but not to the notion that they should simply play the role of housewife.

In fact, Lulu wanted badly to start her own family. "I don't want to just play the role of son, taking care of my parents when they're older. I want to be a daughter too," she said. "My little dream is to get married, to have kids, to live out our little lives happily."

In a way, she was emblematic of the three highs. She was well educated, well remunerated, and held a position of power within the brand of cosmetics she and her team sold. Her standards for herself were mercilessly high. Her standards for a partner were equally high. Her representatives believed that was why she remained single.

"Chinese men are intimidated by her," one agent said. Lulu herself had trained this agent, who became a star saleswoman. Her monthly income had already surpassed that of her husband. She did her business entirely from home. Boxes of products were stacked up in their living room and package slips covered their coffee table. "Men like to feel powerful in the relationship. They like to feel like they are providing, like they are the patriarchs," the agent told me. "Lulu is very feminine—we sell beauty products, after all. But she is a shrewd businesswoman."

As in many cultures around the world, Chinese masculinity has proven to be somewhat fragile. During all the years I asked Chinese men what they were looking for in a woman, the men's replies consistently revealed they were intimidated by women who outearned, outsmarted, or outclassed the men. The men's ideal continued to be traditional gender roles, a Confucian household where men occupy the dominant role. By all measures by which men are valued, Lulu ought to have been the most sought-after person in the marriage market. Instead, the national media have recast Lulu and women like her as rejects.

Chinese society and the Party are sending these women mixed messages. As higher education has become essential to securing a job that can pay for city life in China, more and more women are delaying marriage. More than half of those enrolled in higher education in China are women. On one hand, they must get a college education to be competitive in the workplace. They work their entire childhoods for the opportunity to get into a good college. Then, a few years after they graduate, they are supposed to be ready to make their career a secondary priority and get married and form a traditional household. And their entire love life—from first boyfriend to marriage—should ideally take place between ages twenty-two and twenty-six.

Stories like Lulu's are common: a high-powered, high-earning woman refuses to settle, and Chinese society tries to push her into the box of what womanhood ought to mean. But stories like Wendy's are common as well. She is not a winner in society and must deal with an overinvolved community that tells her she should shift her priorities. Like the many single Chinese women I've met who are in their late twenties, Wendy wants to get married. She has an idea of marriage that is foreign to her highly practical parents. She wants to love the person and to commit herself to that person for the rest of her life. Most women described for me a romance novel, movie, or TV show—for Wendy it was Hugh Grant in *Love, Actually*—and said they wanted to have a love like *that*, not a practical union. These women want love and happiness.

三

A few weeks before Spring Festival, I was struck with a mean, high fever. Wendy still had not moved out, and neither of us brought up the landlord's request for her to leave. Outside it was below zero. For three days I hid beneath two blankets sipping hot water ("Cold water is bad for your stomach!" Wendy reminded me) and watched daytime Chinese TV, a smattering of reality dating shows, singing competitions, and a ridiculously high concentration of anti-Japanese made-for-TV war-of-resistance-against-Japanese-aggression movies.* The dating shows were filled with couples but little romance, not like the Hugh Grant films Wendy liked to watch. I slipped outside when I needed to eat. Twice Wendy brought me rice porridge.

---

*This is how the Chinese refer to what the West often calls the Second Sino-Japanese War (1937–45), beginning with the Japanese occupation, most famously including the Rape of Nanking, and extending to the end of World War II.

My room was dark; it had one bulb hanging from the ceiling. Some ambient light filtered over the brick wall outside my full-length window. My TV was bulky, a middle-market leftover from the era before flat screens. The floors were a varnished dark wood. Although Wendy insisted that the wood was fake, those varnished floors were my favorite part of the apartment, offering a welcome sense of warmth compared with the hard linoleum and tile in the rest of the place. I slept on strips of processed plant material that were tightly woven together and attached to a sturdy wooden frame, somewhat like a taut hammock or a stiff trampoline. This type of bed was traditional and an inexpensive alternative to a mattress. It was comfortable enough and a level up from my previous mattress, which was nothing more than slats of wood. The old-school style of the bed was another anachronism in what would otherwise be a sort of rundown apartment. The TV was connected to a karaoke machine that came with the apartment. Of the ten apartments I looked at before taking this one, three had these machines included for free.

On the advice of one of my colleagues from school, I peeled, sliced, and boiled the hell out of a bunch of ginger and drank the water slowly until I fell asleep. It was a traditional method for breaking a fever, and my colleague had guaranteed it would break it with force.

Hours later, sweating, shaking, freezing, and burning, I received an urgent text from Wendy that woke me from my fever dream: *I'm in jail.* Sure I was hallucinating, I drifted off again.

When my fever finally broke hours later, I took a look at the text again and panicked. I got up, wrapped myself in one of the quilts, and walked the six paces through our linoleum dining room to Wendy's door. Light leaked out from under her doorway. I knocked, and after a moment I heard, "Come in."

That night Wendy had gone to see a man she had dated several times. All I knew about this guy was what Wendy had told me: "He is rich and appears on TV from time to time." She called him Boss Guo.

It turned out that for the past seven years, Boss Guo, who was married, twenty-five years Wendy's senior, with a son the same age as Wendy, had been seeing her on the side, making Wendy not only a leftover woman but also a little third. Boss Guo had bought Wendy a small place in the Chinese countryside in lieu of having to house, feed, and raise the two fetuses that Wendy had aborted. (Terminating a pregnancy is easy in a nonreligious country with a family planning program.) She had tried life in the countryside, which in China lacks whatever charm the word might connote in the West. Rural China represents the past, the undeveloped, and the poor. For Wendy it represented banishment. That was how she had come to rent my extra room for $86 a month.

Now Wendy was pregnant again. For the past three weeks, Wendy had tried to get in touch with her lover, sending texts and making calls to no avail. Boss Guo had told her he would be away for three weeks on business in Sanya, Hainan, a tropical island in the South China Sea. Wendy smelled a rat, and her situation—she was then two months pregnant—had demanded decisive action. She told all this to me just after being released from jail.

Earlier, while I was sick in bed, Wendy had told me, "I'm setting out to search for him." No one at his workplace would say where he was. She went to the police and asked for his home address, which they for some reason supplied, a detail I do not fully understand to this day. Wendy then went to his home but, "not wanting to disturb him or his family," waited outside by the gate. Sure enough, Boss Guo was at home, not in Sanya. The family dutifully ignored the shadow milling by the gate, and Boss Guo did not come out for hours. When he did, it was to greet the police, whom he had summoned.

The police took both Boss Guo and Wendy to the police station where Wendy told all. Smile, my landlord's daughter, later explained to me, "What Wendy has done has stirred up a major crisis of *face*."

面子, *mìanzi*, or "face," is a mixture of reputation, personal pride, and social standing. By revealing her participation in this illicit affair, Wendy had deliberately besmirched the reputation of this well-known local businessman. He lost face. But Wendy lost face too. Wendy had made public her affair with a man twenty-five years her senior, a successful businessman and the provider for his family. In an attempt to maintain face, the man denied any and all involvement with Wendy, claiming: "I have never laid a hand on her. . . . I have been involved in no pregnancies in the past." Wendy did not budge.

The police demanded an immediate but informal solution: Boss Guo was to give Wendy 500 RMB—about the amount of Wendy's rent for a month—to "handle the immediate problem." They wanted Wendy to abort the fetus she was carrying. But Wendy was having none of it—she was done with the years of silence, secrecy, and the steady abuse for being a leftover woman. Wendy wanted to talk—and she demanded to be heard by more than just a foreign roommate or a sympathetic friend.

"The media told me they want to help me," she told me the day after the altercation with Boss Guo and the police, as she washed her hair in a big ceramic bowl in our bathtub. (Our bathroom sink was not connected to pipes. We used it as a toilet paper holder.) "I need to speak. I cannot continue to hold my problem by myself." She looked high-strung but relieved and determined. She had put on her nice red sweater and her pants had no wrinkles. With a final look around the apartment to see if she'd forgotten anything, she grabbed her keys and set off on her electronic bike for the police station. The next day more reporters came to our apartment. I was aware that if Smile's parents thought Wendy's living arrangement with me was strange, the local media would find her an especially easy target. I locked my door and pretended not to be home. An hour later they left, and I thought that was the end of it.

Two days later I got a text from Smile, who asked: *Did you know Wendy is pregnant??? My whole family just saw her on TV. My parents are very, very upset.*

Smile's text confirmed that people had indeed heard Wendy. She had been busy these past few days. I had not seen her and knew she was around only because I saw a light under her door early in the morning and some half-eaten rice porridge she had left in the sink. I had also overheard her talking on the phone about Boss Guo to her close friend who owns a tea shop. Wendy often went there to listen to her friend play *guqin*, a classical Chinese stringed instrument, and to play with her friend's daughter, who considered Wendy an aunt. Based on Wendy's responses to the phone conversation, it was clear her friend was pleading with her to let the whole thing go. Wendy said that she would not and that she would stand up for what was right.

But the media did not agree that Wendy was in the right. By Western measures she was, although she was complicit. Boss Guo had seduced Wendy with promises of loving her and wanting to elope with her. He had cheated on his wife, seriously harmed and maybe ruined his family, impregnated a lonely impressionable woman, and then denied it. This man was despicable.

But none of the people I spoke with saw it that way, and that's not how the media reported it. Confucius preached the importance of the family unit. Each member of the family plays an important role: The husband is the patriarch, the wife supports him, and the children obey and respect their parents. The most important part is that this unit is just that—a unit. It is a major cornerstone of Chinese society.

Wendy's going on local TV destroyed a family unit. Her motivations for doing so were not clear. The Western romantic in me says, "She did it for justice." The Chinese pragmatist, however, might raise a few questions, particularly about the motivations of a poor woman with a rich lover.

The media, along with everyone I talked to afterward, pointed to something more malicious in Wendy. They all pointed out that she didn't need to go to the media to get a settlement from Boss Guo. Having a mistress is such a common occurrence that such settlements are almost a matter of course in China, especially when the man is wealthy. All Wendy accomplished by going on TV was to ensure the destruction of a man's face and family. People felt Wendy deserved to suffer for what she had done.

A week later the landlord asked me to move out. Smile explained that her family had been "uncomfortable" with the whole scandal. They came the next day to handle the contract, and Uncle Peng, Smile's father, slipped me an envelope with the security deposit. "I am sorry for you," he told me. His accent was thick, but he spoke slowly so I could understand. "In China, some people are good and some people are bad. I believe it is that way in America too, but I do not know." He motioned toward Wendy's suitcase with his head. "Here, you have found a bad person. We are not all that way." Smile shrugged. Her mother looked at me unhappily. Spring Festival was right around the corner, and those few hundred RMB from me would have been useful.

Weeks later the media had lost interest. They had gotten their story and moved on to the next scintillating bit of local news.

At the same time, the city announced the renovation of an old residential area as a tourist district. This turned out to include the apartment Wendy and I had just vacated. The government would be tearing down our old building and turning it into a tourist district. I ran into Uncle Peng at a local restaurant, and we ended up having a meal together. "I can only hope the government gives us a good amount for our apartment," he told me. He barely touched the food.

A bit shaken from the experience, I moved into an apartment by myself at the southern gate of the university. I was farther away from the canals and the student street I'd come to love in Suzhou.* Months later I would leave the city for good, heading west to Chengdu, the center of China's "Develop the West" program and what I was told was one of China's new boomtowns.

A few weeks before I left, at about the time the apartments were to be torn down, a missionary from Texas led Smile, as she explained it to me, to "find the Lord in Heaven and to be saved by his good graces." She began going on church outings and tried to convince her parents to join the faith. The next and last time I saw Uncle Peng he looked as if he'd aged ten years, his life made disastrously more complex by his few interactions with foreigners.

The last time I spoke with Wendy, she had yet to reach a settlement with Boss Guo, and it was not clear that she would ever reach one. He had continued to deny her allegations, and Wendy's lack of

---

*I was once reprimanded by a friend from Beijing while telling him how it pained me to move away from that apartment in Suzhou. His family had moved out of the Hutong district, the narrow street alleys that have come to be emblematic of "old Beijing." He told me, "You foreigners, especially journalists and academics, come in and want to learn about China, who China is today, where China is going, right? You all move into our historic districts and old buildings that we're all trying to move out of. Tell me this: is China going in the direction of the Hutongs? Of the run-down apartments by the canals? All of you living in those parts distorts your understanding and coverage of China."

public and personal support seemed to have sapped her strength to continue her stand against him.

With nowhere else to go, Wendy moved into a third-floor office in Boss Guo's business. She did it partly out of protest, a statement that she would not simply disappear, and partly out of necessity. Boss Guo did it out of necessity: if she would not go to the countryside, he would have to provide someplace for her to live in the city. She had a simple cot and TV. But the place got more sunlight than our ground-floor apartment had, and there was a sink with running water. The best she could now hope for was monetary support to raise this child. Boss Guo had denied her the emotional support she had been looking for. He had made it clear that he did not want Wendy and that she would remain a leftover.

As the chill continued to bite the air in her converted office space–bedroom, Wendy sat wrapped in her coat at a small table with her laptop open. The glow from a British romance danced across her hardened features. Her habit of leaving the windows open had followed her. Her breath thickened and seemed to cloud the cramped room. A suitcase lay on the ground half open. This spring festival, she was unsure if she would go home and see her parents.

7

Double Eyelids for Double 11

Conspicuous Consumption and the Biggest Consumer Holiday in the World

On an early winter night, seven of us sat in plastic chairs around a large circular wooden table in the courtyard of a bustling Sichuanese restaurant. A hole the size of a watermelon had been cut out of the table's center to make room for the gas burner visible just beneath the brim, suspended on a wooden shelf below the tabletop. The day had been pollution free, and a few stars twinkled in the night sky above Chengdu. No one at the table noticed. In the darkness, Xiao Qi and Yang's friends sat still, elbows propped against their sides, hands lifted, and faces held inches away from their smartphones. The light from their phone screens washed over their facial features, giving them an ethereal glow.

Xiao Qi sighed. He had invited everyone to join him for lamb stew, and, with the exception of his girlfriend, Yang, his friends had spent the entire night with their faces buried in their phones. Yang paid them no mind. Eyes closed, she nestled deeper into the crook of Xiao Qi's arm in his padded winter jacket, her long raven hair falling down his chest. The couple did not often get this kind of privacy—the single-sex dorms at their university did not allow members of the opposite sex into the building. Even if Xiao Qi sneaked past the guard, a sixty-year-old auntie who bore a discomfiting resemblance to Yang's imperious grandmother ("every time Xiao Qi walks me back, she stares at him like he's a dog!"), the other three students in Yang's cramped dorm room hardly made it a private space. Yang was taking advantage of the tech trance of the other diners to get some quality time with her boyfriend.

Chinese pundits and comics call Xiao Qi and Yang's generation of young Chinese the 脑残, *nǎo cán*, "the brain-dead" generation. Members of the post-90s generation are mostly digital natives, very much in sync with the face-in-phone stereotype of millennials around the world. As of 2016, 85 percent of Chinese between ages eighteen and thirty-five have smartphones, compared with only 43 percent of those over thirty-five years old.[1] (In the cities, age notwithstanding, an impressive 88 percent of city dwellers use smartphones.)[2]

On this night Xiao Qi and Yang's friends at the table were doing justice to the stereotype. I scanned the restaurant. Sure enough, the entire courtyard was filled with silent tables as patrons thumbed away on their smartphones.

From within the maze of wooden tables, a short, stout elderly woman in a grease-stained apron appeared, hoisting a heavy metal pot and quick-stepping her way toward us, her shoulders bunched tight under the load of the stew. Her practiced hands placed the pot on a metal rack over the gas burner before she reached underneath to flick it on. Flames began to lick the bottom of the pot. The old woman told us to enjoy our meal in heavily accented Sichuanese dialect, then sped off to the kitchen, weaving through the crowd to get there.

The smell of slow-cooked lamb broth and coriander soon

reached my nose as waves of steam from the pot glimmered under the lights suspended over the courtyard. Just beyond the courtyard walls, cars sped by and three-wheeled motorbikes with tin cabs ferried commuters from the subway station to their apartment complexes. Lamb stew is said to warm the whole body and stock it with nutrients to keep you hearty through the cold months. Tonight's lamb stew invitation had signaled winter's arrival in this gateway to western China.

Xiao Qi and Yang kept stealing kisses. From the corner of his eye, their friend Renée, a young filmmaker and aspiring director, kept peeking at them. He coughed. They continued to canoodle. He coughed louder. They ignored him. Finally, Renée blurted out, "I can't be near them anymore! Their cuteness is making me physically ill." He looked toward Rebecca for support. She did not so much as look up from her phone to acknowledge Renée had spoken.

Rebecca was twenty-three and a recent returnee to Sichuan Province. She often went by her English name, which someone had given her while she was working in Shanghai. Everyone knew Renée had a crush on Rebecca. In response to her silence, he tousled his long hair and went back to his phone. I could see it was opened to Tantan, the Chinese dating app. Renée chose his English name for the same reasons he kept his hair long and a trim goatee, more in a Japanese style than what is popular in Mainland China. "It makes me seem more mysterious," he had told me.

Brain-dead or not, the entire clientele of the restaurant was engaged in excessive phone activity. I disrupted the cuddling couple to ask Xiao Qi, "Is today some sort of brain-dead national holiday? What's the deal with all of the phones?"

Xiao Qi raised his eyebrows. "Don't you know what tomorrow is?"

I shook my head. I did not. Without looking up, Yang pointed to the TV mounted on the concrete wall in the courtyard. The news anchor on CCTV's nightly news was doing her evening report: "With Singles' Day right around the corner, Chinese singletons are fervently scanning the web, determined to find love and happiness . . ."

"Tomorrow is Singles' Day," Xiao Qi said with a grin and pulled Yang a little closer.

I looked at Renée's phone screen. He had found a match on Tantan, and now he was considering how to start the conversation with her, typing a sentence and then deleting it until he settled on "Happy Singles' Day^_^."

"Like Valentine's Day?" I asked.

"Similar but inverted," Renée said. "Valentine's Day celebrates that you have a girlfriend. Singles' Day reminds you that you don't."

Motioning at the room full of people glued to their devices, I asked, "So everyone here is scouring Tantan for a date?"

Xiao Qi shook his head and motioned to the TV once more.

"Shoppers everywhere are getting their purchases ready for Singles' Day to take advantage of the steep discounts. This year Alibaba will have tens of thousands of vendors making discounts. Jack Ma [Alibaba's founder] expects to break the global single-day spending record yet again, and this time in record speed."

The special reports on Singles' Day would air all night long.

"Singles' Day is our major consumer holiday," Xiao Qi said. "Everything on Taobao [Alibaba's online marketplace] is put on sale for twenty-four hours. They're all on their phones using the Taobao app and planning what they're going to buy."

"On Chinese Reverse Valentine's Day, everyone just buys things?" I asked.

Xiao Qi nodded before motioning toward Renée, who was

laboring over what to write to his match on Tantan. "Others are searching for . . . distractions."

Renée cursed under his breath, turned his plastic stool away, and cast another furtive glance in Rebecca's direction. She rolled her eyes and pivoted her chair to face the other direction.

二

Singles' Day, *Guānggùn jié*, translates literally as "Bare Branch Day." The four lonesome ones in the date—November 11, or 11/11—refers to China's singles, still-bare branches without their own family tree. Singles' Day's humble beginnings date to the early 1990s and a group of college guys from Nanjing. These young men had one thing in common: despite their best efforts, they were still single. Each year on 11/11 the singletons would get together. The holiday grew modestly in popularity over time through word of mouth and, eventually, online forum chatter, and then nurtured annually by beer, karaoke, and commiseration. No one aspired to be invited to attend again the next year.

Two decades later, in 2009, Jack Ma, the founder of Alibaba, reinvented Singles' Day after it caught his eye. Without Christmas to drive sales in China, Ma was searching for a way to boost Taobao's revenue between Chinese National Day in September and Chinese Spring Festival (better known as Chinese New Year), which, because of the fluctuations of the lunar calendar, typically occurs somewhere between early February and late April.

China has roughly two hundred million single citizens older than eighteen.[3] They are playfully called single dogs. If they formed their own country, they would be the sixth-largest nation in the world, ranked between Brazil and Pakistan. It would undoubtedly be an island nation. China also has the largest online matchmaking business in the world, Baihe, which has 220 million registered accounts. Should these single dogs form an island nation, it would be one of the few countries in the world that nearly all citizens would be doing their damnedest to leave.

Alibaba transformed Singles' Day into a one-day shopping bonanza. It started with twenty-seven vendors who agreed to slash prices for a twenty-four-hour period. It grew almost uncontrollably.[4] Within only three years of its introduction, Singles' Day had broken the global single-day spending record for any holiday, eclipsing Black Friday and Cyber Monday combined.[5] (Singles' Day sales were nearly three times America's two biggest shopping days combined in 2015.)[6] Just five years after Ma turned it into a spending holiday, Singles' Day had grown to *twenty-seven thousand* vendors. Years after that, the number had swelled to over forty thousand and included global vendors.[7] In 2016 online sales on Singles Day alone were more than Brazil's total projected e-commerce sales for the year.[8] Alibaba did its first billion dollars' worth of sales in five minutes.[9]

Singles' Day and Taobao presaged a new era for Chinese consumption. In 2014, during the twenty-third hour of his record-breaking Singles' Day, Jack Ma stood in front of a crowd of employees and reporters and proudly proclaimed, "Witness China's online shopping and consumer demand . . . Today, we can see strength and vitality within that demand. We've just used a novel way to bring that demand to the surface."[10]

What many marketers, competitors, and amateur anthropologists want to know is, well, how? Chinese families are famously big savers. Urbanization has forced families to spend more money on city living, but the Chinese household savings rate remains about 30 percent of disposable income. (The United States just celebrated an increase to 5.5 percent.) By the numbers the Chinese Born After '90 generation is different from previous generations. In 2000, when Xiao Qi was only eight years old, only 4 percent of Chinese families were considered middle class (households earning 60,000 to 229,000 RMB—US$9,000 to US$34,000—a year. By 2012, when Xiao Qi was a sophomore in college, the number had exploded to 68 percent.[11] Still, when Western marketers write about Chinese millennials, they describe them as if they are a pack of unicorns, magical and elusive.

When Jack Ma and Alibaba were able to coordinate more than forty thousand vendors to slash prices on name-brand, high-quality items from all over the world in every single category of product, Double 11 sparked nothing less than fervor—fervor to the tune of $5 billion in an hour, as of 2016.[12] This one holiday offered many complete worlds of products—shoes, clothing, technology, furniture, and even cars—at half the regular price.

On a normal day Alibaba ships seventeen million packages worldwide; the week after Singles' Day, it shipped nearly 650 million. The company estimated that it had deployed 1.7 million delivery personnel, 400,000 delivery vehicles, 5,000 warehouses, and 200 airplanes to get everything where it needed to go.[13]

The days leading up to Singles' Day in China are focused mayhem. To participate in Singles' Day without preparation, Xiao Qi explained, is like "trying to conquer a city without a map of its walls and gates." I laughed. Xiao Qi cocked his head and raised his eyebrows. He wasn't joking.

三

Singles' Day aside, China actually has two Valentine's Days, the traditional one, called Qi Yi, and the adopted Western holiday.

Compared with Singles' Day, neither has gained any real traction in modern China. Pundits have described Singles' Day as a form of mass retail therapy, a drowning of sorrows in discount sales. While that may be the case to a certain extent, Singles' Day also thrives because it offers a genuine solution to the problem it poses: singledom. Jack Ma's Singles' Day has been so successful financially because it plays a clever psychological trick. Whereas Valentine's Day is an opportunity to celebrate what you have, Singles' Day provides an opportunity to get what you want.

It is said in China that when a woman is searching for a man, a real catch is 高富帅, *gāo, fù, shuài*—"tall, rich, and handsome." The punch line is "but, actually, tall and handsome you can do without!" That leaves rich. Yang explains, "What am I supposed to do with a tall guy? Will his height put food on the table? And handsome? Too handsome and too many other women will be interested. I'll have no sense of security with him out and about."

The saying for men is that they should find someone who is 白富美, *bǎi fù měi*—"pale, rich, and beautiful." And of course the punch line is "but, actually, pale and rich you can do without!" That leaves beautiful, so young women like Yang feel tremendous pressure to participate in one of the fastest-growing markets in China: beauty products.

Both sets of requirements—tall, rich, and handsome as well as pale, rich, and beautiful—originated as satire in online forums, biting commentary on China's shallow standards of attractiveness. Now news anchors for the major state-sponsored television network reference these descriptions as social fact.

Renée neatly summarized the correlation between Singles' Day and mass retail: "We Chinese like to have nice stuff. Girls like guys with nice things. Nice things translate to a good income. Good income means you can provide a stable life. Everyone wants a stable life. So I bought this stupid iPhone."

Chinese analysis of Singles' Day orbits around this type of consumer semiotics; it focuses not on what a product can do but what it represents. What does a new car *represent*? What does an iPhone *symbolize*?

At the most basic level, the ability to buy and then have a certain phone, wear a certain brand, or drive a certain car symbolizes security. Chinese matchmaking remains heavily gendered. For Chinese women seeking a match, few factors are more important than what China's bevy of TV dating shows and romance series refer to as 安全感, *ānquán gǎn*, a sense of security or feeling of safety. The sense of security that women seek from men is often financial. Parents in particular emphasize the importance of finding someone who can provide a "sense of security" for their daughter. Several decades ago the word *ānquán gǎn* did not mean what it does today; it is a modern euphemism, the byproduct of a culture in which financial security was not a guarantee and some people became wealthy while others struggled to make ends meet. Every dating site and marriage market in China posts three basic statistics: age, height, and income. The first two are fixed, though the spikes in plastic surgeries certainly attempt to ameliorate these genetic constraints. The third—income, or at least the perception of income—is more malleable. With Singles' Day's many deals, a young man like Renée can boost his perceived value at half the price.

Renée was looking at a denim jacket with a white fur collar from Levi's. I asked him if he knew whether it was real. "Ha! Of course it's fake. The real one costs twice as much," he replied. "But our fakes in China can be very good. We made the real ones to begin with, am I right?"

Taobao became overwhelmingly popular because China's young

people are aspirational, but they're not yet wealthy. Taobao offers them the brands, looks, and types of products they want at a steep discount. More than 60 percent of the goods on Taobao failed to meet China's retail-goods standards, according to the Chinese State Administration of Industry and Commerce based on a random sampling. (Taobao retorted that the survey only selected 51 products out of the more than 1 billion they had on sale.)[14] Even if Chinese young people do not have much money, Taobao allows them to buy fashionable clothes and high-performance electronics without breaking the bank. The goods aren't always real, but they are within reach and often of similar quality.

Renée pointed to his Abercrombie jeans and said, "The best fakes are often made in the real factory, maybe by an enterprising night manager. Often an expensive material is swapped out for a cheaper lookalike. The important part is the brand names. Those all look real."

Anything and everything is available on Taobao—from name-brand clothes, both real and knockoffs, to electronics, bespoke suits, locally harvested honey, or Tibetan jewelry. In the six years following the creation of Singles' Day, the number of packages Taobao delivered annually increased from one billion to ten billion. Seventy percent of the Born After '90 generation who buy online prefer to use Taobao.[15]

Taobao is also democratic. Competition is fierce and users obsessively rate their purchases. The best products naturally rise to the top. Taobao fundamentally changed purchasing power in China by making it possible for people to buy that Gucci belt knockoff while they were still making the equivalent of US$500 a month at a low-level tech job.

For the real stuff, everyone knows to buy from Alibaba's T-Mall, where 85 percent of the products are genuine, or from Jingdong, Alibaba's massive e-commerce competitor. However, Jack Ma's e-commerce buying platform reigns supreme. The combined sales of T-Mall and Taobao mean that Alibaba has 75 percent of China's e-commerce market. Amazon, in comparison, accounts for less than half of the e-commerce market in the United States.[16]

"Fake or not isn't a big deal," Renée continued. "We want an OK quality and brand names. Taobao allows us to get that most of the time at a discount. And on Singles' Day everyone slashes their prices. The sales are better than any other time in the year." As he spoke, Renée used his Taobao phone app to add the denim jacket to his e-cart for checkout. The cart was crammed with items he would buy after midnight when the sales began.

四

On the eve of Singles' Day it felt as if everyone in the entire country was standing by their phones or computers, waiting to push all their bookmarked items into their checkout bin. Friends teamed up on group chats to scour for and swap information about the best upcoming deals. Entire blogs devoted to shopping strategies for Singles' Day circulate spreadsheets that compare the best deals on laptops and the prices of different phones offered by competing platforms. Masses of Chinese buyers had reserved an entire year of big-purchase shopping for this one day in November.

Singles' Day attracts everyone, not just singles. Xiao Qi and Yang would be buying too. Xiao Qi wanted to replace his old, beat-up jacket. Yang would buy a new pair of winter boots.

Yang also planned to buy something else on Singles' Day.

She clicked on an ad a friend had sent her: "Double Eyelids for Double 11!"

Yang had become convinced that she would not be beautiful enough to keep Xiao Qi without "double eyelids," a new beauty trend in China, like a six-pack or a light skin. The double eyelid fold is a horizontal crease in the skin of an eyelid that appears when someone who has it opens and closes their eyes. While it is something I had never considered, it has become an obsession in China. (Someone who has had the surgery looks as if she's had a minor eye lift.)

I learned more about the craze at the Guangzhou Beauty Conference, the twenty-fifth biggest beauty expo in the world. The Disney World-esque crowds flock from all over Asia and around the world, packing into five multilevel hangars. Hotels fill up months in advance. I met a woman named Lily who ran a company that sold double eyelid stickers. She promptly sat me down in a chair on a small stage so she could use me as a sales gimmick.

"Close your eyes," Lily instructed after I was seated. Fifteen young women hovered around us, watching intently.

Lily stood over me like a doctor performing an examination for a theater of med students. Gesturing with a closed pen, she pointed to my eyes. "Watch what happens, ladies. OK, open them slowly."

I complied. Lily raised her voice sharply for effect, gesturing toward my face. "There! Do you see it? The double eyelid fold." Lily pointed at me with her pen for the benefit of the crowd. "Foreigners have the double eyelid, even young men. We Chinese do not," Lily explained.

Lily was in the business of eyelid stickers, small strips of plastic about a third of the size of a piece of litmus paper that you can stick on your eyelids to cause their skin to fold over. This creates a double eyelid effect. "Most Chinese are cursed with flat features, eyelids included," Lily declared for the crowd. "Our eye stickers help solve the curse Chinese women live with that even foreign men like this don't have to worry about! The effect is a deeper, more complex look. The stickers and the double eyelid add dimensionality."

Lily's major competition is double eyelid surgery. She explained that the decision to get the surgery was partly a financial one. "What, do you expect a Chinese person to not do the math? A lifetime of stickers or a few-minute operation? Easy decision. I can't compete with women or men willing to do the procedure, and with little social stigma it becomes more and more popular all the time."

There isn't much social stigma around body enhancement in China. Eyelid stickers are commonplace, and products like colored contact lenses are daily wears for many young people who want to stand out in a populace with predominantly black eyes. For the aspiring Chinese, "self-improvement" of this sort has become normalized. Who is to say that a minor surgery is going too far?

"We live in a face-centric society," Yang said, citing a popular bit of social commentary about selfie culture and Chinese social media, where people take daily close-ups of their face to share with their whole network. "I know I am pretty, but my single eyelids make me feel very average. Xiao Qi is handsome, and his job is fairly good. Other girls probably would be interested in him. The double-eyelids procedure gives me my own 安全感, *ānquán gǎn*, sense of security."

Yang paid for the procedure by using an online voucher—she paid on Alipay, Alibaba's e-wallet—on 11/11.

A week later she took a two-hour train ride from Chengdu to visit the Chongqing Plastic Surgery Clinic. From the banks of the Yangtze River the sign for the clinic blinks like a hotel's.

The procedure for double eyelids is quick. There is almost shockingly little to do. Two quick incisions on the eyelids, and the scarring will cause the crease.

Just like that, Yang, like thousands and thousands of other young women, now met a standard of beauty that didn't exist in China a few decades ago.

五

China's galloping GDP has always had an invisible running partner—China's rapidly rising social expectations. In a country that thirty years ago had a per capita GDP of less than US$200, notions about what it takes to lead a "good life" have mutated faster than China's economy. TV shows and movies showcase the latest trends in China's development. The chasm between the expectations of Chinese young people—their dreams of the life they'd like to lead—and their financial reality is often bigger, broader, and more harrowing than any other such gap in the world. They suffer the frustration that comes from sitting at a roadside stall and eating a dollar plate of fried rice while a Ferrari zooms by.

Rebecca had just moved back to Chengdu from Shanghai. There, she had worked at a Korean barbecue restaurant downtown. She was twenty-three, from Anhui Province, and single. She had moved to Shanghai for the opportunities. "I didn't actually know of any specific opportunities, just that everyone in the country says Shanghai is one of those cities where you can make your dreams come true," she told me. Rebecca's dream was only to make it big in a modern city. Anhui had no big cities, and few in the world could rival the glitz and glam of the coastal metropolis of Shanghai.

Rebecca didn't have a lot to offer the job market. "I graduated from a three-year trade school in Chengdu," she told me. "I could have gotten a decent job back home, but then I would have had to stay in my tiny hometown or a fourth- or fifth-tier city. I'm young! I wanted to experience the big city for myself like I'd seen on TV." When she had trouble finding and keeping a job in Shanghai, she came back to Chengdu, one of the fastest-developing economic hubs in China.

Despite her job troubles, she was determined to buy an iPhone on this Singles' Day.

How on Earth does someone making US$500 a month afford an $850 phone? Rebecca's parents were not wealthy. Rebecca borrowed only a little from them for rent and food, because she didn't want to place undue financial pressure on them. "This phone I want to buy myself!" she asserted proudly. So she waited for Singles' Day, when the phones would be somewhat less expensive.

Two of China's most popular media personalities and podcasters, Liang Dong and Wu Bofan, devoted a show to the question: "How do servers at an average Chinese restaurant afford that iPhone they are using to snap selfies of themselves at work?"

On the surface it makes little economic sense. Although iPhones are assembled within China, they are more expensive there than almost anywhere else in the world. While an unlocked iPhone cost $649 in the United States, the same phone was $851 in China.*

iPhones also cost Chinese consumers a greater percentage of their income than they do shoppers in other countries. The cost of an iPhone is more than five times Rebecca's monthly rent. A server in California who works full time might make about $30,000 per year. That server might be able to cover the cost by scrimping for

---

*"The lock is really a software code that's put on the phone by the manufacturer as per the requirement of the carrier that sells the device. And the lock is meant to ensure that the phone can't be used on any other operator's network until a different software code is entered to unlock the device." Marguerite Reardon, "Ask Maggie," *CNET,* August 15, 2013, https://www.cnet.com/news/confused-about-locked-vs-unlocked-phones-ask-maggie-explains/.

a few months. If Rebecca doesn't eat, pay rent, take the bus to work, pay any bills, or spend any money whatsoever for a month, she still cannot not afford to buy an iPhone with her month's earnings.

Dong and Wu hypothesized that people who cannot afford an iPhone insist on buying one because the Born After '90 generation is intensely aspirational, and they want to be living their best life now. Someone who makes 3,000 RMB (US$440) a month will never be able to afford a car. Buying an apartment is even less of a possibility. An iPhone, then, is the nicest big purchase they can afford that feels loosely within reach.

In Shanghai growing numbers of women were looking to buy their own apartment. Doing so is a statement of independence, especially for urban women who are choosing to pursue their career rather than marry young. Rebecca had considered saving for an apartment but quickly ditched the plan. "It just would never have been possible without huge help from my parents," she said with a shake of her head. But an iPhone? If she saved diligently, maybe took out a small loan, or went on a payment plan, the luxury of an iPhone could be hers. It was her reach-for-the-stars purchase, her pride-and-joy investment, and her way of reveling in the moment. "I could save for a lifetime for an apartment to enjoy when I'm old, or I could save for half a year to enjoy myself now," she reasoned.

Chinese young people possess a new determination to enjoy themselves today, a "be here now" mentality that's become pervasive. Rebecca didn't want to save for an apartment and become what she and millions of others called 房奴, *fáng nú*, "apartment slaves." Her parents emphasize delayed gratification, but she wants to live fast while she is young.

And so iPhones sell wildly, although they are a financially insane purchase for the vast majority of China's youth. It is a luxury they can have now.

六

Xiao Qi withdrew his arm from around Yang's waist and scribbled, "An entire year's planning begins in spring" on a piece of paper. This Chinese proverb dates to 500 AD. When farmers first harvested rice eight thousand years ago, they initiated a proud agrarian culture in China that today produces and consumes about a quarter of the world's rice. Planting begins in spring, and so Chinese rice farmers must work especially hard to set up a proper foundation upon which the year's plantings—their livelihood—can grow. Dreams of bumper harvest must take root in spring.

In the abstract, the proverb is about youth. Youth in Chinese is 青春, *qīngchūn*, literally "young spring." I once watched as a teacher at a middle school in Jiangxi Province wrote that idiom on the blackboard and had her forty students write it one hundred times in their notebooks. Her message? The seeds of a person's fate are sown in the spring of their life; work hard now so your future can blossom.

Xiao Qi added the character 节, *jié* (festival) transforming *spring* to *Spring Festival*, commonly known as Chinese New Year, and by far the most important Chinese holiday, like Christmas amplified. "There," he said, admiring his modification. "A whole year's plans depend on Spring Festival. It is good to update these sorts of proverbs, am I right?"

Perhaps Jack Ma's greatest stroke of genius in creating Singles' Day was its place on the calendar before Spring Festival. The holiday is the only time when nearly everyone in China returns to their hometown and to their family. It is one of the largest human migrations on Earth; in 2014 the Chinese booked 3.6 billion one-way train tickets for the festival (the China Railway Corporation does not sell round-trip tickets).[17]

Renée blinked several times at the idiom Xiao Qi had written on the napkin before turning to the rest of the table and asking, "What is he talking about?"

Xiao Qi replied, "You're buying a new comforter for your parents. You're buying two vitamin sets for them for the next year. You've got sneakers for your dad and a purse for your mom. You've got booze for your uncles." Renée continued to stare at the proverb. Xiao Qi added, "The point is that these are not items for Singles' Day; these are purchases in preparation for Spring Festival."

Just as China's is a culture of treated meals, it is also a culture of gift giving. The vibrant gift economy, as it is called in China, is both an expression of love and a social necessity. That's why the master stroke of Jack Ma's Singles' Day may be its timing. Because Singles' Day always arrives close to China's most important holiday, the country can do all of its Spring Festival shopping at a major discount.

Going home means facing the fusillade of questions from the 七姑八姨, *qīgū bāyí*, the seven aunts and eight uncles discussed in chapter 4. Last year, on a seven-day trip to his hometown for Spring Festival, Xiao Qi tracked how many times people had asked whether he had a girlfriend. It came to 107.

This year Xiao Qi described the process of going home as a sort of championship lap for him. He had the answer to the big question always asked by his parents, who now would have an answer to the big question asked by his relatives, who would have the answer to the big question the neighbors would ask: Are you seeing anyone? He had a wonderful girlfriend. They expect to get married. His job is alright and his future looks fine, even bright. Because he had a reply to the one major question on the community's mind, he was at ease.

Because he was pursuing a nontraditional profession, Renée's homecoming promised to be much more difficult than Xiao Qi's. "How will you ever make money as a director?" his aunt would ask. "How can you ever find a girlfriend without a better income?" his uncle would ask. "When am I going to be able to hold my grandson?" his mom would ask.

So Singles' Day provided three opportunities. Singles' Day purchases might prove to be bait for finding a steady girlfriend or boyfriend before heading home. (Through Taobao you can pay for someone to accompany you and pose as your significant other during Spring Festival.) Because Chinese believe they can use Singles' Day purchases to improve their appearance, they also believe that these purchases improve the perception of your life in the city. People often marry someone from their hometown, so Singles' Day provides an opportunity to impress the neighbors at half the price. Finally, buying great presents for all your relatives is an expression of magnanimity that they will use to gauge your financial status. Win. Win. Win.

七

Alibaba's headquarters is in the ancient Chinese capital of Hangzhou, a two-hour ride on the bullet train from Nanjing, where those college guys started Singles' Day.

Back in 2012, the pens, pencils, binders, folders, staplers, and notebooks in the stationery aisle at a Chinese supermarket were dominated by an instantly recognizable visage, and it wasn't Jack Ma's. The late cofounder and CEO of Apple, Steve Jobs, was the king of the back-to-school section.

Young students should aspire to be like America's greatest innovator, the notebooks were saying. Then, in 2014, Ma took Alibaba to the New York Stock Exchange and broke the record for world's largest initial public offering. It made Jack Ma a hero of innovation in China. Today Ma's face presides over the stationery section, and he has been immortalized in documentaries, dozens of biographies, and on the rubber eraser of #2 pencils.

Taobao has turned China into a country of entrepreneurs. For college students and young adults like Xiao Qi and his friends, Taobao was something of a club—"for us by us." Hundreds of thousands of small resellers populate Taobao, and many are young people trying to supplement their income. They are able to get inventory—phones, wallets, handbags—at wholesale prices by making monthly trips to Hong Kong and bringing them across the border in luggage to avoid paying the various taxes that were imposed on large retail stores.

E-commerce has done so well in China in part because Chinese consumers are natural early adopters. In 2016, 82 percent of Singles' Day purchases on Taobao were made through its mobile app compared with only around 25 percent three years earlier.[18] China's apps, especially for smartphones, are in many ways much more advanced than those available in the West. Yu He, an exchange student at San Francisco State, once told me, "Compared to how easy it is to buy with Taobao and Jingdong, it honestly feels like your companies here don't want my money."

八

We finished the stew and headed to a nearby cafe. "Fast, reliable, cheap Wi-Fi," Renée assured me.

When the clock struck midnight, the shoppers were unleashed. The crowd at the café shouted out their buys as they were confirmed. A minifridge. Pu'er tea, a gift for Xiao Qi's parents. A Xiaomi cell phone. One year's worth of Korean face-moisturizing masks to repair skin and maintain that youthful glow. Huawei computers. A pair of Nikes for Wang's dad. Two pair of Nikes for her. A couple two tables down bought a car—a Cadillac, no less—at half price. They hugged and jumped, hugged and jumped.

I watched online as the sales streamed in to Alibaba headquarters. In the first eight minutes Alibaba made its first $1 billion in sales for the day.

Xiao Qi bought Yang the winter boots she had wanted so much. Yang bought Xiao Qi the new winter jacket he needed, replacing the one she'd spent so much time nuzzling. Xiao Qi bought a Xiaomi phone for his mom. He bought his dad Puma shoes to ease the pain in his feet. He also bought a briefcase-sized box of vitamins for Yang to give to her parents on Chinese New Year, a common gift for those for whom you are trying to express caring and consideration. "This is a gift for in-laws," Renée noted. "Is there something you want to tell us? Is there a wedding proposal on the way?" Xiao Qi socked him in the arm. He had still not met Yang's parents.

Rebecca bought an iPhone for herself, vitamins for her parents, and a variety of Sichuanese delicacies to bring back to her friends and family in Anhui Province. "The spice is going to make them cry," she said with a smile. No one quite understood how she afforded it, but Yang said she saw stacks of instant noodles last time she was at Rebecca's apartment.

Renée bought expensive boxes of vitamins for his parents, good booze for his uncles, and fancy tea for his aunts. "I get that they want the best for me, but the questions are a real pain in the ass," he said. "Truthfully, they make me feel like I'm failing here by going after my dream. These gifts ought to show them that I'm doing OK."

In the States, 2016's Cyber Monday had raked in just shy of

$3.5 billion in twenty-four hours across all companies and all buying platforms, easily blowing past initial estimates and last year's record.[19] By 1:00 a.m. shopping sites like Taobao, Tmall, AliExpress, and Tmall Global had poured more than $5 billion in sales into Alibaba's coffers.[20]

When Yang went home a few months later, her parents took in her eyelids with a quizzical look. "What beautiful boots!" her mom said, an artful diversion. "Where did you get those boots?" Yang's dad asked.

"Actually, someone bought them for me."

"Who?"

Yang handed her parents the yearlong supply of vitamins Xiao Qi had gotten for them. "The same person who got you these."

They looked at each other, looked at the box of vitamins, and then looked at Yang. Her mom smiled and laughed excitedly. Her dad shrugged and scratched his head. "When will we be getting to meet him?"

8

Test Monsters Dream of Innovation

Will China's Superstudents Reinvent Their Country?

When Lin Lin sat down at the table, her eyes surveyed my tape recorder and notepad in one deliberate sweep. "It is a pleasure to meet you," she said in lightly accented English. She slipped her backpack straps over the back of her chair, placed a book with a light blue cover on the table, and promptly rested her hand on top. A portrait of a young woman peeked out from beneath her fingers. Before I could get a good look, her résumé materialized on the table for my perusal. The server arrived. Lin Lin ordered an apple juice.

I was interviewing Lin Lin because I was working on behalf of the Columbia University admissions office. My small role was to speak with students, primarily in western China, who had made it through the first few stages of the college admission process. After each interview I wrote a report, one of many components that comprise the strange alchemy of a Columbia University admissions decision.

"Your SAT scores are quite good," I said, looking over her materials. "Was taking the test in English difficult for you?"

The young woman across from me smiled broadly, revealing a full mouth of braces. "The test portion was OK, but I struggled with the writing portion."

I looked down at her résumé. She had gotten a perfect score. In fact, she had gotten a perfect score on the whole test. Of the nearly 1.7 million prospective college students to take the test that year, Lin Lin was one of the 583 who had earned a perfect score—2400. And she took the test in her second language.*

"Of what achievement or experience are you most proud?" I asked Lin Lin.

"My book sales and my scholarship fund," she replied. The young woman pictured on the book cover beneath her palm was, in fact, Lin Lin. *Love You on the Moor*, a book of poems, written in English, inspired by the Victorian authors and poets she loved to read in middle school, was published when Lin Lin was fifteen.

Lin Lin had spearheaded the advertising and sales efforts for *Love You on the Moor*. She began with a book sale at school. She explained, "I was really nervous because I worried that the students would not accept my poetry, which took me years to complete. However, I convinced myself to give it a try, because, after all, the worst that would happen would be failure. I did lots of preparation work beforehand, practicing a sales speech and making a roll-up banner." On the day of the sale she gave a rousing speech in front of her homemade banner and sold 325 copies to a student body of only eight hundred. Riding high on that success, she contacted Dangdang, one of China's biggest online booksellers, and asked it to sell her book on its site; she used the sales she made at school to demonstrate the book's

*The College Board denied my request to see countries of origins for all testers who scored perfect marks, and I couldn't help but wonder how many came from China.

potential. Dangdang agreed. With the proceeds from the book sales, Lin Lin started her own scholarship fund in rural Chongqing, sponsoring the high school education of four exceptional students from the rural village of Ersheng.

Chengdu, her hometown, was the center of China's Develop the West strategy, an attempt to mend the economic fractures riddling China. Due to quick and uneven development, the economic distance between a city like Chengdu and a village like Ersheng was staggering, better measured in decades than miles.

"Why did you select these prospective majors?" I asked.

"My dream to study economics and political science is rooted in funerals," she told me.

I blinked and asked, "Your dream is about funerals?"

"Funerals," she repeated. "In the rural areas in my home province, Sichuan, people have to save as much as possible for huge one-time expenditures, like big surgeries and traditional grand funerals. Their income is low, and their land yields inconsistent results, often quite meager. Whenever someone dies or get sick, these families shoulder a large economic burden."

"The Chinese urban-rural wealth gap seems like a problem best studied in China. Why not consider Tsinghua or Peking universities?" I asked.

Shrugging, Lin Lin swept the hair out her eyes before explaining, "I've considered those options. My dream is to study at a university that promotes . . ." Lin Lin looked up in thought, sifting through her expansive files of English words and phrases. She was also the third prizewinner of CCTV's *Star of Outlook English Talent Competition*, beating out tens of thousands of contestants nationally, "critical thinking and innovation. Plus, Chinese universities are not the best in the world. The best are in America. I want to go there."

—

In recent years, people all over China have become fluent in the soul-searching language of dreams. While ambition has always been native to China, the self-centric idea of dreams has not always found a place in China as it had abroad. Surprisingly, the Chinese government had a hand in normalizing dreaming.

President Xi Jinping first introduced the Chinese Dream to his country in 2012. It has since come to epitomize his administration. When he first enunciated the idea, he kept it vague. Xi explained obliquely that the Chinese Dream meant "the great rejuvenation of the Chinese nation." The word *rejuvenation*, though, doesn't capture all its meaning. It can also be translated as "renaissance." The idea was abstract and profound; the president of a nearly 1.4 billion-person country was urging his people to dream.

As time passed, the notion of a Chinese Dream became increasingly personal. Teachers began to ask their students to write papers about *their* Chinese Dream, and the best might be featured in local news. On China's hit TV series *Voice of China*, the host suddenly began by asking contestants, "What is *your* Chinese Dream?" TV reporters covered the heart-wrenching story of a student from a disaster zone who made it to a province-level science fair and won first prize; they praised the winner for "actualizing *his* Chinese Dream."

It takes guts to dream sincerely, and China is also in a so-called pre-ironic phase. People are not jaded about the idea of dreaming, nor are they discouraged from speaking from the heart. Debbie Ho, a popular post-90s podcaster who is a Peking University student and originally from Tibet, told me, "Say what you will about China and Beijing, but at least it is a place where no one will laugh at your dreams."

Eventually, President Xi became clearer about what the Chinese Dream means for the country. He announced the "Two 100s," goals to be reached by the centennial anniversary of two pivotal moments in Chinese history. The first is to become a "moderately prosperous nation" by 2021, the hundredth anniversary of the founding of the Communist Party. At the crux of this goal is doing away with poverty and improving the standard of living for China's poorest people; Xi wants to double China's 2010 per capita GDP (then about US$10,000) by 2020. For stability's sake the Communist Party wants to bring wealth and prosperity inland and out west. The second 100 is to become a fully developed nation by 2049, the hundredth anniversary of the founding of the People's Republic of China. These are to be the pillars of China's modern renaissance.

The Two 100s are based on a new vision of China's economy, which, under Xi's direction, is straining to become more innovative. To beat poverty and become a developed nation, China needs not just manufacturers but also scientists and entrepreneurs.

The government began this search for innovation by trying to fix the systems that destroyed it—namely, corruption. The aspirations of Chinese once were limited by their station and standing with the local government. Pew Research quantified that helplessness in 2015 when it reported that Chinese say the single biggest problem in their country—more than polluted water, unsafe food, or hazardous air—is government corruption.[1] Only those with the right connections could enter the guarded doors to success. In an era of dreaming, it made sense that the other pillar of Xi's administration has been his well-documented anticorruption campaign, which he introduced almost concurrently with the Chinese Dream.

But some dreams of Chinese young people began to drift overseas. A piece of punditry that circulated widely in WeChat circles jibed, "Young people's Chinese Dream is to leave China and study abroad in America!"

When Xi introduced the Chinese Dream in 2012, nearly a third of all study-abroad students in the United States came from China, a full three times more than from India, which has a larger college-age population than China and similar education ambitions. The number of students China sent abroad increased on average just under 20 percent a year between 2007 and 2016.[2] By 2015 more than half a million Chinese students were studying abroad, bringing the total number of Chinese students outside China to almost a million, a third of which were in the United States.[3] The Chinese Dream seems to increasingly revolve around other countries, especially the United States.

It seems strange. Why does a political party deeply invested in information control allow young minds to be shaped abroad? The Chinese government, if it chooses to do so, has a dozen different ways to eliminate, restrict, or, at the very least, severely hamper efforts of students to study abroad. Visa restrictions would be a one-stroke solution if the Party were so inclined. But it has not been. The government is even passing legislation that encourages students to study overseas.

What role does America—and countries like the UK, Australia, Japan, and Canada, all with large Chinese study-abroad populations—play in China's plans for rejuvenation? For renaissance?

☰

First Lady Michelle Obama arrived in Sichuan Province in 2014 amid much fanfare. All the local and national media covered her visit: Mrs. Obama visits the panda conservatory; the First Lady tries tai chi with students; Michelle speaks with local high school students.

Obama visited Chengdu No. 7, one of China's four "national model high schools," a designation bestowed by the Ministry of Education in 2009. It also happened to be eighteen-year-old Ju Chao's high school, and Ju Chao was tapped to give the speech welcoming America's first lady. Ju Chao, a senior from Chengdu, then was in the process of applying to colleges abroad. We met when I interviewed him for Columbia. He was a natural choice for the speech—the president of the school's Model United Nations Club, an honors student in science, and a standout English speaker with charisma. Still, he was nervous. In his Columbia college application essay he had described some of his emotions when he was called to his principal's office and greeted by Beijing officials, who briefed him on the speech he would prepare:

> *Due to the strict diplomatic codes, I had to pay great attention to my words. "No, you can't say 'warmly welcome.' Just 'welcome.'" I was cautioned many times about minor details. Like dancing with shackles, I tried to squeeze in some of my own ideas besides conveying Beijing's message, which occupied most of the space.**

In addition to Columbia, Barack Obama's alma mater, Ju Chao then was applying to a half-dozen other top American universities.

Ju Chao groaned as he recalled the essay: "My writing voice sounded so uptight. What was my problem? I needed to relax." He whisked two pairs of chopsticks out of the red plastic container on the table and handed one to me. Then, with a sly grin, he said, "Pretty cool, though, eh? The First Lady listened to me speak."

---

*Both Ju Chao and Lin Lin offered me their admissions materials after the admissions process had been completed.

Ju Chao's dream of studying abroad had begun when he was ten and his father read to him from a science magazine. "My father read to me about the Apollo mission. It was such fantasy, so far outside of the 'get up, study, go-to-sleep' pattern here. My dad loved to read it to me, and I loved to listen." Columbia, he told me later, was not his first choice—that was the Massachusetts Institute of Technology, which the Apollo article had mentioned repeatedly.

During his interview, Ju Chao had evidenced a cheerfulness that had startled me. The other students had looked pained, laboring in English to convey they were thoughtful, responsible college candidates. But Ju Chao seemed completely at ease. His enthusiasm was infectious. When he began talking about his interests—astrophysics and space travel—his wide-open features lit up.

Ju Chao's English was more fluent than Lin Lin's, more colloquial. He told me he had honed it since he was fourteen by taking online courses provided by Coursera and edX from some of the best universities in the world. (According to Coursera, the site has more than one million registered users in China.)[4] By the time I was interviewing him, Ju Chao had already taken two semesters of college-level courses in his spare time, all while maintaining his high school grades and schedule. The first class he completed was titled Justice and given by Harvard. The next seven were from MIT, including Introduction to Aerospace Engineering: Astronautics and Human Space Flight.

I asked Ju Chao if his parents had pushed him to take the courses. He raised his eyebrows and smiled, "My parents can't speak English. Do you think they know what Coursera is?" He shrugged. "I was just curious, I guess."

Ju Chao was also one of the best SAT testers in the world. He was ten points shy of a perfect score, placing him among the 810 best SAT testers globally that year.

I asked Ju Chao why he didn't want to go to Tsinghua or Peking universities. He said that if he did go to school in China, he would try to go to the Beijing University of Aeronautics and Astronautics.

"Our universities are getting better for research, but there is still not a great reputation for promoting new ideas," he said. "Plus," he added with a grin, "neither was used as a base for Launch Control."

So Ju Chao, like Lin Lin, wanted to study abroad, and the government was allowing him to do it.

四

"How did you prepare for the writing section?" I asked Lin Lin. What I really wanted to know was, how did you beat the SAT?

Forty-five days before she was to take the test, Lin Lin recognized her greatest weakness was writing. She was surprised to realize that the writing section would be her Achilles heel, but a weakness is a weakness, she reminded herself, and went about strengthening it the best way she knew how—methodically. Every morning for the next forty-four days, she woke up fifty minutes early to write a practice essay, culminating with her forty-fifth and final essay on test day, which was perfect.

The best Chinese test takers all use the same specific strategy to prepare for any and all tests. It is called 题海战术, *tíhǎi zhànshù*, or "the sea of questions strategy." That was how Ju Qiao and Lin Lin both beat America's formidable college entry exam.

The sea of questions strategy is to learn the content of the test through the test itself, to throw yourself into the deep sea of test-prep questions until you've learned to swim. Ju Qiao explained, "For the SAT, I had never taken the classes. I just went through the problem sets, because that was the most direct way for me to get familiar with the problems. All the answers are in those questions." Ju Qiao's study strategy was to buy practice tests and take them, then buy test-prep books and read them. The best testers in China take the practice tests repeatedly until they are ready to take the real test.

The danger of throwing anyone into the sea is, of course, drowning. The psychological strain of the sea of questions strategy is sizable. It takes supreme comfort with being consistently wrong for a long time. All the colleges to which they applied also required Lin Lin and Ju Qiao to take the SAT II (formerly the achievement tests), and both decided to take American history. Ju Qiao did it because he wanted a challenge. Lin Lin chose US history because she wanted to learn more about the country in which she would be studying.

Because he had never taken a course in American history, Ju Qiao answered every single question incorrectly on the first practice test he took. "Every single one," Ju Qiao grimaced. "But after I got them all wrong, I knew I'd never do as badly again." He tested again and did better. The time after that he did even better.

Both said that familiarizing themselves with the types of questions, the way questions are asked, and then the timing for the test was the most important preparation. Ju Qiao would read the standard high school history book at what he called hyperspeed and then dive into the tests. "All the facts are there in the test," he asserted.

The SAT II would be the most formidable major test either had ever taken in English, so learning test lingo and test strategy was just as important as learning the content. The difficult part of the math section of the SAT I and of the subject tests was the English idioms used to ask the questions.

"How old were you when you learned the relevant math for the SAT II physics test?" I asked Lin Lin.

She laughed, pulling her shoulders up by her ears and looking around the room. "Thirteen," she said.

When she was sixteen, she transferred to a boarding school that was famous for having students who studied extremely hard and administrators who ran a tight ship. The dorm room lights shut off promptly at 10:40 every night. Teachers recommended each student have a flashlight for studying in the dark.

I asked Lin Lin if she was happy there.

She laughed awkwardly.

"Actually, I don't know how to explain, when you stay at school and then you study all day, it's not as hard as you imagine. I mean, before I transferred to this school, I heard other students were really hard working and I was afraid that every one of my classmates would study until 1:00 a.m. and I would be the only one who went to sleep early. After I transferred to this school, I found that the students were not so scary and hardworking, and that it's okay if you get up early because it's a routine that is set for you and you just have to follow it. You don't have to decide anything."

She thought for a beat before concluding with a nod, "It's kind of natural."

Ju Qiao made a deal with his parents. When he was fifteen, he told them he wanted to go to college abroad. He wanted to learn more about space than he thought he could at a Chinese university, he said. They agreed but only if he secured a scholarship for half the tuition. So he hunkered down to work on his English. Doing that, Ju Qiao knew, meant he would have to find opportunities to practice English in Chengdu.

Ju Qiao spent almost every Friday night of high school hanging out at two flagpoles outside the Sichuan University gymnasium and speaking English with strangers. He took me there once. A small crowd had already formed in the shade of the gymnasium, which towers over the parking lot and has a roof that resembles that of the Sydney Opera

House. Ju Chao mingled comfortably in the crowd. By the time darkness fell and the streetlights buzzed to life, people were swarming like bees, gathering, dispersing, and then reforming again in tight-knit groups around the flagpoles. This was English Corner.

Cities and towns all across China have English corners. They have only one rule: you must speak English. Sometimes, in a big city or on a larger campus, a foreigner comes along, and a group hoping to practice with the genuine article orbits around that person. The attendees are mostly Chinese—college students, high school students, mothers with their children, grandparents with their grandchildren, and a curious array of hobbyists.

When I was in Hohhot, the capital of Inner Mongolia, a group of grinning college students converged on me. They were desperate to know—in English, of course—where I was from and what I thought of the local cuisine. At the English Corner in Guangzhou, the mother of a seven-year-old boy told me that exposing him to English now would no doubt help him get into a good university and secure a good job in the future. The seaside port city of Ningbo, the mountain metropolis of Chongqing, and even a tiny village on the border of Sichuan and Yunnan provinces all have some permutation of the weekly English Corner.

Sichuan University's English Corner is one of Chengdu's biggest. In winter a canopy of umbrellas protects the crowds from the steady Sichuanese drizzle. Spring brings bigger crowds and fewer clothes; the corner felt much more like happy hour than a language group. Humidity weighs on the summer learners as they fan themselves through dense hours of small talk in English. Fall brings the new school year and, with it, new faces. Without fail, Friday nights roll by with accented accounts of global warming, basketball games, World of Warcraft, or different processes for making noodles, and there's always the ironclad fallback—"Have you eaten dinner yet?"—depending on the level and bent of the speakers.

Almost everyone there was chasing a dream. A twenty-two-year-old senior studying chemical engineering at the university explained, "Study abroad in America has been my dream for years. I must study hard, work diligent, if I am to pass the TOEFL [test of English as a foreign language] and become admitted." A seven-year-old, still in her blue-and-white school jumper, stood with her mother at the edge of the circle. "I too want to go to America!" she exclaimed.

"Why?" I asked.

"Because . . . I like pizza!" The dozen or so crowding around us laughed. Her mother nodded approvingly.

五

The first time I went to Tsinghua University, the first student I met, an undergraduate named Zhou Jia Li, told me not to apply. "You'll hate it," she said after I mentioned I was considering doing graduate work there.

I asked her why. "All the students here are test monsters," Zhou said.

The common complaint among Chinese students, parents, educational professionals, and, later, these students' bosses is that the culture of rigorous testing creates only exceptional test takers. Chinese students have more incentive to be terrific test takers than to be problem solvers, to be better bubble fillers than innovators, better crammers than creators. Too many of China's young minds have been, as Ju Chao put it, dancing in shackles.

The Chinese college admission system relies solely on *gāokǎo* scores. The system doesn't expand to incorporate other factors because of the difficulty of finding an alternative method of comparing the qualifications of nine million college applicants every year. At best the process is geared to producing what people were increasingly calling test monsters. The retired boss of a Sichuan engineering firm once complained to me, "Tests are meant to reflect an understanding of a specific topic. All my engineering graduates used to understand was how to take a test on engineering."

The Chinese Communist Party is a party of plans, so it seems natural that it would plan how to make young Chinese more innovative. The Party's thirteenth Five-Year Plan charts China's trajectory from 2016 to 2020. The first section after the introduction is titled "Implement Plan to Propel Development of Innovation." The articles within the section are:

1. Strengthen Science and Technological Innovation
2. Deepen Advancement of "Masses of Entrepreneurs, 10,000 Innovations" [this is a directive designed to stimulate innovation and entrepreneurship]
3. Construct a Systematic Mechanism to Encourage Innovation
4. Implement [the Plan] "Development of Outstanding Talent"

All of China's economic plans express a desire to change the economy from one that boasts "Made in China" to one that brags "Created in China," and the plans envision that Chinese will be both the administrators and employees of these companies.

China's problem is that its education system doesn't produce innovators, so the government is sending top students to the schools that do.

The personal dreams of Lin Lin, Ju Chao, and the hundreds of thousands of others who hope to study abroad fit into China's national dreamscape. As part of its mission to develop "outstanding talent," the Chinese Communist Party explicitly discusses creating opportunities back home for study-abroad students to incentivize them to return. At least for now, study abroad has become an indispensable part of China's pursuit of innovators.

China has plenty of precedent for looking abroad to gather the tools for economic reinvention. In the early 1980s, China wanted to become a self-sufficient, modern industrial country. But it knew nothing about modern industry. It had spent the previous three decades lionizing the farmer-peasant as the bedrock of society under Mao. Although farmer-peasants know a lot about hard work, they know little about smelting steel—or making sneakers, clothes, computers, and appliances. China then opened its doors and invited the world's top industrialists into the country. Volkswagen, Nike, and Gap came into China with all their manufacturing know-how. Apple, Samsung, and General Electric moved in too.

In the short term, these companies got China's inexpensive labor. In the long term, however, China got all their manufacturing techniques. The Western press called it intellectual property theft. China called it speed-learning the industrial and technological revolution it had missed in the nineteenth and twentieth centuries.

China is now doing the same with international education. Just as Chinese learned industrialization from the world's industrialists, they are trying to learn innovation from the world's foremost innovators.

It's not new, either. Since the late 1950s, foreign universities have played an indispensable—and intentional—role in China's development plan. Wang Lang, an exchange student from Suzhou who was studying in Australia, put it this way: "For core technologies like rockets, guided missiles, and even higher-tech railroads, countries obviously would not send their scientists and technicians to teach us, so we had to send our students to developed countries to study."

China has championed these study-abroad students as pioneers of change. Deng Jiaxian, the father of China's nuclear program, or the "Two-Bomb Forefather" as he is known in Chinese history books, developed China's first uranium and hydrogen bombs. He received his doctoral degree in physics from Purdue University in 1950 and is credited with giving China a basic sense of safety, despite its being surrounded by nuclear Russia, North Korea, India, and Pakistan, as well as US-supported countries.

China's various titans of modern entrepreneurship also trace their company's beginnings to time abroad. Robin Li, the CEO and founder of Baidu and sixth-richest man in China, got his master's in computer science from the State University of New York at Buffalo and worked at a company that was developing an early search engine before he returned to China. Jack Ma says he was inspired by his first exposure to the Internet during an extensive stay in the United States. (He had wanted to study abroad but famously received ten rejections from Harvard.) Zhang Xin, cofounder and CEO of the commercial real estate development company SOHO and the third-wealthiest self-made woman in the world, got her master's degree in development economics from Cambridge University and worked at Goldman Sachs in New York before moving home and changing the way buildings are constructed in China's biggest cities.

Chinese students are no longer the test monsters of the past decade, since Chinese higher education underwent reform in 1998. Mauro Ferrari, president and CEO of the Houston Methodist Research Institute, which is in the forefront of cancer research, told me half his researchers are Chinese. "The language of science has already changed to Chinese. Obviously, written publications still remain dominated by English, but in the actual lab, doing the actual research, Chinese is on top." This is in Houston. "There is an illusion that Chinese testers are rigid and not innovative. That used to be true. The students we are getting now are simply not that way."

The more professors I asked about the Chinese students they were teaching, the more I found professors in awe of their students' combinations of talents. Although Chinese students remain notoriously insular on US campuses, their exposure to the outside world and Western-style classes had helped them couple their famous diligence with curiosity and intellectual dynamism.

The study-abroad bargain means that China forfeits close control of its young peoples' intellectual diet. It also means losing money when some of its wealthier citizens leave China. In the short term US universities are also getting a major boost from the tuition paid by Chinese students; the *Yale Economic Review* estimates that in the 2011–12 academic year alone, Chinese students spent approximately $5.4 billion on tuition and housing at American universities.[5] American institutions also benefit by hosting some of the most dedicated students in the world because they facilitate research and amp the competition among researchers. In the long term, China's best minds are learning to innovate, which puts China closer to realizing its dreams.

A month after I interviewed Lin Lin, I spent several days about three hundred miles outside Chengdu in a friend's small hometown in the mountains. I was there for several days to celebrate a holiday with my friend's family, but I ended up spending much of my time taking part in a funeral procession for their next-door neighbor. Much of the town had come out take part in guarding the soul, 守灵, *shōu*

lǐng, of this respected member of the community. Chinese keep vigil over the body of the deceased until they have been buried, alternating who keeps watch day and night. During the procession joss paper—冥币, *míng bì*—the currency of the afterlife, is burnt almost constantly so the deceased can prosper after death. (Chinese believe in the afterlife more as a continuation of their life on Earth rather than either a heaven or a hell. Practical as always, Chinese tradition knew they'd need money for their activities after death.) The immediate family puts in the longest hours during the vigil, but they invite the entire village to take part. I couldn't help but think of Lin Lin and her dreams. A dozen mahjong tables were set up throughout the house. The sons and cousins walked around offering mourners trays stacked with food and expensive cigarettes.* They held an extravagant banquet for practically the whole village. On the day of the funeral, the professional grievers they had hired wailed and shrieked and played horns to send off the deceased. All in all, the funeral costs were more than the family's annual income.

"Funerals and illnesses. These enormous one-time expenses can ruin the fragile livelihoods of people living out in the village," Lin Lin had said. "I want to help them solve that."

America is a sort of dream incubator for Lin Lin, a place to learn, push, and grow. Her goal remains back in China with the poorer people of the countryside. China's top 1 percent owns a third of the wealth in the country, according to a recent report from Peking University.[6] China's Gini coefficient, the metric used by the United Nations to measure internal inequality, was 0.49, far above the "warning line" of

---

*China has a taxonomy of cigarette brands that everyone recognizes: the workingman's cigarettes, the government official's cigarette, the festive cigarette, and so on. The cigarettes handed out by the sons of the deceased were far too expensive for the humble village.

0.4 and just a hair away from the 0.5 demarcation line of "highly unequal." (The United States is 0.41, and Germany is 0.3. Of the big countries that the World Bank tracks, only Brazil and South Africa have higher Gini coefficients than China.) A bevy of national directives, including China's most recent Five-Year Plan, identifies the wealth gap as a primary area for China to seek to improve in the near future.

Lin Lin's dream is in sync with China's. Because she grew up watching Chengdu become a first-tier city while the humble wood houses and tilled earth of the rice paddies in her grandparents' hometown remained the same, the wealth gap was a problem that affected her personally. Her success would be the country's success.

Ju Chao's dream was a little different: "I want to go anywhere where I might be involved in a space program." China's commitment to space exploration is part of its determination to become a global tech leader. When Ju Chao watches TV, whether the news or science fiction, China's space program looks more and more formidable. If he had to make a decision today, he said, he'd like to work for Elon Musk, but he is open to opportunities back home.

The fear for China has been brain drain, which is what happened in the 1980s and 1990s when the best and brightest who went to study abroad didn't go home. China was then at the beginning of its modern development. Wages were low by international standards, and the government was not supportive of people who wanted to innovate—researchers, academics, creative entrepreneurs, and thinkers. The opportunities for them were better in the United States.

Now, China is putting a tremendous amount of effort into creating an environment that will lure the innovators to return. Ferrari, of Houston Methodist Research Institute, explains: "Chinese researchers come on a two- or three-year deal, a type of exchange, and then they go back. It is already a well-developed exchange system that has their top researchers cycling through our system. We train them and benefit from their great skill. Then they go home."

By 2015, according to the Chinese Ministry of Education, 70 to 80 percent of Chinese students were returning, a believable number, considering the small number of US work visas available after they graduate.[7]

When the possibility of getting a visa to work in the United States began to look precarious, Robin Li of Baidu encouraged international entrepreneurs in Silicon Valley to go to China.[8] For Chinese students looking for opportunities at home, the government has created policies to help them start businesses and receive funding. Or, in the case of someone like Ju Chao, funding for China's national space program is increasing faster than the other major space programs in the world, particularly those of Russia and the United States, and makes far more launches per dollar spent than NASA, despite the latter's funding still dwarfing China's.[9] It is an appealing choice.

Chinese students have returned home for pragmatic reasons. Zhou Jia Li, the young woman who told me not to apply to Tsinghua University, was then in the process of applying to graduate schools in the States. She wanted to see the world. Two years later, and six months shy of her advanced degree in mathematics from New York University, Zhou felt she had gotten what she came for. "America's population is small. Comparatively, the playing field isn't as happening as it is back home. In terms of opportunity, China's market is so big, and there are so many consumers, it is kind of a no-brainer. Once I'm finished studying, and maybe after an internship getting knowledge and experience, I will move back. I want to raise a little capital and start my own business. I'm not sure what to do yet, but anything is OK as long as I'm working for myself."

An opinion piece that circulated widely in study-abroad WeChat circles described the temptation of the start-up scene back home. "Even if we could graft the channels of resources and networks of contacts to our lives abroad, we'd still have to tack on a major markdown in value," the writer noted. Whereas these young Chinese would be seen as the best and brightest back home, abroad they'd be just normal college graduates, young workers with accented English who need a hard-to-get visa that allows them to be employed. They'd always be outsiders abroad, wrote the author, an international student who planned to return to China after graduation. His peers' lives abroad had a discernible upper limit.

Also, the opportunities back home felt big and real. The opinion piece continues, "The surging waves of start-up frenzy back home will, one after the other, trigger inner turbulence for those of us abroad. Open up your WeChat Friend Circle and see, today, that an old classmate has started a business; tomorrow, a former colleague has gotten several million in funding. They can do it—why can't I?"

七

Against my advice, Columbia University rejected both Lin Lin and Ju Chao. I asked the admissions office why. Near-perfect testing is expected of Chinese, Korean, and Singaporean students, I was told. It is what they do to set themselves apart that makes the difference.

That was tough to take: Lin Lin was a self-published author with her own charity, and Ju Chao had been the student ambassador to Michelle Obama and was a self-motivated student of astrophysics.

Maybe they both looked like test monsters. Also, Lin Lin and Ju Chao had applied the same year that major cheating scandals were making news in Korea and China. The Chinese students accepted by Columbia that year all came from more recognizable high schools, places with well-established credentials. The two students I'd championed had also applied for financial aid, and Columbia's admissions are not need-blind for foreign students.

Lin Lin was upset, even angry. When she got in touch with me, she asked why she had been rejected. Did Columbia have a quota system for Chinese students? How was this decision fair? She had worked hard to be able to study at one of the world's elite universities and believed she had earned her spot.

Lin Lin's mother attributed her daughter's rejection to the murkiness of the admissions system. She wrote to me, "[An SAT score of] 2400 has little advantage over 2300 or 2200 in admission officers' eyes. In fact, 2200–2300 is an easy grade that could be earned by many ordinary Chinese students, so how can they judge and pick really excellent students by using an easy test?" She echoed a popular belief that Western universities have far higher standards for Chinese students applying in the arts than in the sciences. Popular reasoning had it that the latter were more likely to become distinguished in their field and reflect well on their university.

The successful Chinese candidates I met after I returned to New York were all exceptional in their own right. Each came from one of the handful of Chinese high schools whose names I recognized. They were in international schools with International Baccalaureate programs; from an admissions officer's perspective these are the most transparent and trustworthy schools, least likely to pass along a bogus transcript, but they also are the most expensive and the most exclusive.

After getting rejected by Columbia, Lin Lin couldn't decide whether she should go to a Western school with no reputation in China or the University of Hong Kong, widely regarded as the Harvard of Asia. She asked me what I thought about the University of

Hong Kong, where I had studied abroad. "Are the education styles similar at all?" They're not, I regretted having to inform her.

Lin Lin eventually chose the University of Hong Kong and began her study in economics and political science. "The best American universities didn't want me," she said. "I wanted to be in a community with some of the smartest people, even if they're just the best in Asia."

Ju Chao received a scholarship to the Minerva Schools, an education start-up founded by a former Harvard dean in San Francisco, an initiative meant to disrupt the overly expensive elite education system. "Our first year is in San Francisco, and then every semester after that we live in a new country," Ju Chao told me excitedly. All the classes at Minerva were online, led by elite professors teaching remotely. They were highly interactive and the class size was small. All the students would live in dorms, and the professor would beam in. Because all the students' faces were on screen, and the professor could call on them at random, each student sat fully engaged. It lacked a human touch, but for Ju Chao, who had been taking online classes for years, it was a perfect fit. "I've always wanted to be part of something cutting edge, something experimental," he said. "Plus, we really get to see the world."

In addition to his coursework, which takes Ju Chao only about twelve hours a week to complete at his blistering pace, he does another ten hours of coursework for an edX class. "Advanced astrophysics is more difficult than any of the classes I'm taking at school," he said. "But, hey, it's not going to learn itself, right?"

9

The Good Comrade

Being Gay in the Middle Kingdom

Two meaty bouncers stood guard outside Destination's concrete gate. They checked bags, backpacks, and purses, of which there were several, before allowing clusters of men to make their way into the stone courtyard outside the club. William chuckled as he watched the bouncer sift through his backpack, knowing the check would reveal only lube and condoms. On the subway ride over, William had insisted he was not on the prowl that night. He preferred Funky for that, but the owner of the trendiest gay club in Beijing had closed its doors during the Chinese Spring Festival so he could go home and see his parents. Therefore we chose Destination. Voted trendiest comrade club back in 2008, Destination had matured to popular. From outside the gates the vibrations from the club's bass pounded through Beijing's gray sidewalk, the *thump-thwap-thump-thwap* quivering up through the soles of my shoes.

Comrade, *tóngzhì*, 同志, literally means "someone of the same ambition, dream, or aspiration." The address is emblematic of Mao's

China during the Cultural Revolution, which saw all Chinese citizens transform from being neighbors, cousins, brothers and sisters, and even spouses into political allies.

Today the term *comrade* no longer refers to Communist revolutionaries; it has been co-opted by China's gay community to describe its members. Posters pasted on the walls of buildings along Beijing streets no longer read, COMRADE, SHATTER THE OLD SOCIETY, BUILD THE NEW! Instead, a poster inside Destination asks, COMRADE, HAVE YOU BEEN TESTED RECENTLY?

A hundred or so men milled in the courtyard outside the club. Brightly colored outfits began to poke out from under thick winter coats. Within the courtyard walls no one risked being seen by a co-worker, family member, or neighbor while waiting to enter the well-known gay bar on one of Beijing's crowded bar streets. The secluded courtyard served as a depressurization chamber, a type of cultural air-lock that facilitates the transition from Beijing's gray-skied world to the sultry red burn behind the club doors. Tall, short, heavy, thin, femme, butch, built, glitz—the full array of looks, types, and attitudes inched forward in line, everyone posturing and checking out other clubbers with feigned indifference. Yet a significant number, what William called day walkers, displayed no style at all. "You wouldn't be able to pick these boys out of a lineup of straight guys. Your gaydar might not work so well in China," William told me while he scanned the crowd.

William, who was in his early twenties, was one of the youngest in line. He stood tall, his posture sturdy. A black T-shirt clung to his well-muscled shoulders. By early morning he would peel it off on the dance floor. William was a philosophy student at Sichuan University, one of the best in his class. He wore his hair in a bun secured with a dark wooden hairpin on top of his head. "Not like your dirty hipsters," he explained. "Like a Song Dynasty scholar." Take out the pin and his hair would fall over his broad shoulders. Will had been to the gym a few hours earlier. "I wanted a pump before hitting the dance floor."

We finally reached the ticket counter. When the heavy doors pulled open to let someone in, waves of bass rolled out and tingled the nerves on my cheeks. The doorman was handsome and manicured, dressed in a sleek black suit with a black shirt unbuttoned to show a smooth chest. The pink-orange club light glinted off his swooping hair and reminded me of a Taoist painting of an ocean wave at dusk. "Two, please," William said. On the wall behind him a large poster on the all-black wall announced: BEAR HUNTING, WEDNESDAY NIGHT and featured a bulky half-bear half-man leaning suggestively against a wall. William pointed to the sign and yelled, "God, I wish it was Wednesday!" Then, turning to me, he added, "Don't forget: tonight, steer clear of potato hunters. They're everywhere!" With that, he shoved me toward the door, and we squeezed into Destination.

二

Two weeks earlier William and I had pushed into a bus in Chengdu at rush hour.

William was born in 1992. At that time in China homosexuality was regarded as a crime against the state and a psychological disease by the Chinese Society of Psychiatry. From 1979 to 1997, the first twenty-eight years of post-Mao China, male homosexuality was criminalized as hooliganism, 流氓罪, *liúmáng zùi*. Hooliganism was a type of catchall criminal charge for what the Communist Party deemed morally unsavory activity. It became emblematic of China's "severe crackdown," which began in 1983, against the moral laxity associated with opening China's doors to the world and foreign influence. Acts deemed hooliganism included premarital sex, dancing to Western music, sexual harassment, petty theft, disturbing the peace, fighting in public, and engaging in homosexual sex, among others. The punishment for hooliganism could be lifetime imprisonment or even death.

Gays in China tells stories from the antihooliganism days about comrades who gathered in parks, public restrooms, under bridges—any public place that got dark enough at night to afford some privacy. Older comrades tell stories about love affairs cloaked in anonymity, furtive romances consummated quickly in the dark, movements rushed, voices low for fear of being caught. They set up their own types of sexuality speakeasies in cities as safe spaces to sit, talk, and feel normal for an evening; everyone understood that flirting, much less hooking up, was out of bounds. "If you lived in the countryside, which most people did then, you were living on an island," an older comrade told me. Today Internet forums have largely supplanted that normalized space. So when William said he wanted to take me to a gathering, I had no idea what he had planned for us.

When William was a young boy growing up in Beijing, he had not known what homosexuality was. "It was brought up casually in the news, movies, the media," he said. "They would mention 同性恋, *tóng xìng lìan*, but I never knew what it meant. Does it make you sick? Does it hide under your bed? Will it take you to jail?"

Chinese use the same word, tóng xìng lìan, for gay and lesbian. The first character means "same." The second character primarily means "sex" or "gender." The third character means "to love." The problem is, the character for *gender* sounds the same as the character for *surname*. Both characters are pronounced with a falling fourth tone. In written Chinese the difference is as small as a changed radical on the left side of the character—性; 姓. When first meeting someone in China, it is polite to ask what their honorable *xìng*, their honorable surname, is. Though it sounds identical, you are not asking, "What is your honorable gender?"

Because he had never seen the word for homosexuality in writing, William misunderstood the two characters completely. "Eventually, I sort of understood that it was two people who had the same surname and so would have a special bond. We would joke around at school with other classmates, 'Your last name is Zhao. My last name is Zhao. We are *homosexual*!' "

William was five when the government abolished the antihooliganism law in 1997, but that did not change the way people talked about sex. Chinese sex education is notoriously sparse. Ye Su, a twenty-two-year-old lesbian from Jiangxi Province, told me, "Our sex-ed teacher, the school nurse, wouldn't talk about it with us. She put on the [video] *Mysteries of the Human Body* and then walked out of the room." When I asked what her parents had told her about sex, she said, "My mom told me she found me in the dumpster."

Chinese society firmly discourages experimentation and relationships among young people. But there was a loophole. Because no one ever even mentioned LGBT issues, they were uncharted moral territory. William had his first homosexual sexual encounter, oral sex with an older classmate, before he knew what homosexuality was. "We all knew that sex was bad, something for adults when we were younger. But we also knew that sex was something you had with a girl. We truly did not know what we were doing was a sexual act."

The Chinese Society of Psychiatry removed homosexuality and bisexuality from its *Chinese Classification of Medical Disorders* in 2001. Notably, the psychiatrists failed to strike gender dysphoria from the list of psychological diseases, and it remained on the list in 2017.

William was in elementary school when being gay no longer meant having a psychological disease, but that did not change the way his sex education teacher would describe homosexuality. All the way through middle school, William remembered, the school nurse would tell students that being gay was "akin to being mentally retarded, having something psychologically wrong with you."

He probably would have believed his teachers, he said, were it not for the Chinese sexologist Li Yinhe, one of the most famous intellectuals in modern China. William read in detail about homosexuality in her book, *Their World: A Study of Homosexuality*, originally published in 1992, when he was 12 years old. He had found it tucked away in a Beijing bookstore and sat down and read it right there, too afraid to buy it and take it home.

三

China probably has the largest homosexual population in the world. Specific numbers simply do not exist, but experts estimate that 3 to 5 percent of China's population, or forty to seventy million people, are homosexual.[1]* China is not a religious country by

---

*According to Gallup, fewer than 5 percent of Americans identify as gay or lesbian. See Garance Frank-Rutka, "Americans Have No Idea How Few Gay People There Are," *The Atlantic*, May 31, 2012, https://www.theatlantic.com/politics/archive/2012/05/americans-have-no-idea-how-few-gay-people-there-are/257753/.

nature, so neither sin nor God stands in the way of full social acceptance for the homosexual community in the Middle Kingdom. And yet, according to surveys from Danlan, one of the biggest Chinese gay men's social networks, only 3 percent of China's gay male population are fully out of the closet to everyone—friends, parents, and colleagues. A full one-third have not told another soul. For lesbians the numbers are only slightly higher: 5 percent are fully out; 80 percent have come out to some friends; and only 9 percent have not come out to anyone.[2]

For decades Li Yinhe had dared to talk and write about life behind the bedroom door when sex before marriage was still a crime and homosexuality could get you locked up for life. A hero in the gay and lesbian community, she continues to push a measure to legalize gay marriage, an issue she first broached in 2003. As one friend told me, "If you are LGBT in China, Professor Li's writings likely taught you about who you are."

As I discussed in chapter 5, Li Yinhe graciously met me for tea in Beijing. The professor, born in 1952, is nearly the same age as the People's Republic of China; she was born three years after Mao won the civil war against Chiang Kai-shek and his Nationalist Party. She is short with close-cropped graying hair and big glasses and has a heavy Beijing accent. We settled down to talk in the second-story tea room.

"You can learn a lot about the way Chinese people see the world from the way they see homosexuality," she said. "In Chinese history people didn't look down on homosexuality as unnatural, as going against the laws of nature or God. They saw it sometimes as silly, sometimes as a shame, and mostly as a missed opportunity. 'A healthy young man like him should be making children, not messing around!'

"In China, we have a saying," Li Yinhe continued, intoning one of the most quoted lines of Confucianism in modern China:

不孝有三，无后为大*

This sentence comes closest to Chinese scripture. It describes the importance of family continuity. Morally speaking, not having children isn't just a personal choice: it makes you a bad person.

The saying has become particularly relevant since the one-child policy was abolished. Throughout all the discussions I've had about Chinese culture, this Confucian principle stressing the importance of children has been brought up more than any other law or value. A young man from rural Shaanxi said to me at a gay bar in Chengdu, "Westerners drink the blood and eat the flesh of their God every Sunday—and they say *homosexuality* is unnatural! Chinese are far more practical: Where is the next generation?" Chinese men who decide not to come out of the closet most often cite pressure from the family as the reason.[3]

Professor Li said Chinese culture teaches people to deal with sexual urges by suppressing them. Confucius famously said that when he turned seventy he could finally follow his heart's desires without violating his moral code—it took him that long to train his body's impulses to fall into line with the ethics he taught. China's gay community chooses to suppress their sexual orientation or at least conceal it. Li Yinhe believes that 80 percent of China's gay male population, twenty to thirty million men, marry women.[4] Another of China's pioneering sexologists now retired from the University of

---

**Bùxiào yǒusān, wǒ hòu wéi dà:* "Of the three major violations of filial piety, not producing a successor is the gravest."

Shanghai, Liu Dalin, has gone so far as to say 90 percent of male homosexuals in China marry women, compared with 15 to 20 percent of American men.[5]

四

At the beginning of the summer of 2012 Luo Hong Ling, a lecturer at Sichuan University, heard her new husband's phone buzz while he was in the shower. She answered it and found a text message from a man she did not know. Official reports later said the text was of a "dubious nature."

Like many couples, she and her husband had been introduced by mutual friends. Luo Hong Ling was quite familiar with the tradition of matchmaking—the title of her master's thesis was "An Inspection and Comparison of 'Matchmakers' in Chinese and Korean Literature." But married life was not what she had imagined. She sought help in online forums. After her online friends learned that she and her husband had been intimate only a handful of times in their several months of marriage, they told her she might be married to a comrade.

As Luo flipped through her husband's phone, she was shocked to find that he had accounts on several gay social apps.

Twenty-five days later, on an early summer morning, Luo Hong Ling sent out a status update on Sina Weibo, a popular microblogging website: "This world is truly exhausting. Might as well end it all."[6] She then walked up thirteen stories to the roof of her university apartment complex and leapt to her death.

The media picked up her story, and the net erupted in outrage at her husband. "He tricked her, lied to her, all just to protect his identity from his family!"

Luo's parents took her husband, Cheng Mou, to court, leveling a charge of *piànhūn*, "scam marriage," an accusation originally written into law to protect those whose spouses have stolen marital assets, typically money or land. This was the first time a scam marriage had been associated with what Chinese call simply "gay wives," *tóng qī*, women who unknowingly marry a gay man. But from a hard legal perspective, Cheng Mou had nothing tangible to gain from the marriage. He did not steal property or money, nor did he entangle Luo Hong Ling's family in business-related debt. What Cheng Mou had gained from the marriage was an opportunity to not disappoint his parents, to be a good son. With no evidence of stolen property or money, the court rejected the case.

Marriage is often the gravitational center of a Chinese person's life, the vehicle for creating a family legacy, and family is the social fabric of traditional China. For tens of millions of Chinese women like Luo Hong Ling, their gravitational center is based on a scam.

五

As our bus headed north through Chengdu, William began to talk about the Internet and how his parents had learned he was a comrade.

The first email from within China was sent in 1987. It said, "Across the Great Wall, we can reach every corner in the world." Internet became available to the public in 1994.[7] Because of his family's connections, William's was one of the first homes in his neighborhood with a desktop computer connected to the Internet. He was about twelve when his mother noticed that his Internet history led to the Friend, Don't Cry website, one of the earliest forum websites in China—and devoted entirely to explaining homosexuality. He found the site poking around on the internet after discovering the work of Li Yinhe. "More than anything else, it was a site that told me, for the first time in my life, really, that being gay is a real thing," William said. The forums were especially useful. "The forum described gay lifestyle, the feelings involved. But it was the stories that hit home. I saw those and was like, 'Oh shit, I've been gay this whole time.' "

William's voice rolled out smooth and deep. His Mandarin was crystal clear and extremely standard, unlike most of the Sichuanese-tinged Mandarin spoken in Chengdu. "It was a new age, an Internet era, and I didn't understand how to cover my tracks," he recalled. When his mom asked him about his use of the site, William explained it away as curiosity, saying, "I just wanted to understand the peculiar gay society better." The China of 2003 was experiencing a surge of interest in the novel field of psychology. To William's rational, academic mother, his curiosity was intellectual and therefore justifiable.

Then he got worse at covering his tracks. When he was fourteen, his mother found his chat history on QQ, a social website with a chat function similar to instant messaging. He was part of a gay group chat with weeks and weeks of gay-related conversation. William once again fumbled through an excuse. Then, a year later, his mother looked through his texts and found him sexting, talking dirty in a text message, with a classmate.

"After they caught me for the third time, there was no getting around it." Will prepared a pot of his father's favorite tea and set it out on the living room table. Then he called his parents together and told them he was gay.

"My dad didn't say one word, just leaned back and stared at the ceiling. My mom said, 'If you're sure, we can only accept this. We've already prepared ourselves.' "

Our bus pulled to the side of a bridge to let passengers off. William bounded off the bus and into Chengdu's packed bike lane. Electronic mopeds whizzed past. He breathed deeply and exhaled, nodding his appreciation. "The air is good today. Good for practice."

We had arrived in the old part of the city, the less developed northeast. The southern end of the city had turned into a high-tech zone during the previous five years, with glimmering steel and glass climbing higher and higher above the concrete apartment buildings erected years before.

"You know mapo tofu?" William asked, as we weaved through the foot traffic on the sidewalk. I nodded—he was talking about one of Sichuan's most internationally renowned dishes: tofu set in a numbingly spicy chili and bean sauce and cooked with fermented black beans and minced pork. Legend has it that the tofu used in this dish is named after a *"MáPó,"* a pockmarked grandmother who used to sell it from her shop. "The pockmarked grandmother originally lived a few blocks away from here," William said, gesturing north. I blinked at Chengdu's hazy skyline, trying to imagine a ruddy grandmother hawking her spicy specialty in a time before these concrete apartments and metallic high-rises dominated the nightscape.

Soon William's determined gait whisked us across the bridge, dodging electronic bikes and street vendors selling knock-off iPhone cables and selfie sticks that they had laid out on tarps on the side of the street. Chinese music from the 1990s blared from a portable amplifier providing the beat for rows of dancing middle-aged women who were getting in a streetside aerobics workout after dinner. A car honked, a child cried, and then William slipped around a corner and out of sight, engulfed by the activity of a Chinese city at night.

六

After William had come out to his parents, days passed before his father voiced any reaction. Finally, he pulled William aside to ask one question: "What have you planned for kids? What about the next generation?"

William shouldered a particularly consequential role in his family. Grandfather Zhao had had three sons, a major point of pride. "With so many sons, it should have been easy to continue the family line. Plus, that many sons would mean my grandparents were well taken care of as they aged."

Then the one-child policy changed everything for the Zhao family. Now those three sons could have only one child each. Two already had daughters. Only William's father produced a son, making William the sole hope for continuation of the family line.

William was gay but nonetheless responsible for producing the next generation. His dad had thought the issue through. The issue wasn't marriage or spouse but bloodline and genetics. "You've got two options: adoption or a surrogate mother."

William was relieved. The conversation meant his parents would not try to force him to get married. He too wanted children; he wanted to take part in the Chinese tradition of family, of having a child to continue the Zhao family line.

Father and son agreed: A surrogate mother was clearly the best option. That way, the genetic material would still be Zhao, and their bloodline would remain intact.

Many comrades William knew were less lucky, including the young man he was seeing at the time—his gym mate and friend with benefits named Josh. In China the word for friend with benefits is 炮友, *pàoyǒu*. 炮, *pào*, means "firecracker" or "cannon." 友, *yǒu*, means "friend." It's a new word, invented out of necessity.

Josh was twenty-five; gay, not bi; smart; handsome; and, by the often transparent system of matchmaking in China, exceedingly eligible (read: tall, rich, and handsome). Josh's parents had been pushing him to get married.

Marriage is a family affair in China—parents take an active role, and then grandparents, cousins, second cousins, and the so-called cousins a family acquires through long friendship. Josh's family saw him as their pride and joy, and they talked constantly about wanting to "hold our grandson"—a Chinese set phrase that parents leverage to urge their children to have kids. In Chinese sitcoms about wacky marriages, the story lines are less about the ins and outs of a couple's relationship and instead focus on the balancing act of the young couple that wants to pursue their passions and careers while their kooky parents want to hurry up and "hold our grandson!" Josh's parents would call him regularly, not to ask how he was doing but to cut right to the chase: "Do you have a girlfriend yet? We want to hurry up and hold our grandson!"

One day Josh's mother called him and announced: "It has all been arranged. We're coming to Chengdu today." Sure enough, his mother arrived that afternoon. In her wake came Josh's father and another family made up of two parents, a grandmother, and a very pretty daughter. "We're going to lunch," his mom said. Josh knew better than to disobey his mother and break the plans.

They all had lunch, and Josh, like a good son, went through the motions in public. In private later that day, he had it out with his mother.

"I'm not ready. Let me figure this out for myself," he said. "It's the twenty-first century." His mother wouldn't hear of it.

Her reaction forced Josh into a workaround. China's LGBT community has had to adapt to deal with social pressures, especially those around the issue of marriage. The most popular solution has been a 形式结婚, *xíngshì jiéhūn*, or "shape marriage," or an "appearance" or "formality marriage"—a marriage that looks traditional but lacks any substance. They're often called mutual help marriages.

A shape marriage is the union of a gay man and a lesbian. After the discussion with his mother, Josh, William's pàoyǒu, reached out to a lesbian friend. The two were considering marriage just to stave off the pressure from both sets of parents.

"The hardest part is that his mother is doing this because she loves him," William noted. "She's doing it because that's what good Chinese mothers do. It's what they've always done. It's tradition."

七

One of the stories most read and passed along from the gay-oriented website Friend, Don't Cry was often described to me as required reading for Chinese comrades. "Two Peking University Comrades' 10-Year Love Story" is about two hardworking young men, Ted and Fred, who meet at Peking University.* They fall in love and decide to study abroad in America. They win places at Columbia and Notre Dame, respectively, and keep up a long-distance relationship. After graduation, Ted gets a job in finance on Wall Street, and Fred moves to New York so they can be together. They travel during vacations from work, posting romantic pictures of themselves at the Grand Canyon, by the fountain at the Monte Carlo Resort and Ca-

*It has now been circulated in so many different permutations under so many names that pinning down the original is impossible.

sino in Las Vegas, and sitting in the Rocky Mountains. Then they get married.

That's it. The story isn't about revolution or radical acceptance, fame or abrupt fortune. It is about a peaceful couple who work hard and make a successful life of their own, no shortcuts, no excuses, but also no pressure or intrusion.

Many of the comrades I interviewed expressed the simple desire to not have their sexuality derail their efforts to achieve their dreams.

Ted and Fred were more fiction than fact to most comrades. Chinese pop culture seemed to have no one who was publicly gay and happy, gay and successful, gay and proud. Because China had criminalized homosexuality for so long, the public sphere had no gay role models. William and other kids his age could not see homosexual men or women on TV (except on the news), in movies, or in business.

"In mainland China it used to be that there weren't any role models in the LGBT community. No one stepped forward," Li Yinhe told me. "Hong Kong, though, had one."

I had a pretty good idea who that was. "Zhang Guo Rong?" I asked.

"Yes, Zhang."

We shared a moment of silence, unsure how to proceed. If what Li was saying was true, China's sole hero in the LGBT community had committed suicide in 2003. Zhang was a singer and actor, extremely popular both on the mainland and in Hong Kong. Because of his popularity throughout China and extending across the globe, he was voted the third-most-iconic musician of all time, behind Michael Jackson and the Beatles, in an online poll by CNN.[8]

In 1997, the year Hong Kong was returned to China and the hooliganism law was lifted, a Chinese investigative reporter outed Zhang. His sexual preference became a national issue at a time when most Chinese still believed homosexuality was criminal and perverse. The country had reeled in horror at this news about Zhang.

Six years later, Zhang committed suicide by jumping off the Mandarin Oriental hotel in Hong Kong. People often speak of his suicide as a warning to China's public figures: life outside the closet is dangerous, even life threatening. A friend of mine from Guangzhou Province explained, "Zhang was exceptional, outstanding, charming, and gay. In the end he was killed by public opinion and media. If *he* couldn't come out, who could?"

In lieu of a national role model, the Chinese LGBT community found inspiration abroad, and few people were more recognizable in China than Apple CEO Tim Cook when headlines in 2014 read, "Tim Cook: 'I'm Proud to Be Gay.'" China was stunned. Cook was quiet, considered "normal," and had achieved success on a global scale. His sexuality had not derailed his ability to achieve his ambitions. He was both Ted and Fred from Friend, Don't Cry.

Cook's sexuality was a major eye-opener for conservative Chinese who still believed homosexuality was a disability. China had long considered Apple a standard of excellence and innovation. Could its leader really be gay?

After the Tim Cook revelation, message boards hummed. Homophobic trolls posted nasty comments about Cook: "No wonder the iPhone 6 can't stay straight." Netizens fired back: "What phone are you using to post this comment?" The response? "I have to comment using my computer now!" But the gay community was ready for that one, riposting: "Your computer? You can thank gays for that too! Alan Turing was also gay!"

Cooke's coming out either energized or coincided with a normalizing of LGBT life within Chinese society, especially in big cities. People no longer had to search far and wide to find signs of gay or lesbian community life. Gay representation in the media was increasing. For a while on WeChat, the hashtag #hestoogoodtobestraight was getting a lot of play after several articles featured the hunks of the gay community. One popular Weibo blogger posted, "They stay in shape, they groom themselves, they know how to dress. Man of your dreams? Too bad. Definitely gay."

Rong, a young man I met on Blued, a social app for gay men in China, had recently moved from distant Gansu Province to Chengdu. There he found he wasn't looked down upon for his style, interests, way of talking, and mostly not for his sexuality. In fact, he was considered cool. "We're interesting, curious, and modern, like Korean soap operas or something. We're *in*—the most tapped in to what's hot, what's cool, what's fashionable," he told me.

Popular TV shows began to include quietly gay characters. Most often the role was the stereotypical gay best friend of the female protagonist. This character was never explicitly homosexual on the show itself, but each actor managed to convey the sexual identity of his character nonetheless. Media conglomerates under the watchful eye of the government could not openly acknowledge the gay community, but they also were not ignoring it.

This half-acceptance was what upset William the most. The government had never said that it supported the LGBT community—but recently also had been careful not to condemn the LGBT community, either. "It is their full lack of acknowledgment that kills us," William ranted to me. "We were invisible. We didn't exist."

In China, to be ignored by the government is often to be permitted. When Li Yinhe last asked the State Council to consider her LGBT marriage law, she told me, she was not rebuffed for its lewdness but questioned about its necessity. "Why do we have to be leading the world on this?" the government officials asked her.

Meanwhile, the government was quietly accepting China's changing sexual landscape, at least to a point. China's early Internet was more heavily controlled than it is today, but even in the mid- to late 1990s the government had not censored Friend, Don't Cry. Back then radio talk shows in China that approached the topic of sex were beginning to proliferate, like the famous *At Night You're Not Lonely*. Years later it came to light that these shows were sponsored by the Communist Party and that their genuinely popular and sincerely beloved hosts were Party members. They worked for the government. Still, they delivered something essential: an introduction to sexuality in the modern world. It was a way for the Party to disseminate information without publicly condoning acts that many Chinese still considered shocking. The Party and the media talked endlessly about how China's economy was changing, how skyscrapers, train tracks, and highways were remaking the landscape. Friend, Don't Cry and government-funded talk shows about sex were tacit acknowledgments that Chinese attitudes about sexuality were evolving too.

Today the Chinese homosexual community is gaining recognition as a market opportunity. "There are more than seventy million LGBT people in China," said Geng Le, CEO of Blued, the world's most popular gay networking app, "equivalent to the UK's population."[9]

Blued's CEO hoped that the business opportunity represented by China's LGBT community would make them understood in the term the rest of China could understand: money. Although many Chinese were still getting used to the social implications of recognizing China's gay community, no one needed time to adjust to the business opportunity.

Grindr, the top gay social app in early 2014, boasted more than five million users worldwide.[10] Blued had two million users at the time, not bad for a two-year-old app. It was a proud moment for Geng

Le, and it signaled a very real awakening to China's "Pink Market." Geng Le was feeling cocky, so confident in fact that he declared Blued soon would have ten million users. Pundits scoffed.

As of late 2016, Blued boasted twenty-seven million registered users.[11] It is easily the largest LGBT app in the world. The size and scope of Blued has opened up conversations in China about the market potential of the Pink Market, and so it has earned the comrade community a bit more acceptance and normalization. Plus, they created an online space that wasn't confined to China's more progressive cities. Clubs like Destination found their place in Beijing, Guangzhou, Shanghai, and the other big metropolises, but apps like Blued have created a gay community across all of China.

八

In the club Destination, I quickly learned that a potato hunter is a Chinese person who is looking to hook up with a foreigner, gay or straight. "Because, um, Westerners eat potatoes." I sipped a Long Island iced tea as I navigated the different floors, watching men dance and play a popular dice drinking game, hand drinking games (intricate versions of rock, paper, scissors in which the loser has to take a drink), and any other type of drinking games someone knew. Heavy techno boomed through bulky speakers.

Here in Destination, no one seemed psychologically imbalanced, as the Chinese textbooks used to say, unless a healthy sexual appetite merited that classification. Security guards were posted around the room to make sure things didn't get out of line. They didn't have to intervene once. Compared with other big clubs in China, Destination, at least from a drama perspective, was tame.

We left the club at two in the morning. On the way out we passed a Chinese day walker who was making out with a Caucasian guy who looked to be eastern European. William rolled his eyes. "Potato, hunted," he said, then added, "You Westerners have terrible taste in men. Did you see that guy?"

We entered the courtyard as we emerged from the club. William put his black shirt on again as well as his heavy coat, and we talked as we reentered into Beijing's gray night. Haze glowed under the streetlamps as we sat on the curb and waited for the car we had called through one of China's Uber-like phone applications. William was going back to his parents' apartment. They had not asked where he'd be spending the evening, and he hadn't offered any information. I then asked William a question I'd asked most comrades in China, once I felt they wouldn't object. Of all the social issues, from scam marriages to Li Yinhe's attempting to get marriage legalized in China, which did he think was the most important?

William did not hesitate. "Education," he said. "Our sex education doesn't teach us anything about sex, and its treatment of comrades remains terrible. I don't want any young boy or girl to grow up like I did, not knowing who they were or why they felt the way they did." With that, he got into a cab and went home to his parents.

10

Learning to Play

From Eating Bitter to Eating Hotpot

"Food is the god of the people," Zhang Wei intoned. With that, he gracefully scooped up a soup dumpling, cradling the delicate casing gently between two chopsticks so as not to puncture it and lose the broth within. We sat in a lunch canteen in Suzhou, an ancient capital of China and one of two "earthly paradises," according to Chinese literary history. A Suzhou native, Zhang had promised to take me to all the best local eateries that remained from his childhood. He took me to traditional restaurants, stalls, and eateries around the city, expounding on the merit and complexity of Chinese food culture. Zhang spoke of food passionately, detailing how each province and each town has its own food culture, and how there really are "four big cuisines" within China, Shandong cuisine in the North, Cantonese food in the South, Sichuanese food in the West, and, of course, Jiangsu food, of which Suzhou is the capital, in the South.

The place that day was authentic and low key, an "old one-hundred names"—the phrase used to refer to the common people—eatery:

plastic cafeteria chairs and simple tables for easy wiping, casual and food forward. Bamboo baskets stacked at Dr. Seuss-like angles reached just below the ceiling fan, towering over the middle-aged and elderly men and women in white smocks who were mincing meat, packing it with chives, folding it into its delicate casings, and then storing it into a bamboo basket to be steamed. Each basket contained four tender *xiǎo lóng bāo*, better known as soup dumplings, one of China's most famous culinary exports.

Zhang looked at me appreciatively, confusing my intense gaze for intellectual curiosity in his culinary lecture. (I was actually studying how Zhang gripped his chopsticks to support the dumpling without breaking the thin skin. A sad puddle of precious meat broth had pooled in my vinegar dish.) Zhang Wei reinforced his spiritual observation, by noting, "Back when you were worshiping Zeus and Thor and whatever, we Chinese had food."

In China food is the first luxury, the Ur-indulgence, and the core of the Chinese pleasure center. All other sources of fun are derivative.

"Food is the god of the people" comes from *History of the Former Han Dynasty*, finished in the second century AD.[1] The line was meant to be more Machiavellian than culinary, a comment on the importance of keeping the populace well fed to ensure stability.

Today, food remains the god of the people to at least some degree. On Friday mornings when I would bike to the local wet market, a large collection of stalls that sell fresh meat and produce, I could usually guess the price for half a kilogram of pork (the usual unit of measure in Chinese markets—it's just over a pound) from the expressions of my neighbors as they walked or stormed into the morning light. "The Pork Index," as it is sometimes called, is known as one of the best indicators of happiness in China. It is often used as a stand-in for the Consumer Price Index, as China consumes half of all the pigs in the world. Sixty percent of all the meat consumed in China is pork. (Poultry is second at less than 20 percent.) China's taste for pork has changed its agrarian culture. Since the early 1990s corn production has jumped nearly 125 percent, while rice has increased only 7 percent, according to the World Bank. The spike in corn production is not to feed the people but to feed all of the nation's pigs.[2]

However, the question has since gained a psalm-like status for Chinese foodie academics, serving as historic justification for China's intensive pancultural commitment to eating.

Zhang Wei lifted the soup dumpling to his mouth and bit a tiny hole in the noodle, like a vampire bat making its small incision in a victim. With a flourish he added, "And, 'food is the god of the people' is written on all the hearts of the Chinese people!" He then placed the dumpling to his lips, tilted his head back like he was taking a shot, slurped the broth from inside, and relished its flavor before fitting the dumpling into his mouth and scouting the next one.

二

Food is the most basic organizing principle of Chinese culture. Wang Xue Tai, author of the bestseller *The Chinese World of Food* (2012) and *Chinese Culinary Culture* (2006), writes, "From a multitude of perspectives, the very soul of Chinese culture is linked to food in a thousand and one different ways."[3] Chinese academics consider the lofty centrality of food to every aspect of Chinese culture a social fact. "If you don't understand Chinese food," a philosophy professor from Sichuan University once lectured me as he brandished a well-marbled morsel of pork between his chopsticks, "you don't understand China."

Every culture must ask itself, "What tempts humanity?" The West has the concept of the seven deadly sins, temptations or pitfalls that also tacitly acknowledge how humans are likely to stray.

China's temptations are fewer: food and sex. When discussing human nature, Chinese scholarship often reflects on one quote from *The Works of Mencius:* "Eating food and having sex is the nature of human beings."[4]* They are not *within* human nature; they are human nature itself.

Within popular Chinese philosophy is a group of scholars who say the fundamental difference between China and the West is merely the difference between food and sex—the West is driven by the desire for sex, whereas China is driven by food. Wang Xue Tai, who also wrote extensively about Chinese humor, explains, "The West is characterized by male-female lust and passion . . . Here in China, we have food."[5] In *Culinary Principles*, the Taiwanese professor Zhang Qi Jun explains how comparing the Confucian Classic of Ritual with Western religious and philosophical texts makes clear that people in the West are driven by a desire for sex. Zhang points to original sin as the benchmark. In an interview recording played for me while I was in Taiwan, Zhang explains: In the story of Adam and Eve, the apple is a metaphor for the temptations of the flesh. In the Chinese version, it wouldn't be symbolic—just food. They'd eat the apple, then eat the snake, too.

As a nation, China thinks and feels with its stomach. To strain or toil at a task is to "eat strength" (*"chī lì"*). To be well received in business or by society, you "eat fragrant" (*"chī xiāng"*), or good-smelling, food. For instance, "People of real learning and strong education eat fragrant wherever they go." Chinese who had converted to

---

*食色性也: *Shí sè xìng yě.*

Christianity, beginning in the European Age of Exploration from the sixteenth to the eighteenth centuries, are said to have "eaten foreign teachings" (*"chī yáng jiào"*). When my friend Xiao Huai tried to hit on a young woman and got shot down, he was made fun of for "eating closed door soup" (*"chī bì mén gēng"*). When Chinese media admonish the younger generation for being too soft, they call them the Strawberry Generation (*"cǎoméi zú"*). The critics say that, compared with the older generations, which are hardened by years of "eating bitter," the young generation can handle only "the sweet tang of privileged fruit."

China's young people have inherited China's millennia-long deep appreciation of food. Now that the young generation has a bit of disposable income, food is an intuitive outlet for their expanding desires. While China is quickly becoming a more sexual nation, it already is a well-developed gastronome.

So it should come as no surprise that China is the ultimate food-porn nation. *A Bite of China*, a documentary TV series about food that is most aptly described as the *Planet Earth* of Chinese food, earned thirty million views on Youku Tudou, China's biggest video site, for the first episode alone. The second season has been streamed more than two hundred million times. And that is discounting those who watched when it aired live. Two hundred million views for a program that takes ultrahigh-definition shots of Chinese people harvesting and preparing food. With the ultratight closeups of glistening sauces and gurgling soups, it is difficult to deny that China has eroticized its food better than anywhere else in the world.

My Chinese uncle* would tell me, "Eating for us Chinese is the

---

*Not to be confused with my Chinese godfather, my Chinese uncle is a man named Chungliang "Al" Huang. He and my dad have known each other since they were

closest we get to religious congregation. It is the most sacred part of the day," as he heaped more wok-fried Fujianese-style bamboo shoots onto my plate.

Like the Indian parable of the many blind men, each of whom touches only one part of an elephant, such as a tusk or a haunch, and then describes the elephant as something entirely different, I was often left confused by the multitude of meanings in a Chinese meal. Over the years I had learned food could be a tonic, a binding agent, a family therapy session, a warm embrace, an olive branch, or a battlefield.

Even when I was unable to grasp a meal's implication, I always felt the weight of its importance. Slowly I learned to eat a second bowl of rice at my friend's house to show his mother I liked the food, but I also learned not to ask for rice in the early stages of fancier dinners because doing so meant I wanted to fill up and get the meal over with. When a host poured the tea, I learned that tapping with two fingers on the table shows appreciation and never to tap with two knuckles, which is considered grossly overly courteous. I also learned that people in certain provinces, such as Fujian, care far more about tea etiquette than people in other provinces. I learned that a friend who messed up and then invited me to my favorite grilled fish restaurant intended it as an apology, even though he never apologized. Also, offering to split the bill is often an insult, a signal that you don't want to owe the other person anything and you don't want them to owe you. Real friends are bound by owing and being owed favors small and large, the exchange of 人情, *rénqíng*, "actions done for friends," the give-take

---

young. He has known me since I was a child. Uncle Al is a Tai Qi master and calligrapher. Several months after I arrived in China, he invited me to take part in a Tai Qi retreat he was leading in the mountains of Wu Yi, Fujian. He is also responsible for giving me my Chinese name.

currency of China's economy of relationships. These small friend debts are essential—they are a commitment to see the person another time to return the favor. I learned that saying thank you is unnecessarily formal; a real friend does not need to be thanked. Most important, I learned that sharing everything is the magic in a meal, that the invitation to eat together can turn a hostel room full of strangers into compatriots, and that even—or perhaps especially—in a generation of single children, community is an ideal to be protected and pursued.

Oddly, China's reputation abroad can run contrary to its true foodie nature. Chinese are notorious within the travel adviser and hotelier community for not eating local food when they are on the road. It became so bad for their public image as travelers that President Xi Jinping chastised his people in a speech he gave in Singapore in which (in part as a sign of goodwill to Singapore and their increasingly China dependent economy) he instructed the Chinese to "eat less instant noodles and more fresh seafood" while traveling, a reprimand you wouldn't expect would be necessary for a nation of gourmands. Real foodies travel with their stomachs leading the way.

The problem with foreign food for many of my Chinese friends is almost always the same—it is too *not Chinese*. Although young people were being exposed to more food from the outside world, European foods were still not part of their weekly diet. When this generation of Chinese were young, their parents did not stop at the Indian restaurant for lunch or order in Italian on Sundays. They ate Chinese food, most often the food from their own province. In middle-class and wealthier circles, Western food was a trendy luxury and a novelty. The most popular foreign foods continued to originate in Asia—Japanese sushi and Korean barbecue. Although they are tossed together as Asian fusion abroad, they were still foreign to the Chinese palate.

Zhang Wei, the expert dumpling eater and peddler of food philosophy, had been away studying in France, and when we caught up with each other on his return, the first thing I asked was how he enjoyed the famous French cuisine.

We sat at our favorite lunch counter, as he prepared to slurp down some soup, meticulously measuring how much vinegar to drop in beforehand.

"How was the food in France?" I asked him.

"It was so-so," he replied courteously. By so-so he meant no good.

"French food is *so-so*," I muttered in disbelief. "What didn't you like about it?"

He put down his spoon and thought before replying, "Everything was too . . . hard." He considered the question for another few seconds, eyes wandering toward the kitchen behind us before nodding, confirming his answer.

My puzzled follow-ups yielded no other information; the food was just too hard. It had never occurred to me before, but most Chinese food is soft. Meats are cut in thin, chewable strips; there are no hard rolls; and rice and noodles don't require much chewing.

Foreigners eating Chinese food find that texture is the number one problem. Flavor is never the issue. Sautéed tofu tastes great but oozes in the mouth. For foreigners visiting China the number one problem is that the food is too *soft*.

So instead of enjoying what many believe to be the finest food destination in the world, my foodie friend Zhang Wei ate instant noodles while in France. Toward the end of his tour of France, he got really desperate and ate local Chinese food that had been adapted for the French palate. "How can a man who has never been to Sichuan

Province cook Sichuanese food?" Zhang Wei complained. The vast majority of early emigrants from China to the West came from the southeastern provinces of Fujian and Guangdong, which boasted major ports. Most French Chinese chefs come from these two provinces. The same is true in the States. So when they are cooking spicy Sichuanese food, or, as it is often romanized, Szechuanese food, they actually have never eaten the real thing themselves.

As a Westerner, I thought at first that my Chinese friends lacked interest in foreign food perhaps because they just didn't like it. But in time I saw that the Chinese image of foreign food is that it is fatally flawed—it is simply too *not* Chinese.

三

It sounds simple, but leisure is one of the defining differences between the post-90s generation and their parents. They have it; their parents did not. What we're witnessing now is a generation that is moving away from bitterness and learning how to play.

In making a list of all the things young Chinese people like to do, I couldn't help but feel like I was putting together a Tinder profile or, in the case of China, a Momo or Tantan profile, for an entire generation.

> *Hi, I'm 22, single, like eating out with friends, karaoke on the weekend, shopping online, badminton with friends and love, love, love to travel!*

Rob Gordon, one of American millennials' favorite soliloquizing lonely guys from the movie *High Fidelity*, says, "What really matters is what you like, not what you are like. Books, records, films—these things matter. Call me shallow, but it's the fuckin' truth." By the Rob

Gordon metric, Chinese young people's passions, hobbies, interests—how they like to play—reveal something essential about who they are. How does a generation of single children growing up in China's pressure cooker educational system cut loose? How do young adults living in multigenerational households or in dorms with four roommates create their own space? How do a brutal housing market, low starting wages, and fierce competition for jobs change the way people spend money? How do young people brought up by a generation defined by "eating bitter" search out life's sweetness?

Fei Fei, a twenty-two-year-old from Chengdu, explained to me over dinner that the biggest difference between her generation and her parents' generation is that "we have different Needs," with a capital *N*. We were with several of her friends in a fish restaurant in the club district of Chengdu. Fei Fei gestured across the room to the server wheeling our cart of food through the crowd, her frame and the cart silhouetted against the sleek black walls alive with swirls and slashes of multicolored graffiti. "Maslow's hierarchy of needs talks about filling your stomach and keeping warm before being able to think about other needs," she noted.

China's young generations have become enthusiastic amateur psychologists in an increasingly introspective China. Much of psychology is intuitive for Chinese; for those who have had to maneuver the complex web of *guanxi*, their network of relationships with government officials and business people, understanding concepts like emotional intelligence is second nature. In an English-language discussion class I taught to thirty-five people at my night school in Suzhou, no one needed an explanation of EQ alongside IQ. It is a cultural imperative.

Similarly, Chinese young people have tried to understand why they want different things than their parents, an imperative that springs from the cultural mandate to honor their parents. Wanting something different feels like they are being disrespectful, so many have turned to Abraham Maslow's hierarchy of needs for an explanation. According to Maslow, humans must satisfy their need for food, water, and shelter before they are motivated to fulfill their need for belongingness, esteem, and, eventually, self-actualization.

"It makes sense," Fei Fei continued. "Our grandparents and parents were brought up when China was poor. My grandparents were obsessed with food, finding enough and having enough to be able to survive." A lock of hair worked free of Fei Fei's beanie. A heavily ringed hand—rock star chic—brushed it back. Music pulsed in the restaurant. It was 9:00 p.m. The wait for a table was still an hour. "We're not interested in basic needs—food, water, shelter, right? At what point can we enjoy our lives now? We're only young once."

Amid the pressure and uncertainty of modern China, Fei Fei's generation is absolutely determined to enjoy themselves. Whereas delayed gratification, the ability to eat bitter, once was the hallmark of Chinese students and workers, an attitude of 活在当下, *húo zài dāng xìa*, "be here now"—that is, live in the moment—has moved in. China still values the ability to eat bitter. But this young generation insists on enjoying the sweetness of youth while they can. Their parents, for their part, are encouraging their children to enjoy life more as they go, to live a better life and enjoy childhood more than they did when they were young.

Fei Fei raised her glass of dark beer. "Today we have booze, so today we are drunk!"*

Her toast is a line by an unknown Chinese poet from the Tang Dynasty (619–907 AD). It is perhaps the classiest way of declaring

*"今朝有酒，今朝醉!": *"jīn zhāo yǒu jiǔ, jīn zhāo zuì!"*

the millennial battle cry familiar in the West, the generation's justification for living in the moment: YOLO, You Only Live Once.

We all clinked glasses, tucked into the fish we had ordered, and, true to our word, proceeded to get drunk.

四

Community has become a priority in impersonal urban China, so, bolstered by increasingly steady jobs, hobbies have taken a central role in city life.

My Chinese uncle often pointed out that the defining characteristic of a Chinese meal is that you can't eat one alone. Sure, some fried rice and noodle dishes are meant to be solo affairs, but a real Chinese meal needs to be enjoyed with a community. Young China, which could have been known as "the lonely generation" because of the one-child policy, has a driving hunger for connectedness.

Chengdu is brimming with clubs and societies. Every hobby has a citywide group formed around it. These clubs organize on WeChat or even Momo. They have shirts that feature their club logo. They get together and take selfies with the shirts on. They make banners. They get together and take selfies under the banners. Gather, grin, repeat.

Chinese post-90s also seek a sense of individual identity. China's rapid urbanization has spawned more than one hundred cities with populations of at least one million people. For a generation that mostly populates crowded urban spaces, finding a sense of self can be challenging. It is hard to feel like an individual during your morning commute in a packed Chinese subway car. The types of communities they choose to be a part of help define who they are as they navigate a foreign city, often far from their hometown.

Dozens of these groups invited me to participate. I tried the

Chengdu Crossfit Society, Chengdu Billiards Boys, Chengdu Fixed-Gear Bike Squad, Chengdu Basketball Club, Chengdu Foodie Friends, See the World Weekenders, Chengdu Friends of Charity, Groovy Movie Mania, and a dozen or so more. For each group I tried, three to fifteen other groups met around a similar central theme.

The hobbies young Chinese choose, rather than the work they do or subjects they study, can come to define how they see themselves. Some are dabblers, but a mounting number are ultraenthusiasts and superfans. Something about the personality, a level of dedication perhaps picked up in the tedium of memorization, makes my Chinese friends and their generation the most intense hobbyists I've ever encountered.

Compared with the other groups, the Block Dash Crew was fairly pedestrian. BDC was a running club. Members would meet on weeknights and some really early weekday mornings and run ten-kilometer jogs around different parts of Chengdu. College students and recent graduates ran with BDC. What set them apart was their business savvy. They'd managed to get a bevy of sponsorships. All the group leaders—stylish, attractive twenty-three-year-olds—raced around in the newest Nike gear.

BDC partnered one night with a new high-end noodle shop to sponsor a run. All runners who participated would get a free sweatshirt and bowl of noodles. Chengdu is famous for its spicy, saucy, delicious noodles. These high-end noodle shops were beginning to pop up all over the city, serving not only Sichuanese noodles but also Japanese udon or ramen, Thai curry noodles, Vietnamese pho, and noodle dishes from all over China. They were doing well, as noodles are an intuitive entry point to foreign fare for Sichuanese. Skeptical, I thought their glitzy signage and prices five times higher than local shops' were a rip-off.

Before we met, the group sent out a text about the air quality for the night, a 73 on the Air Quality Index (AQI), which measures the particulate matter (PM) and its diameter. PM 2.5 is particulate matter that is 2.5 micrometers or less in diameter (a human hair has a diameter of about 100 micrometers). These types of particulate matter are produced during fuel combustion. Because Chengdu is surrounded by factory towns, most of us had an app that tracks AQI. Outdoor athletes and commuters alike are in the habit of checking the AQI in the morning, like checking the weather. Air quality of 73 was fine—not great, not bad. Even so, a few people of the fifty people who showed up brought masks to protect their lungs.

We started off. In a Chinese city center at night, low-lying bad air bounces and refracts the light from the megamalls, office buildings, and restaurants. It is like holding a flashlight to a colored plastic water bottle—bright beams of light dilute into a duller glow. We ran and talked through the ethereal city. As we ran, a swarm of fixed-gear bikers pedaled by us towing a speaker system and blasting Chinese pop. They wore jerseys that read CHENGDU BIKE SQUAD. We ran past the English Corner. A group of college students, members of a photography club, had also partnered with BDC, and now they circled us on mopeds, one person driving and the passenger facing backward to snap candid shots. Even the elderly were gathering. Beneath a highway overpass, on a raised concrete platform on an island that separated the nighttime traffic, a large group of elderly Chinese men in tank tops and sandals fanned themselves as they listened to a local opera singer through a portable amp. Other packs of aunts and uncles glided around city squares to ballroom music, while others still did choreographed exercise routines.

I ran next to a young man named Guo Yu. He worked in information technology at a media company. He was a twenty-four-year-old white-collar worker who had just gotten married. Guo Yu's wiry frame, light step, and smooth gait gave him away as a serious runner. Around the eight-kilometer mark I struggled through my end of the conversation amid labored breathing. Guo Yu's voice remained even and clear. BDC was Guo Yu's second, less-serious running group. Like me, he had been enticed by the free sweatshirt. He usually ran on Fridays anyway, especially when he was training for a marathon.

"Have you run a marathon before?" I asked Guo Yu.

He nodded in the affirmative: "I ran one three days ago."

I turned to him, blinking, making sure I had understood. He glided along beside me, smiling back at my searching look.

"And you're already training for another one?"

"That one is next week," he responded. Two marathons, two weeks.

"How many marathons have you run this year?" I asked.

"This next one will be my sixth." It was early May.

We ran silently for a few dozen meters; he was gliding along, I was reconsidering the way I live my life. Then another question occurred to me.

"How long have you been running?"

Without so much as a glance at me, Guo Yu responded, "About a year and change now."

I stopped in my tracks. Guo Yu flipped around, jogging in place, still smiling, waving for me to keep moving.

Fifteen months ago, someone Guo Yu used to play computer games with had picked up running. It was in the middle of a fitness craze in China, driven more by social media and showing off a lean figure than by health. After seeing more and more people take up running and watching an ultramarathoner on a Chinese TV show explain how distance running can hone a person's self-motivation and will-power, Guo Yu had decided to try it.

China's respect for endurance sports is owed in part to its history. Every child in China learns about Mao's Long March, when he and his Red Army trekked fifty-six hundred miles in a year to avoid defeat by the Nationalists in 1935. The Long March was a testament to Mao's ironclad willpower, a feat that continues to inspire awe and command respect. It also bears a striking resemblance to running marathons, long-distance biking, and winter swimming, all of which require extraordinary mental strength and fortitude, the bitter sports, if you will.

"Had you ever played any sports before?"

"No, not really."

"How long did you train before your first marathon?"

"Two months."

After his first run with Block Dash Crew, Guo Yu had started running every day. Running became his social outlet. He would run every night with friends or with clubs. Running became who he was.

"I had no context or expectations for what was possible or what wasn't. After two months of running, I ran a marathon," he told me. "Two weeks later I ran another one. I thought, so what?"

I asked if he knew that he sounded nuts. You could do that sort of thing back home—from zero miles to 26.2—but people would make a YouTube video about it, and it would become an inspirational meme on the Internet: "IT Nerd Runs Toward New Life." And then to run six marathons in six months—it was beyond my comprehension.

Guo Yu's explanation reminded me of a conversation I'd had with

Yu Jiawen, a young entrepreneur in Guangzhou. Jiawen is a well-known Chinese entrepreneur. Through frequent TV appearances he became known for his boyish appearance and fearless attitude, as well as the great success of his mobile platform, Super Schedule, a social app that allows students to see the schedules of, and interact with, other students in their classes. It quickly turned into the most popular way for students to find their classmates and start to flirt. In a conversation at his headquarters in Guangzhou, Jiawen told me with a big grin, "We tried to create a platform for classmates to interact and it became the largest dating app in China."[6]

Jiawen spoke to me about the unique moment entrepreneurship was enjoying in China. Over tea in his company's Guangzhou headquarters, Jiawen explained, "It was only when foreign investors told me what I was doing was incredible that I began to think I couldn't do it. Otherwise, I wouldn't have noticed."

Because China has a remarkable lack of precedent for start-ups, or for runners, for that matter, few people put limits on what they think is possible. Part of that comes from a lack of experience—it takes a roomful of chatty mediocre runners to make running a marathon feel out of reach. Another part of that, though, is the contemporary Chinese mind-set: If I work hard, why can't I be successful, especially if all the factors are within my control? Systematic hard work over time, like marathon running and coding? No problem.

For China's "Me Generation," as its post-90s are often called, finding a sense of self can be taxing in cities whose very existence seems to negate individuality. Finding meaning in what can feel like a rat race for an apartment, a car, a kid, and more, more, more can be spiritually draining. Chinese hobbyists put their heart and soul into their passions. Building a community around something you love, and giving yourself the emotional space to love something immaterial, provides immense meaning in a changing society.

Jiawen's passion was coding and entrepreneurship, so he threw himself into his work. His job became his social life. Working nights and weekends wasn't an issue; he was used to a limited or work-oriented social life, so he had nowhere else to go. For Guo Yu and the dozen or so other flash marathoners I've met, what they threw themselves into was running.

That type of intensity creates an especially loyal, though distant, sports superfan. One of my roommates, Huan Huan, would set his alarm for 2:00 a.m. and then stay up until 4:00 in a red Arsenal jersey to cheer on "his" soccer team on the other side of the globe. Some offices started to allow young employees to work a special nocturnal schedule during the World Cup soccer madness that gripped China so they wouldn't fall asleep at their desks. Hou Wei walked around Sichuan University in a Steph Curry Warriors jersey at all times. Curry's small stature and supernatural work ethic have earned him legions of fans in China. Hou Wei's roommate had a poster of the US basketball player DeMarcus Cousins, then of the Sacramento Kings, taped above his desk. Whenever Hou had to take a test, he would light incense to Cousins, whose name transliterated to Chinese means "God of the Exam." NBA superfandom has gotten so intense in China that the scoreboard for playoff games always has a Chinese ad, an effort to reach fans in China like Hou Wei and his roommate.

Some brands have even recognized and capitalized on this Chinese urge to join a hive.

Few brands have done it better than Nike. Nike was already making all the coolest running clothing. All the best Chinese running apps were Nike's. The problem was, Nike didn't have any Chinese runners. In the late 2000s, participants laced up at the starting line at the annual marathon in Shanghai held only a patchwork of runners.

Nike put its effort toward creating a running community, not toward selling shoes. The company sponsored a BDC event and events like it all across China. Nike created free apps to track how far you were running and share your progress on WeChat, Weibo, QQ, and Renren. The company turned running into a social and competitive experience; people wanted to outrun their friends and colleagues and share their accomplishments on social media. Nike supplied all the free sweatshirts, sweatbands, posters, and promotional swag. BDC runners plastered WeChat with pictures of its members running in Shanghai, Chengdu, Beijing, Taiwan, Hong Kong, and even Japan.

The company understood that running culture was a perfect fit for Chinese young people. When all entrepreneurs around the world were claiming meditation and daily exercise lead to success, running was a fit. When all the new TV shows and magazines were featuring sexy bodies and six-packs, running was a fit. When young people were looking for a release, running was a fit. When young people were looking to learn how to endure in the absence of a societal mandate to do so, running was a fit. But they were also looking for community, so Nike helped build one.

Chinese college students and young professionals ate it up. In 2015, one hundred thousand people applied for a spot in the Shanghai marathon, which had room for only twenty-three thousand runners.

After the BDC event that night, we all sat down to eat fancy noodles. And, despite my lingering doubts about authenticity, I have to say they were excellent.

五

Given the pressures of their lives in China, young people fervently seek avenues of escape. Urban density and multigenerational homes make personal space hard to come by and a valuable commodity. Dorm rooms usually have four occupants. Places like McDonald's and KFC, places that don't charge to sit and won't accuse their customers of loitering, are invaluable resources for young people without a private space to call their own. Those secondary spaces become their own little universe for young people, out of the orbit of family and schoolwork and outside the gravitational pull of responsibility. But sometimes those little universes are too small. They certainly cannot compete with the vast and dynamic gaming multiverse.

No other industry has gained as obsessive a following in China as online gaming. A hundred and thirty million Chinese play multiplayer computer games. They pack Internet bars, rooms lined with rows of computers and comfy chairs that offer high-speed Internet and gaming equipment—a mouse and a headphone—for little money.

In China, gaming has thrust itself into the mainstream largely because of people like Chu. I met Chu during my thirty-six-hour workathon in an Internet bar while doing a rush translation job. I had been hired to translate and localize the entire script for a smartphone game I called *Honor Quest: Steam & Magic*, an adventure game in the style of Lord of the Rings. My computer was broken and I had a tight deadline, which was why I spent thirty-six hours straight in an Internet bar, translating Chinese into English lines like, "Quick, speak! Remember, your words decide your fate!" "What kind of magic could control Titans, the War Machines, and the minds of mankind?" and "These are the Desert Dwarves. Allow me to make an introduction."

Chu, who was twenty-two, was there playing *League of Legends*, one of the most popular games in China. The game earned such a loyal Chinese following that the largest Internet company in China, Tencent, the company behind WeChat, acquired full control of Riot Games, including *League of Legends*, in 2015.[7]

Chu was an engineering student at a local university. He went to the Internet bar outside the university gates five days a week. "[I come here] whenever I can," he told me. "It allows me to zone out, not to have to think about jobs, school, family, girls, or whatever else is happening."

Chu was on a computer to my left. On my right was another young man who also was playing *LoL*. His gaming handle was LiuBei, named after the Chinese warrior hero from the book (and game) *Romance of the Three Kingdoms*. LiuBei was twenty-five, married, and a graduate of the local university. He had started a job as a chemist at a local factory. He went to the Internet bar several times a week to blow off steam after work. "Through the game I can zone out, let my mind go blank, and forget about the stresses of the day," he told me. "Plus, it is a way for me to keep up with friends from school and from home. We all play the same games and plan times to play together."

Neither Chu nor LiuBei ever played an organized team sport growing up. Their *League of Legends* teams were the first long-term team experiences of their lives. "I don't feel like my classmates really get me," Chu said at about hour eighteen in the smoke-filled Internet bar. "These guys have known me for years. We've been through things together, we have common experiences and interests." Chu paused. "We've even gone to war together," he laughed. "They get who I am." People like Chu and LiuBei live all over China. Some are less educated, some are more educated. Some are employed, some are unemployed. Many are factory workers, and a surprising number of white-collar, banking and investing, or marketing employees still link up to play intense first-person shooters or participate in deeply immersive multiple-player role-playing games.

While I was living at Outside Island, I often saw young men and women huddled around a phone watching videos together, *oohing* and *ahhing* as if watching a title bout. Then I would realize they were watching highlights from international gaming tournaments. They weren't even playing the games—they were e-sports spectators.

Gaming offers the least expensive diversion from life in China, an escape into cyberspace that is even further removed from reality than a karaoke box or a big meal. Not including the four meals of instant noodles, three cans of Red Bull, chips, processed sausage, and duck neck, the thirty-six hours cost me US$29.

LiuBei told me, "I'm married and am a white-collar guy now. My mom lives with my wife and me. She [his wife] is expecting a baby. Mostly, I work. Sometimes, it is nice to just let my mind go blank, you know?" *Click-click-click-click-click* persisted in the background. "It's a bit of escaping reality, but is that such a bad thing for short periods? My wife is OK with it. She handles the finances, and this is cheaper than smoking or drinking, right?"

China is full of puzzles to solve. Why is everyone in China such a great singer? Why do people love karaoke? These questions would keep me up at night. I once told my parents on the phone that I feel as if every single person in China is a talented singer. They did not believe me, so I stopped a student outside the library, explained to him that my parents hoped to hear a Chinese song, as they'd never heard one before, and he happily serenaded my parents, who listened from thousands of miles away. He sang "Within My Voice," a drippy pop love song that was the number one hit at the time.

When looking at these puzzles, there is a tendency to throw up your hands, say, "That's weird!" and stop there; there is something satisfying about cultural novelty that would be somehow diminished by an explanation. For instance, when I first went to China, I thought I would make a small business of correcting mistakes in English. Signs, pamphlets, menus, business cards—the glaring spelling and grammar mistakes, I felt, made for good comedy but poor business. "Why don't they just fix it?" I thought. When I got a job posing as a foreign client for a photo shoot for a paper producer's corporate pamphlet, I seized the opportunity to pitch my services to the CEO. The pamphlet would, after all, be written at least partly in English. Between pictures I talked to the boss, who was there to oversee the photo shoot. The CEO looked at me with raised eyebrows before finally telling me, "We don't have any clients outside of China." I was startled. So I asked him why his old pamphlet included copy in English. It turned out that the English served the same purpose as my picture in the new pamphlet: to make the company seem international and modern. None of its clients actually relied on the English. Spelling and grammar? It made no difference.

These small disambiguations occurred almost daily when I first got to China. But as time went on, there was one mystery whose deeper logic would simply not reveal itself to me. That was karaoke. Its existence and near-unanimous popularity confirmed that I did not understand something absolutely fundamental about China.

China's obsession with karaoke reminded me of a classic science fiction short story by A. E. van Vogt called "The Weapon Shop" (1942). In it, shops selling gleaming, high-tech guns begin to pop up overnight all over the fictional Empire of Isher, which spreads across our solar system. At first citizens are outraged at the presence of violent wares in their peaceful towns. But those who enter the shop leave ideologically changed. Vogt reveals the shops themselves to be independent political entities, islands of revolution within the Empire of Isher. The selling of weapons was just a convenient front.

That is how I used to envision karaoke joints, known as KTVs; nearly every block in any Chinese city has at least two. They constituted a violent imposition on the peaceful scenery of my social schedule. Everything in my body would scream at me, "No, you're not meant to go sing garish pop hits in a dark room and drink weak tea on a Friday night!" I believed it with every fiber of my being. So when, day after day, night after night, I was invited to go sing karaoke, I figured I was missing something crucial.

KTV shops have a collection of private rooms that rent by the hour. I figured those dark black boxes with leather couches, bejeweled walls, and flat-screen TVs must have a secret purpose, like the weapons shops in Isher, islands of political impunity or revolution that I was too dense to access.

Long karaoke sessions have become the social glue that binds relationships, especially in government and business. When you walk into a karaoke room, you enter an explicitly private space within which people are expected to let their guard down. China has no other spaces where custom dictates checking pride and formality at the door.

At my first job in China my Chinese coworkers went to karaoke together almost every Friday. I could avoid it for only so long. We took taxis to a nearby shopping mall and walked into a midlevel KTV.

Others I would visit over the years would be mind-bogglingly upscale, with crystal chandeliers, dazzling in-room light effects, and offerings of high-end food and alcohol. Most were like this one: a high-gloss lobby and a small army of attendants to bring food like kettle corn, peanuts, sunflower seeds, or even barbecued duck neck and soft drinks and alcohol to your room at the push of a button.

KTV offers one of the few private spaces in China that one can buy for cheap. As Joy, a whip-smart, somewhat reserved young woman with whom I worked, told me, "There are multiple people in our homes. Our dorms are packed. We even have to shower in a hall full of people. Restaurants are overrun with people. Where else can we have privacy with our friends?" A private karaoke room is one of the few second spaces in China that you can truly call your own, even if just for a few hours.

Six of us piled onto one of the leather couches in the dark room. Several young women immediately went over to the flat screen's control panel on the side of the wall and began to choose a playlist. Before long, music began to stream from the surround-sound stereo system, and Joy jumped between two other coworkers to snatch up the microphone, yelling, "It's my song, it's my song!" On flickered the music video for the number-one pop hit at the moment, "Within My Voice."

Still remember us once walking side by side together past that
bustling alley
Even though we were strangers, just passing by each other,
we still felt each other
One look, one beat of the heart,
one unexpected delight. It's like
a dream that was destined.

Karaoke's popularity has a formative impact on the Chinese pop music industry. Chinese musical artists intentionally gear their music to create karaoke hits. Most music in China is freely accessible—free to download one way or another on apps or on your computer—so karaoke popularity is one way for artists to skyrocket up the charts and make money through licensing fees. Karaoke chains buy the rights to songs and music videos. At the time "Within my Voice" was such a big hit that people didn't get tired of it. I'd heard the song a hundred times in fifty days, and that was while avoiding karaoke.

Joy's rendition of "Within My Voice" was, not surprisingly, pretty damn good. The linguistics community has offered an explanation of why the average Chinese speaker is a better singer than native speakers of other languages; it has to do with the higher occurrence of vowels and vowel combinations in Chinese than in other languages. Vowels are easier to enunciate clearly and with more resonance, and a lifetime of such pronunciation, alongside more opportunities to sing, leads to better-trained voices. On top of that, research suggests that the tonality of Mandarin and the necessary heightened tonal awareness means Chinese speakers are much more likely to have absolute pitch than English speakers.[8]

After she put down the microphone, Joy fielded the question I would ask all my friends whenever I was forced to sing karaoke, a question whose answer I was sure would unravel the other cultural mysteries of China: What do you love about KTV? Behind her, the other employees hovered around the touch screen song menu, scrolling, laughing, and pointing excitedly when they found a song they liked. During lulls in the music Joy gave me an explanation I would hear time and again during the next three years. She said, "We have lots of pressure at work. We have pressure at home. We aren't able to let that pressure out in our daily lives. It isn't 'Chinese' to do that. Karaoke is a release."

China places a tremendous amount of value on 含蓄, *hánxù*. It means "subtle," "implicit," or "contained," and it is a term often used to describe the characteristics of classic Chinese poetry. When referring to people, it means "reserved." For young people especially, the modalities of expression in China and the hierarchies in the office make for a bottled-up life.

Work hierarchies also tend to be more stifling in China. The distances between bosses, managers, and staff are greater in China. Regular staff members, like Joy and her coworkers, are not supposed to exercise autonomy within a work unit. Opportunities for self-expression are limited throughout the week. In a study titled "Consuming Karaoke in China," the author breaks down karaoke's functionality: Political (a private, democratized space separate from the hierarchies of society), Personal (release of tension), Community (builds comradery amongst employees and friends), and Class. Karaoke offers a space at least relatively detached from those social constrains. As Gil, a colleague at the school, would tell me, "We are all here making asses of ourselves. There is something tremendously unifying about that."

Over the years I saw that the dark music rooms, lit only by videos, served as therapy sessions countless times. In a culture that doesn't encourage showing emotion, karaoke becomes, as Joy said, a release. When a friend of mine from Henan, a server in a local restaurant where I often ate, was fired and had to go home and restart his life, he took me and other friends to KTV, where he ripped Chinese rock ballads of pain and sorrow until he cried. The next day, with his belongings crammed into cheap plastic sacks for the train ride home, his eyes were dry as he said goodbye, and his face was as expressionless as when he washed the dishes. When a friend gets fired, Chinese go to KTV. When a friend gets promoted, they go to KTV. When someone has a birthday, suffers a breakup, fights with his parents, has a baby, or starts a new business—people go to KTV. When Huan Huan's girlfriend broke up with him and he failed the civil service exam, he went to KTV five days in a row, singing his favorite rock songs in the dark with a rotating cast of friends by his side.

Few activities give me as much anxiety as being handed a microphone while a song by Lady Gaga or the Back Street Boys is queued up. I find it difficult to imagine KTV as relaxing. But it soon became clear that, if I were to have a normal social life in China, I would need to get over my reluctance to sing karaoke. I never did figure out how everyone was doing this with a straight face. In the end, though, I ended up going to KTV by myself for a four-hour afternoon session. With a tabletop of beers, thirty or so songs, and a well-oiled rendition of Gao Jin's "My Blood Brother" under my belt, I had at least somewhat overcome my fear of karaoke. I called five friends and we sang for hours. Fei Fei, the young Maslow enthusiast, rushed over to line up her song. She picked up the mic, hushed us, and gave her best rendition of "Within My Voice."

11

Be There Now

One Hundred Million New Travelers Hit the Road

The ice spreading across the sleeper cabin window finally swallowed up the last moonlit glimpse of the outside world. I rocked back into the small foldout seat in the narrow hallway. Now I had nothing to look at except the icicles forming on the seams of the doors between the train cars.

Sitting with me were Feng and Ma, both of whom were twenty-one-year-old college students. Feng sat on the foldout seat opposite me, and Ma had propped himself on the foot of the nearest bottom bunk. We had met in the first hour of the trip. Now, in the twenty-seventh hour of our train journey to Harbin, the capital of China's icy northernmost province, we knew each other quite well. What began with small talk had turned to a discussion of food in hour four, family in hour six, marriage in hour eleven, government in hour sixteen, and sex in hour twenty. By hour twenty-four we were exhausted and had reverted to small talk.

Feng and Ma were college roommates. This trip was their

graduation present from their parents, a sum of money they begged for a semester before they graduated and would receive in a "Red Envelope" of cash, congratulating them for earning their diploma. Feng, the more talkative of the two, had explained that ice was forming on the window because of the temperature difference from inside to outside. He pointed toward the rest of the cabin, which was filled with people heading back to their hometowns in the North from their jobs in China's more prosperous southern cities. Inside, the heavy breathing of the thousand or so sleepers throughout the train created humidity within the train cars. Outside the wind-chill factor put the temperature at forty degrees below zero Fahrenheit, and the winds were whipping the train's steel exterior into a deep freeze.

Feng took out a creased pamphlet. On its front was a picture of Saint Sophia Church, Harbin's most recognizable landmark. Saint Sophia was built in the Byzantine style in the early twentieth century by Russians, who in the late nineteenth century had turned a small fishing village into a city by making it the construction center for the Chinese Eastern Railway; in 1904 that railway linked the Trans-Siberian Railway with Vladivostok in easternmost Siberia. Harbin later became a refuge for Russians fleeing the Revolution of 1917. The church was built of timber in 1907 by Russians, who then rebuilt it of masonry between 1923 and 1932. It features an iconic Russian onion dome and spires, and today is a museum, listed since 1996 as an important cultural relic under state protection.[1]

Harbin, however, has two versions of Saint Sophia Church. The second exists only in winter, made entirely of snow and ice. The church on the front of Feng's pamphlet glowed blue and yellow and orange from within, lit by streams of lights snaked through the large ice bricks and pillars supporting the structure. I asked Feng why he had the pamphlet. Ma rolled his eyes and said, "He's a romantic."

Then Ma used his phone to show me a far more detailed description of the Harbin Ice and Snow Festival, held from January to March each year. Feng pushed Ma's phone out of the way, pointed to the faded picture, and said, "We'll be here tonight."

Like me, Ma and Feng were traveling to China's northernmost province in what was once called Manchuria to see the festival. "Over one hundred thousand cubic meters [more than four million cubic feet] of ice go into making the ice sculptures," Feng read from the pamphlet. "Fifteen thousand craftsmen work around the clock to build the massive city of ice and snow. There are replicas of the world's most famous churches, temples, and statues. They can be six or seven stories tall, lit up like a wonderland by multicolored lights." It is by far the biggest festival of its kind on Earth. Each year more than a million travelers arrive in Harbin during the festival's seventy-day run.[2] The northern city's fusion of efficient Chinese architecture and whimsical classical Russian architecture make the city unlike any other in China. Ma watched me zip my jacket a bit tighter and added, "And, of course, the temperature will be thirty degrees below zero."

Despite warnings from Chinese friends in Suzhou, I had not realized just how cold Harbin would be. As I watched the scenery go from green to gray to white, the windows from clear to frosted to totally opaque, apprehension set in.

I doodled with my finger on the ice on the window. I was more than a little frightened about the cold we were about to face. Jokingly, I asked Feng and Ma, "Remind me why you're going here again?"

Feng inhaled deeply. Like many people I'd met, Feng took on the role of cultural interlocutor when having a conversation with a foreigner for the first time. He took the role seriously. He patiently explained, "Every young kid wants the same thing right now: travel. Our parents lived very constricted lives. When we were young, we lived pretty constricted lives too. For us, travel has become the socially accepted expression of 'freedom.' We want to live in the moment."

What I had meant was "Why are you going to freezing Harbin instead of the beach in Sanya?" Still, Feng's answer made us all think, and the three of us slipped into silence. Behind Feng, a sleeper let out a giant snore and turned over. The train rattled softly as it raced north through the darkness.

We arrived several hours later. Hundreds of passengers hustled onto the platform at the Harbin train station. The first thing to freeze in the bitter morning air was the hair in my nose. Cold pressed in. It singed my eyes. It clogged my throat. In that moment I felt my reptilian brain start to shoot off bursts of warning flashes. I felt trapped in the freeze, claustrophobic in its cold. Around us some of our cabin mates, locals returning home for the holidays, smiled and waved. They wore blazers, loafers, and thin leather gloves, whereas I was dressed in a heavy winter jacket and dogsledding boots.

Feng slapped me hard on the back, breaking the spell. "We can't get into our hostel rooms till noon," he said. "We should check out the Siberian tiger reserve. Do you want to come?"

Grinning, he spat. The spit landed on the platform and crystalized within seconds. "I hoped it would do that," he said with satisfaction and turned to go.

He nodded to Ma, and they moved into the flow of passengers, all laden with gifts for their families for Chinese New Year.

二

By tradition China lionizes the wanderer, the person who has seen the world. As children they memorize Chinese poetry extolling the virtues of discovery on the open road. For the first time in China's history, the precious ability to travel is within reach for growing numbers of people.

China has the largest outbound tourism market in the world.[3] Since the Beijing Olympics in 2008, the Chinese have spent ever-growing amounts on international travel, zooming past the traditional globe-trotters, the Americans, Germans, and British, in 2011. "My mom couldn't get a visa to Australia when she was younger because she was single. They thought she was going to try to marry someone and emigrate or flee underground and emigrate illegally," Xiao Jiu, a twenty-four-year-old brand representative for Qunar, one of China's biggest online travel companies, told me. "I helped a group of ten leftover women book a trip to Australia last week, all single. The Australian visas? Their consulate couldn't give them to us fast enough. Times have changed."

Considering the size of China's population, that China is now the biggest spender on international travel doesn't seem like such a big deal—at least until you consider that only 4 percent of the population has a passport.* Then it's a really big deal, especially when that number is projected to grow to 12 percent by 2025.[4]

Two-thirds of all Chinese passport holders are younger than thirty-five. Chinese are only beginning to travel internationally, and young people are leading the movement. They're not traveling to emigrate or to seek for a better life for themselves or their children, as in generations past. Young Chinese are traveling to see the outside world, because they are curious and, frankly, can afford it.

In 2015, a counselor at a middle school in Henan Province submitted her resignation, which consisted of only ten characters; it soon be-

---

*In comparison, a third of Americans, two-thirds of Canadians, and three-quarters of the British hold passports.

came the stuff of Internet lore. It said, "The world is so big, I want to see it for myself."* The Internet exploded. Aside from inspiring a bevy of job resignations, the simplicity and straightforwardness of the counselor's resignation letter inspired what felt like a vigorous and synchronized national nod of agreement: we want to see the world. For months everyone used the line from the resignation letter to caption their travel pictures. People posted selfies in the office with the wistful caption "The world is so big . . ." In a report released by the Department of Education's Minister of Language, *The State of the Chinese Language, 2016*, "The world is so big, I want to see it for myself" was on the list of the ten most influential Internet phrases for that year.[5]

Most big Chinese trends begin at home. In 2015 Chinese tourists took four billion domestic trips and about 120 million abroad.[6] For the first time in China's history, its people are seeing their country, and the world, en masse. The first place they go is often Beijing. Chairman Mao said you are not a real man until you've climbed the Great Wall, so the nation's capital is the first stop. That is why the first Chinese people that foreigners encounter while on their own sightseeing trips are also coming to a first-tier Chinese city for the first time.

Young Chinese, who have been seeing the world through the Internet since they were small, are especially eager to hit the road. At any given moment my WeChat wall is flooded with dozens upon dozens of articles about travel, such as "Travel Is Not a Luxury; It is Necessity!" They are written, circulated, go viral, then disappear under the next wave of articles: "Dreaming of a 'Say Go, Then Go' Spontaneous Vacation." A host of my favorite Chinese podcast, a twenty-three-year-old student at Peking University, revealed in a podcast his compulsion to look up flights and Airbnb rooms in places he

---

* 世界这么大，我想去看看: *"Shìjiè zhème dà, wǒ xiǎng qù kàn kàn."*

wants to visit. "Before I know it, I'm on C-Trip [one of China's largest e-travel companies], and my fingers are typing in *S-a-n D-i-e-g-o*, and then I'm, like, nope, can't afford it and close the page. But then half an hour later I'm looking at apartments on the beach before I even know how I got there."

During my first year in China, I taught on and off for months at a night school in Suzhou, saving just enough to buy a set of train tickets and take off. China's train routes spread across the entire country, linking the provinces with fast, affordable transportation. That first year alone I spent more than two hundred hours on trains.

One of the classes I taught was Hobbies. The teacher's manual for the course prompted me to ask, "What are your top three favorite hobbies?" I would end up keeping tallies of the answer during the year until I had gathered a hundred.

The number one choice, of course, was eating with friends. Karaoke always predictably ranked near the top. But neck and neck in the standings with karaoke was travel. Because I had not been in China long, I was surprised. My students were usually young college graduates who clocked out of work and came straight to English school. They left at 8:00 or 9:00 p.m., went to sleep, woke up at seven the next morning, and punched back in to work only to repeat the day. Employees in China are guaranteed only five paid vacation days and have eleven paid public holidays. A one-day public holiday such as Tomb-Sweeping Day (when families pay their respects at the graves of their elders), means companies and schools make up the missed day on a Saturday or a Sunday. Two days of holiday can mean a twelve-day week with no break. The unbridled traveling spirit did not seem compatible with the tightly regimented lives of Chinese.

Beyond the practical elements, on the surface, travel struck me as un-Chinese. For most of Chinese history the average person had little to no experience of the outside world. Late in China's history, during the Qing era (1644–1911), Westerners were assigned small swaths of land as trade zones. They were not permitted to enter China's interior. Traders and merchants were among the few locals who interacted with Westerners.

China did not explore the seas. Before and during the European Age of Discovery (mid-1400s–mid-1500s), China stayed home. In its five thousand years China embarked on only one famous series of explorations, seven voyages in the early 1400s. They were led by Zheng He, a Muslim eunuch diplomat and mariner of the early Ming Dynasty. Zheng's first voyage was more an exhibition than an exploration; he presented extravagant gifts to the few countries (including Vietnam, Thailand, and Sri Lanka) he and his fleet of sixty-two ships visited. Zheng has become a point of differentiation for China over the last twenty-five years. Even though among his fleet were ships exponentially larger than the three captained by Christopher Columbus decades later, Zheng rarely resorted to the type of violent, coercive measures taken for centuries by European colonizers, as a *Time* article points out. He did not come back with pillaged gold, new colonies, or even substantial trade routes. Part of the Zheng lore is that one of the most noteworthy prizes returned from his travels was a novelty item, a giraffe from what is now Kenya.[7]

China had been turned inward for so long that the emperor considered outward exploration unnecessary. The empire was already complete. China, as Emperor Qianlong wrote to King George III, lacked for nothing.* The average person left the existence of an outside world to rumor and speculation.

---

*Though there has been some recent scholarship disputing the popular reading of Emperor Qianlong's letter to King George, which argues that the correspondence proves

Hundreds of years later, Feng's and Ma's grandparents and parents still had little to no access to the outside world as they grew up. The first Chinese television broadcast did not come until 1958, and no foreigners lived in Chinese communes. Feng's and Ma's families knew an outside world existed—many of Mao's slogans referenced catching up to England, defeating American capitalists, or smelting iron to bomb Taiwan—but it was almost entirely abstract. Ma's grandparents told him that their only view of the outside world came from a calendar in their neighbor's house. The twelve pictures in their "Fields of Europe" wall calendar made its owners famous locally because they were so worldly. There was intense interest in the outside world, especially as China opened its doors and foreign industries, products, and ideas began to make their way in, but limited access for the average person.

Yet despite China's being so closed off, or more likely because of it, travel was consistently the favorite pastime of my students. May, a young computer programmer, was no exception. When I asked about her hobbies, she said she loved to eat Cantonese food with her friends. She also liked to sing with her friends on the weekends.

Like everyone else in the class that day, her next-favorite hobby was travel.

"What do you like about travel?" I asked.

"I like the feeling of . . . freedom. I like to taste different foods and see the . . . way of life . . . of other people," she continued, bringing her hands to her face as if using a camera. "And I like to take

---

China's arrogance in underestimating the Western empire, Chinese primary school books continue to utilize this narrative as a cautionary device. For the new reading, see Tom Cunliffe, "Emperor Qianlong's Letter Strategic, Not Arrogant," *China.org.cn*, January 30, 2015, http://www.china.org.cn/china/2015-01/30/content_34686142.htm.

pictures of it all!" May concealed a laugh behind her hands. The other students nodded their agreement, smiling their solidarity.

"Very interesting. What are some of your favorite places you've been?"

She cocked her head at an angle, mulling it over. I watched her repeat the words to herself more slowly, think it over after making sure she understood, and then responding, "Outside of Suzhou, I have only been to one other location, Wuxi, to see the"—she looked up, thinking, and then said, "樱花 . . . *yīng huā*?"

"Cherry blossom," a more senior student chimed in. May nodded eagerly.

Wuxi is a city twelve minutes from Suzhou by bullet train. Shanghai was only eleven minutes farther down the track. At twenty-two May had yet to venture that far.

May was neither the exception nor the rule. Many, many young people have traveled within China. Some have traveled abroad. But many more have not traveled at all. For those who had never been more than a dozen or so miles from their hometown—the farmer's son in the mountains of Guizhou; the tea seller in Fujian; the tour guide in Beijing; May, the computer programmer from Suzhou—traveling was a dream to be realized.

Feng, Ma, May, and countless friends inherited a driving curiosity about the outside world. Theirs was the first generation to be able to see beyond China's walls through the Internet, to witness the outside world—not just out of their village but out of their country—in high definition.

"But the place I want to go to most is Harbin," she said. I asked her why, but she couldn't immediately describe it, slipping into what I call "language angst," the frustration of having complex thoughts limited by your simple vocabulary. After class we sat down and figured out how to translate the Chinese words for *ice sculpture*, *chilling cold*, and the feeling of being immersed in a magical, otherworldly place.

三

I gulped as I stood on a skywalk overlooking an expansive cage filled with hulking Siberian tigers. We had come straight to the Harbin Siberian Tiger Park from the train station, with only a quick detour at our respective hostels to drop off our stuff. The park was packed with tourists *snap, snap, snapping* pictures of the beautiful white tigers below. A child got his head stuck in the grate of the fence overlooking the tiger cage. I vaguely remembered reading a story somewhere about how zoos elsewhere in the world build fences significantly lower than the maximum jumping height of big cats, and I hoped that was not the case in China.

Harbin's extreme cold is hard on tech. An iPhone's lithium-ion battery will function at only 50 percent of capacity in temperatures colder than minus 0.4 degrees Fahrenheit. Feng and Ma came prepared. Their phones and digital cameras lived inside their jackets while their hands braved the cold. Ma, the camera photographer, had gloves with removable fingers for handling the camera settings. Feng, the iPhone photographer, had the gloves with padded tips on the forefinger, middle finger, and thumb designed to be used on smartphone screens.

In China, this era has been heralded as the "face-centric society."* Travel captures that part of young Chinese culture perfectly. Groups of travelers with selfie sticks saying, "Qiiiieeeeeezzzi" (Chinese for eggplant) at the count of three—like *cheese*, it forces a grin onto everyone's face—denote you've arrived at a landmark location. Even

---

*看脸的社会: *kàn liǎn de shèhuì*

those who don't document their daily happenings succumb to taking selfies wherever they go. When people are starting a business like a bar, nightclub, or coffee shop in China, the essential questions are: How photogenic is my shop? How pretty are my cocktails? Will someone want to take selfies with this chandelier?

When Feng encountered my reluctance to take selfies, he invoked the famous metaphysical conundrum: "If a tree falls in the forest but no one hears it, did it fall at all?"

I looked toward Ma for help, confused by the non sequitur.

Ma picked up where Feng left off, his pointer finger extended in the air: "Ah, yes, and, to build off said thought experiment, 'If a tree falls in the forest and no one takes a picture of it and posts it to WeChat, did it fall at all?' "

Feng continued, "A subtle point, Professor Ma, and, may I ask, 'If a foreigner feeds a live chicken on the end of a bamboo stick to a pack of Siberian tigers and no one takes a picture of it, did said foreigner really sacrifice said chicken?"

"If the sun sets on your vacation but you didn't take a picture of it, did the sun set at all?"

"If you eat a bowl of noodles larger than your head without photographic evidence, did you—"

"Got it. My hands are going to fall off. Squeeze together. Say 'eggplant.' Good. Let's go."

On the skywalk over the tiger pen, we reached a point where a pack of tigers had gathered. Feng told us to take out our wallets and give him 20 RMB, or US$3.50, each. We complied.

On the way in, I'd seen what looked like a menu on the park's pamphlet. When I was studying Chinese, I had decided early on to spend most of my energies on the spoken language first and work on the written later on. I still studied and did flashcards for hours every day, but I hadn't done the hours and hours of handwriting necessary to learn how to write in Chinese. As such, my writing at the time was worse than my reading, my reading worse than my spoken Chinese, and my spoken Chinese worse than my listening comprehension. I practiced my command of Chinese spoken by someone else all day every day, through songs, podcasts, TV shows, and movies. Even so, I was pretty sure the pamphlet had said, "Chicken: 60 RMB [US$10.50]; Goose: 120 RMB [US$21]; Pheasant: 150 RMB [US$26.25]; Goat: 300 RMB [US$52.50]." I had made a mental note not to eat at the Siberian tiger reserve's restaurant. Those prices were outlandish.

I had it all wrong.

Feng took our collective 60 RMB (US$10.50) and walked it over to an old woman who was wearing a hospital mask and heavy jacket but only thin gloves against the cold. Upon receiving Feng's money, she plucked a live chicken from a Styrofoam tub and bound it to a long bamboo pole. Behind the hospital mask I saw her eyes crinkle into a smile. She then waved me over. Feng and Ma went wild. The other Chinese tourists rushed over, whipping out cameras from beneath their coats.

The old lady grabbed my hands and guided the pole—with the live chicken dangling on the end—through the metal bars of the skywalk fence. The skywalk itself was less than ten feet (three meters) off the ground, and I had the pole dangling over the cage at about chest height. My chest. The old lady showed me how, when the tigers jumped up for the chicken, to push the pole down against the bar. This jerks the chicken end of the pole up, and the tigers, jumping twelve feet (four meters) in the air, come up just short of being able to bat their chicken piñata. My stomach turned. With each squawk of the bird, the tigers squeezed in closer, ready to leap for the kill. The woman handed me the bamboo pole.

If the goal was to prolong the fun to get more pictures and taunt the tigers, I failed. If the goal was to catch a Siberian tiger with a bamboo fishing pole and live chicken as bait, I succeeded, but in the end my line broke and my catch got away with the prize. A massive tiger jumped up and snatched the chicken in its jaws and ran away with the corpse, with the other tigers in hot pursuit, feathers flying, a few drops of blood escaping the squeeze of tigers onto the white snow. Pictures snapped. Game over.

四

The Chinese Communist Party sees travel as a bright spot in the country's still vibrant but slowing economy. In addressing the First World Conference on Tourism for Development in May 2016, Li Keqiang, premier of the People's Republic, said, "China will implement the paid vacation system, improve . . . facilities such as . . . scenic zones and spots, . . . and tighten tourism market regulation, so that Chinese and foreign tourists can have more convenient, safer and happier travel experiences in China."[8] A year earlier the Party had released Tourism Strategy 515[9]; the document outlined the latest comprehensive plan for improving the safety, quality, and oversight of the travel industry in China to ensure its development continues. As Li put it then, "Increasing the speed of the development of the travel industry is a necessary step in adapting to the escalation of consumption needs and industrial structure in China. [Doing so will help China meet] the goals of expanding the job market, increasing wages, promoting the development of the central and western regions, and funneling wealth to isolated impoverished regions." Li also describes a new century of "travel for the masses"—travel in China has shifted from a luxury for the few and is now "a necessary consumption for the general public."[10]

China sees tourism as helping to pull China's more remote regions out of poverty in addition to stimulating consumption. Because of their remoteness, these places are typically more serene than the industrializing areas of China and are relatively untouched. I found that to be true in the villages in the mountains around Chongqing, a leading Yangtze River port in southwest-central China. I was invited to spend a week as a volunteer teaching English to young children at an underserved school. From the center of Chongqing the school was two days of bus rides into the mountains. The region was developing itself as a tourism destination and for good reason: It was absolutely beautiful. The Chongqing city government was helping the local government rebuild a road that ended just outside the schoolyard. Nearby, workers were clearing a large area for construction of a big hotel. An equestrian facility had been built to feature horse shows and pony rides.

The hotel they lodged us in was bizarrely nice, a grouping of upscale villas spread out across rolling hills. But the villas were showing signs of disuse. Dust coated the banisters. Some circuitry was no longer working. Wall mirrors were askew.

An entrepreneur from Chongqing had built the hotel and then left without much thought to maintaining it. The tourists had not yet arrived in large numbers, but his investment was small enough, particularly with government incentives, that it should have been worth the wait. The government provided inducement to build the hotel because its construction—along with building roads and establishing the tourism committee to provide infrastructure for tourism—was employing nearly half the village, including many parents of the schoolchildren. That meant some children no longer had to walk two hours from home to school; their parents could take them on motorcycles and drop them off at school before going to work across the street. Those jobs meant the family would have money for shoes, books, and winter jackets. We had brought down jackets for the children, but many parents toughed out the winters in worn cotton overcoats.

My four companions from Chengdu had hardly ever been out of the city before, and they were initially afraid to go into the hotel villas. This was the quietest, most isolated place they'd ever been. The villa-style hotel rooms evoked the scene of a ghost story or murder movie. The parents of two of these twentysomethings had grown up an hour away in neighboring mountains. When Chongqing began developing during the Great Western Development Campaign, they took their parents, their kids (my friends), and left for the city to find work. Now, their children wanted to sleep in the same room for protection from the unknowns of the countryside.

五

After arriving in Harbin that morning and going to the Siberian Tiger Park, we went to the Harbin ice festival as night was setting in. The lights of the ice festival were said to be prettiest after dark. As with much of China, the scale of the ice festival was imposing, a lifesize wonderland entirely of ice. We saw five-story ice cathedrals lit from the inside, careened down an ice luge run the size of a football field, and rode in a horse-drawn carriage driven by a stoic Manchurian in a mink coat and tall fur hat. We banged gongs outside a

Buddhist temple of ice blocks three feet thick and carved with elegant, intricate wall art. The reproductions included the famous Suzhou gardens; individual ice-chiseled flower petals were lit up in red, blue, orange, and green. Some of the ice installations were sponsored. Caterpillar, the construction equipment company, parked an ice sculpture of a tractor and crane right by the entrance to the festival. The maker of the Angry Birds tablet and phone game sponsored a reproduction of bowling pins several stories high, and about fifty feet away was a twenty-foot slingshot loaded with a bird in the shape of a bowling ball and the size of a Fiat. An ice-dancing show featured skaters imported from Russia. It was so cold and I was wearing such heavy clothing that my feet began to sweat. Then my sweat froze and I had to ask myself whether this event was worth losing a toe. We went inside to thaw and refill our thermoses with hot water.

At the hostel later that night, young Chinese travelers gathered in the lobby, which had a heated floor, so we walked around in our socks. Two young college women were in a corner writing postcards. They told me they were writing poems and allowed me to copy one into my journal. It ends:

Winter grips our eyes, but summer drives our legs,
And northeastern fare propels our chopsticks.
The world is so big, we must see it ourselves.
All the traveler's sorrow fades away,
What better place to rest than this?

It was an adaptation of a poem by the famous Chinese poet and wanderer Du Fu (712–770 AD) that most Chinese have to memorize in grammar school. When I asked, the students said they were writing to their friends back at school a few provinces away. A couple sat reading together on a couch. I asked what they thought of the festival. They said they loved it. What about all the lines, I asked? We had had to wait in line for an hour just to get in. They shrugged. The young man said, "This is our first time ever traveling together as a couple." They cuddled closer on the couch.

For Feng and Ma, their trip to Harbin was as much about the thrill of being on the road and taking pictures as checking out the tourist destinations. They spent an entire late afternoon on Harbin's Songhua River, frozen three feet thick in winter, making sure to avoid the hovercrafts that thundered by giving rides to tourists waiting on the shores. Feng and Ma had their cameras ready just before sundown when the ice fishers pulled out nets full of flopping fish.

The Chinese poet Zhuangzi (369–286 BC) writes that one of the highest ideals in life is being on the road with a full stomach ("Hán bǔ ér xī, gǔfù ér yóu"). Feng and Ma splurged on big meals of northeastern specialties—huge plates of sweet-and-sour pork, a Harbin specialty; smoked and spiced salmon; and stir-fried sausage and cabbage—with flavors worlds apart from the modest southern fare they grew up on. Much of Harbin's food has become a fusion of Russian and Chinese, and the city has the best bread and sausage in China. According to popular Chinese archetypes, northerners also eat more noodles and drink more dairy than southerners and so are taller and more full-figured. Just as Chinese recipes are adapted for Western tastes when they are brought west, even southern China's "northeastern cuisine" restaurants were different than the real deal in Harbin. "The serving sizes were literally twice as big as the ones we'd get back home," Feng recounted, using his hands to trace an oval twice as big as his head. "I don't know how these guys eat so much. The high school girls at the table next to us ate twice as much as we did," he marveled. "The Northeast is something else."

Deeply instilled in Chinese culture is romance about travel. In the Chinese literary world few poets stand taller than Li Bai (701–762 AD) and Du Fu, two wizened men who wandered different paths during the later years of the Tang Dynasty (618–907). Hundreds of millions of Chinese schoolchildren have had to memorize their poems, and with memorization inevitably comes internalization. Both poets were inveterate wanderers, and their poems espouse a deep respect for travel as the path to wisdom and experience.

Du Fu's hometown, Gongyi, was not far from Chengdu. Two years after I visited Harbin, I visited Gongyi. It had, not coincidentally, become a major tourist destination. One of the idioms used most often to describe Chinese tourism is "人山人海," *rén shān rēn hǎi.* It is also one of the most popular idioms to say in translation. If you are ever in a big crowd and say, "people mountain people sea!" (that is, a sea of people), your Chinese friends will love it. I was there with a group from the travel company run by Wei Wei's family, and we waded through the people sea to tour the ancient wanderer's old stomping grounds. I walked with Wei Wei, her cousin, and her grandfather as they recited together Du Fu's ancient words:

I remember the temple, this route I've traveled before,
I recall the bridge as I cross it again.
It seems the hills and rivers have been waiting,
The flowers and willows all are selfless now.
The field is sleek and vivid, thin mist shines,
On soft sand, the sunlight's color shows it's late.
All the traveler's sorrow fades away,
What better place to rest than this?

12

A Young Man and His Party

How the New Generation Sees Its Government

Tom and I returned to our places on the tan leather couches in our apartment. It was one o'clock in the morning. The overstuffed couch on which Tom sat was tattooed with faded blue ink doodles—a giraffe on the arm rest, a stick figure man with a bow and arrow on the seat cushion—clues to a different time left by landlord Wang's grandchild a few years before. Tom shifted his weight several times and then sat quietly, waiting for us to start.

We were tired. For the last few days I'd been interviewing Tom, uncertain what I'd do with all the material but certain we'd both want a remembrance of the last half year of living together. We'd hung four large whiteboards on one wall of our apartment. During the last several months, Tom and I had had long, deep discussions about economics, politics, sex, history, how one ought to spend one's youth, relationships, family, and purpose. As the conversations evolved, we'd draw and plot as we argued about issues, rotating the whiteboards as the conversations became more complex. He studied philosophy and was an expert on Confucianism.

We had recorded six hours of interviews. I had proposed that we take a break for the rest of the night and pick up the thread the next day, but Tom had insisted that we keep going. He was, in part, looking for a distraction. His crush, whom I'll call Cindy, had not replied to his last two WeChat messages. The talking calmed his nerves.

At just twenty-three years old, Tom was a probationary member of the Communist Party. Soon he would join the Party's nearly ninety million full members. He wanted to embark on a career in government because he believed he could be a fair, considerate, thoughtful, and intelligent leader for his people and his country. He was ambitious, capable, intelligent, thoughtful, and proud to be Chinese. He was also, by academic achievement, one of the better minds of his generation, at the top of his class at Sichuan University, the best university in western China. Tom's ultimate goal was to be the mayor of a "small or large town" with a population of one to fourteen million. Power, then, was also a motivator for Tom; politics was a way to be somebody. It was too early to tell if he was on track, but those were his ambitions.

A bottle of *baijiu* rested on the glass table between us. Tom reached over and poured the clear liquor into two white porcelain teacups. We both drank a toast. "Drunkenness," he intoned with mock severity, "reveals what sobriety conceals"*—a well-known business idiom. We clinked glasses.

I asked Tom to turn his phone off so he could focus on our conversation. He looked at his Huawei phone for a moment as if pleading for it to buzz to life with news from his crush, then reluctantly powered down. Cindy would have to wait.

"Let's start with a word association game," I said. "Do you know

---

*酒后吐真言: *Jiǔ hòu tǔ zhēnyán*. Literally, this idiom translates to "After booze vomit/spit out the truth."

what word association is? I say a word and you reply with the first thing that comes to your head. Fast."

Tom nodded and readjusted his glasses on the bridge of his nose.

"Milk?" I started.

"Cake," Tom replied.

"Girls?" I said.

"Marriage," Tom fired back.

"Planes?"

"Fly."

"Kong Qiu?" I said, using Confucius's original name.

"Confucian thought," Tom rejoined, maintaining the rhythm.

"Marriage?"

"Divorce."

"Parents?"

"Kind."

"Money?"

"Shit."

"Russia?"

"Big."

"India?"

"Poor."

"Taiwan?"

"China."

On the table between us sat a Taiwanese history textbook that was illegal to possess in mainland China. I had smuggled it through customs when I returned from a trip to the politically contentious island. Tom and I had spent the better half of the afternoon comparing the Taiwanese textbook with a history primer used in a mainland Chinese high school that a friend's little sister, Xia Xia, had given me when she graduated. She'd grown so tired of my borrowing her books that she'd given me the whole stack. Tom was a history buff and loved comparing the Taiwanese history book with Xia Xia's. Earlier that day, before he dived into the divergent narratives, he had cautiously turned off our phones. "Just in case," Tom had said. "Of what?" I asked. "Big Brother," he whispered, referencing George Orwell's sci-fi dystopia, *1984*. Smiling, Tom then had moved to unplug our Internet modem too.

"England?"

"The Queen."

"Germany?"

"Tanks."

"Japan?"

"Porn."

"North Korea?"

"Crazy."

"South Korea?"

"Kimchee."

"America?"

"Powerful."

"Sexuality?"

"Straight."

"Love?"

"Stupid."

"Autocracy?"

"Stable."

"Tom?" I asked, but I used his Chinese name.

"Hopeless . . . ," he said, gazing down at his inert phone. Tom smiled and ducked a pillow launched from my side of the room.

二

In his own way, Tom was a typical Chinese nerd. He was probably more comfortable opposite a computer screen than a person, a far more capable conversationalist over WeChat than a white tablecloth. He had had one girlfriend early in college. They were together for more than a year, but—and he was quite open about this—they never had sex. Tom also was never interested in visiting a prostitute; although they are not numerous, they certainly are available in China. He was waiting for a real relationship, but it had not come along. Tom was not an extrovert. He also was not tall or rich or handsome, which is what every Chinese mother wants in a son-in-law. He was ambitious, however.

Tom had grown up as the government's plan for modernizing China unfolded. Every five years the Chinese define a new five-year plan, a map for the whole country, including major milestones along the way. Chinese presidents can also set longer-term goals. When President Xi Jinping took power in 2012, he declared two primary long-term goals for the country, the Two 100s (see chapter 8). The first is to turn China into a "moderately prosperous" country by 2021, the hundredth anniversary of the founding of the Chinese Communist Party.*

Tom's dad owned a bakery, where he and Tom's grandfather baked a pastry from a secret recipe that their family had kept for decades. On the strength of his grandfather's pastry recipe, Tom's family had become, in the parlance of the Party, moderately prosperous, middle class with Chinese characteristics. The pastry had a flaky crust with a sweet and savory filling. What kept crowds coming back was the trace of 花椒, *huājiāo*, the peppercorn spice that creates a numbing sensa-

*"Moderately prosperous society" is the translation of *Xiǎokāng shèhuì* used by the Xinhua News Agency.

tion in your mouth and is Chengdu's signature style of heat. The happiest I've seen his grandfather was when I visited the bakery and, unable to help myself, ate a half-dozen of his signature pastries. He smiled ear to ear and sent me back to America laden with boxes of pastries. Those baked goods paid for Tom's high school education at boarding school in Chengdu, a forty-five minute bus away, and the family's new middle-class life. They lived in a new apartment complex with a large high-def flat-screen TV. They had an at-home soymilk machine and an automatic soup maker that allowed bone broth to simmer safely overnight. Their water filtration system and heater provided ten different temperatures for various strains of tea. Their new microwave looked like it could lift off the counter and blast off into space.

Tom's parents were against his commitment to a career in politics. His mom worked in government as an administrator. When she was climbing the ladder in the government system, it was bloated with deeply rooted corruption. The best universities in China were considering Tom for a graduate school scholarship in philosophy. She liked the idea of her son's being a respected academic. "Why can't you just start your own business?" Tom's father asked.

Tom had weighed his parents' considerations carefully and remained resolved to try to make his way in government, certain he could make a positive impact.

Then he met Cindy.

The woman of his dreams came from a middle- to upper-class family, whereas Tom's family had moved into the middle class from considerably less prosperous origins. Cindy had just returned from studying in England at a middling university.

Chinese used to describe a perfect match as 门当户对, *mén dāng hù duì*. It means that two households are of equivalent wealth and stature. Tom told me matter-of-factly that his household had less status than Cindy's; she was not out of reach but a measurable notch higher. Tom hoped to win her over with his intelligence and ambition.

But Cindy had been decidedly lukewarm toward Tom since she met him. They texted back and forth, but she kept him at a safe distance. Whereas her family would have considered a young suitor with government ambitions an appropriate match only five to ten years earlier, in the more constricted government atmosphere of 2016, when the anticorruption movement more closely scrutinized the perquisites of a government job, even the mayor of a city would not earn as much as a middling entrepreneur.

Cindy had told him her stance against government work was about freedom. With so much opportunity now to grab the life you want in China, why join the slow-moving, low-wage bureaucratic government? Her ambivalence had thrown Tom into indecision about his future.

三

Freedom was in many ways a buzzword that cropped up in all my conversations, friendships, travels, adventures, meetings, and even dates in China. Young people craved freedom, talked about it, tattooed the word on their body, daydreamed about it, and went to bed hoping it would stir up from the mists of their dreams.

For about a year, I asked people what freedom meant to them. In classrooms, the library, at bars, while playing basketball, badminton, or mahjong, I'd make a point of asking about freedom. Almost everyone described a sincere desire for freedom, from China's poorest provinces to wealthiest cities, and then went on to explain their money problems or the family pressure they faced.

Tom's generation's attitude about the government tends to be, almost overwhelmingly, summarized by the Ming dynasty idiom "Heaven is high and the Emperor is far away."* More than indignant or displeased, most young Chinese people are simply indifferent. They are focused on other things, and freedom stands paramount.

The freedom most young Chinese people craved was not liberation from an oppressive, restrictive government, but rather freedom from an impossibly demanding set of cultural traditions and expectations, as well as the freedom to determine their own fate. Older generations, including that of Tom's and Cindy's parents, had not always felt as if they were in control of their own fate.

I'd ask, "What about freedom to vote?"

Most people would only shrug. "That'd be nice too." Some would say that, with such radically different levels of development and education across China, their country wasn't ready for it. "Our system works if the leaders are virtuous," Tom would tell me.

One young woman named Jing, a podcast host on a popular program about rock 'n' roll, explained democracy in the context of China's most famous rocker, a Beijinger named Cui Jian.† Cui famously played on a rickety stage during the Tiananmen protests. Some say his song "Nothing to My Name" became the anthem of the entire movement. "Cui Jian's song resonated with people because of feeling small in China, of feeling like an ant in a big anthill of a gazillion people, all trying to run to the top at the same time," Jing said to me. "That is why Cui Jian is still so relevant today. Give us democracy

---

*天高皇帝远: *Tiān gāo huángdì yuan.*

†In *Red Rock: The Long, Strange March of Chinese Rock & Roll*, author Jonathan Campbell writes, "If Western rock blew the minds of young Chinese in the early eighties, Cui's song twisted heads clear off bodies and drop-kicked them across time and space." Jonathan Campbell, *Red Rock: The Long Strange March to Chinese Rock & Roll* (Hong Kong: Earnshaw Books Limited, 2011).

and you're still just one vote in 1.3 bill—" Jing stopped and recalculated, correcting herself. "—nearly 1.4 billion. That isn't having a say. It's an ideal that doesn't mean much on a personal level. Young Chinese just want to feel like we have control over our own lives."

Most frustrating, of course, was the issue of censorship. Cindy's phone was her ever-present companion. Cindy, twenty-two, belonged to the half of the Chinese Born After '90 population who checks their phone once every fifteen minutes.[1] She spent a significant amount of time clicking through links she got through her WeChat content subscriptions or articles and videos that her friends shared. A day in her life might look like this:

Cindy wakes up in the morning and looks at *Fitness Girl*'s daily burst of news, a workout for the day, an article on how to get the so-called mermaid line (the *V* formed by lateral abdominal muscle lines, and de rigueur to be considered a be a hot, fit woman in China). On this particular day she also spends an extra minute or two on a full-length article featuring pictures of the British actor Jason Statham with his shirt off and arrows labeling his neatly delineated muscle groups. She reads an article about travel in Sichuan and forwards it to her WeChat Friend Circle. Then she goes to her internship at the bank. While she is working, her mom sends her a news piece about a local Sichuanese official who's been busted for taking bribes—the state-sponsored newspaper has denounced him for abuses within the Communist Party. Cindy glances at it. Then she watches videos of puppies slipping off furniture and a panda playing in the snow at Canada's Toronto Zoo. She shops for a while on Taobao or Jingdong—70 percent of her generation prefer to shop on mobile. She'll buy a Korean brand—real, not fake—because she cares about quality. Later she reads an article, "Ten Pieces of Dialect You'll Only Know If You Grew Up in Chengdu!" They are mostly curse words.

She'll also read an article about the opening in Chengdu of a new Apple store, the twenty-sixth to open nationwide. She posts another article to her WeChat group that disagrees with the findings of "It's Decisive: 5 Best Hotpot Restaurants in Chengdu."

In the evening, her friends send her pictures of a petrochemical factory in neighboring Pengzhou, twenty minutes outside Chengdu proper. On this day, there has been an accident. The smokestacks were spitting fire, orange-red flames tens of feet high, and producing dark, billowing clouds of noxious fumes. "This is the poison we're sucking in every day. . . . How is the government letting us poison ourselves like this?" she posts to her WeChat, circulating the video. She checks the prices on Taobao of the high-tech air filtration mask she's seen Tom's American friend wear when he bikes across the city; she buys it for less than he paid and smiles as she makes a note to tell him. Then, to make herself feel better before she goes to sleep, she sends the video of puppies falling off the furniture to Tom, then watches it again. At no point during her day did Cindy run into censorship.

The type of censorship that the Party practices in China is often described through the analogy of the "anaconda in the chandelier," described in 2002 by Perry Link, professor emeritus of East Asian studies at Princeton:

> [The] Chinese government's censorial authority in recent times has resembled not so much a man-eating tiger or fire-snorting dragon as a giant anaconda coiled in an overhead chandelier. Normally the great snake doesn't move. It doesn't have to. It feels no need to be clear about its prohibitions. Its constant silent message is "You yourself decide," after which, more often than not, everyone in its shadow makes his or her large and small adjustments—all quite "naturally."[2]

The anaconda in the chandelier was effective censorship of outside opinion in the era before the Internet and before so many Chinese learned English. Cindy and Tom grew up with the Internet and studied English at school for more than ten years.

Despite the censorship, Cindy and Tom have a much better understanding of the outside world than the outside world has of China. They grew up watching Western TV shows that are nonpolitical but jam-packed with cultural content. They grew up reading Western books for class. Tom's favorite movie is *The Matrix*—in fact, many would argue that the only reason Keanu Reeves still has a career at all is Chinese fans. Tom's favorite shows are *House of Cards* and *Breaking Bad*. The last book Cindy read was George Orwell's *1984*. I asked Cindy where she found the book. She told me it was preloaded on the Kindle she bought in China from Taobao last Singles' Day.

Cindy's experience on the Internet as she goes about her day is hardly that of George Orwell's *1984*. She had read the book and understood the parallels with China but moved on. "We all know what is going on with China's government," she said. "We get that we are censored. When we're surfing the web and see that a site has been blocked, it is like being chided by a parent. 'No, this site is too dangerous for you!' It's annoying, but we get what is going on."

People often described impingements on freedom of speech, particularly the scattershot censoring of the Internet, as frustrating, not maddening, and certainly not meriting overthrow of the government. Many who use the Chinese forum site Zhihu comment on Westerners' incredulity that young Chinese don't riot for democracy. Chinese use the modern Chinese idiom 屁股决定脑袋, *pìgu juédìng nǎodai*, to explain why they don't riot. Literally, the idiom means "your butt determines your brain," or where you sit in the world, the education you got, your personal background, largely determines the way you think. From most seats in China, the case for democracy is not always convincing.

Tom's generation has seen ample evidence of democracy's failure as a Western export. Many in China, big media outlets included, point to the Middle East and the Arab Spring and shrug their shoulders. "Maybe democracy doesn't work for everyone," people in China say. "Maybe China's system is better." In 1993, when Tom was born, India and China had the same annual GDP per capita, about US$350. Chinese textbooks point out that the critical difference between the two was political philosophy: India is democratic, and China is . . . something unique. Chinese born after 1990 have watched every year as their country becomes wealthier, more powerful, and more relevant faster than any other country in the world, in history. In broad strokes this young generation believes that their government structure can provide opportunities for them to create the lives they desire.

When Donald Trump campaigned and won the American presidency by claiming that the US government and media are corrupt and controlled by politicians who exploit the system to get rich, millions in China thought, "Wait . . . aren't a corrupt government and a controlled media supposed to be China's problems?" As we watched the US presidential debates, Xia Xia, the recent high school graduate who gave me all her history books, said, "Sounds a lot like what people say about China, right?" Then she shrugged and went back to her phone, mumbling, "I guess all governments are the same."

四

One morning in the spring of 2014, before I lived with Tom, I pedaled along the path to the Sichuan University library. Now that the spring semester was over and students had left the university, I was shamelessly using a friend's university ID to get into the library. Each time I swiped to enter the study room on the second floor, the university librarians would look away from the computer to avoid seeing a lightly bearded American posing as the pretty, smiling Chinese woman they saw on their screens.

As I biked the familiar route to the library beneath the dense canopy of trees lining the campus road, I noticed a gathering of old men in the clearing alongside the library. Nearly every day I had cut through this tree-covered clearing to get dumplings or noodles at the only shop that stayed open when all the students left for vacation. Some called the clearing Old Man Newspaper Alley. The clearing was filled with rows of metal display cases. Tacked on corkboards behind a well-worn plastic covering, the *People's Daily* newspaper was posted every day for the public to peruse at their leisure. Now that spring had sprung, the trees were filled with the chirping of robins and the thrum of woodpeckers.

On this day, a crowd had gathered around a corkboard panel that housed front-page news. I dismounted my bike and squeezed into the crowd, reading over the head of a man speaking Sichuanese so quietly it was as if he did not want to disturb the morning dew. The group was pointing at the headline on the front page: "Xi Jin Ping Warns Peking University Students: If You Want to Get Rich, Don't Go into Government."

People in China joke that foreigners are direct, whereas Chinese tend to be indirect, suggesting or asking or even demanding only through implication. Nothing that Xi said was roundabout: if you want to get rich, don't be a government cadre. But it implied something else: if you are getting rich as a cadre, you're doing something wrong.

"Those officials must be wetting their pants!" one elderly man guffawed, tapping the plastic protector with a bony finger. The group of elderly men belly-laughed their approval.

What did being a Party member mean? The perks of joining the Party in the past were lavish—money, power, and job security. Government cadres were the linchpins of China's "I-know-a-guy economy," the men controlling where economic stimulus flowed on a local and national level. Someone who wanted to start a business had to go through a Party member to get a license. Someone who wanted to build a factory had to go through a Party member to get a government contract. The first millionaires in developing China were the bosses of concrete, steel, and wire companies. Their clients were the government. China's massive infrastructure overhaul after it instituted the reform and opening-up policies meant that Chinese officials controlled who received the infrastructure contracts that all but guaranteed enormous wealth. Brothers, cousins, and then the network of "brothers and cousins" that is created by doing business in China most often received preferential treatment when submitting contract bids. Much of the wealth created by those contracts would circle back to the official. The Beijing-based Horizon Research Consultancy group conducted a survey in 2011, before President Xi Jinping came to power, that showed nearly two-thirds of respondents believed that knowing people with political connections was the primary factor in determining success or failure. John Lee, a professor at the Centre for International Security Studies at the University of Sydney, wrote, "It is no accident that more than 80 percent of the approximately eighty-five million CCP members make up the Chinese middle class and elite."[3]

In addition to wealth, government officials enjoyed tremendous job security. Those with government jobs were said to eat out of an iron rice bowl because they rarely, if ever, got fired. An attitude of "the nail that sticks out gets hammered down"* bred a culture of mediocrity, according to Tom's mother. In a time of notorious social unpredictability, working in government ensured the essentials of life—food, clothing, housing, and a humble though steady salary were all but guaranteed. Then, as the system became bloated with corruption, the iron rice bowl became the golden rice bowl.

The Chinese people loathed the corruption. Chinese regarded corrupt officials—more than crime, pollution, and wealth inequality—as the worst problem in China, according to the most recent Pew Research Center data. People perceived that government officials were withholding autonomy from the common person. When connections, not ability, determine whether you can succeed, what is the point of working hard? However, the same Pew data that said corruption was China's largest problem also found that corruption was the problem Chinese most expected to be reduced in the near future. People believed they were witnessing a change in the way Chinese government works, and that is largely thanks to President Xi.[4]

When Xi Jinping came to power in 2012, he declared that ferreting out corruption would be one of his top priorities. Two days after he assumed the presidency and became head of China's Communist Party, Xi warned the Party that its legitimacy as the country's governing authority was in jeopardy because of what he saw as "endemic corruption eating away at the Party's authority and effectiveness."[5] Xi proclaimed that he would begin an anticorruption campaign, which was dubbed by the media "Tigers and Flies"—the effort to take down corrupt officials big and small alike.[6]

When Xi began his anticorruption campaign, many within China

---

*This phrase is originally from the Japanese saying 出る釘は打たれる, but it is also quite applicable to Chinese culture regarding group dynamics.

believed catching tigers and swatting flies was a power play, a pretense for Xi to weed out competing political factions within the Party and consolidate his power at the top. Few knew the argument better than those in Sichuan and Chongqing.

五

"Do you know Mr. Bo?" asked Old Wang, my landlord, as we sat in the courtyard of his old apartment complex. I looked around at the aunties doing calisthenics led by an iPad propped up on a bamboo stool by the gate. Music echoed off the tile sides of the apartment buildings. Old Wang fanned himself under the hard rays of the summer sun.

"Does he live here?" I asked.

Old Wang threw his hands in the air, a look of exasperation on his face.

He was talking about Bo Xilai. Bo Xilai had been a member of the Central Politburo and secretary of the Communist Party's Chongqing branch. Bo was Xi Jinping's political rival and competition for role of president, the other major politician positioning himself for China's highest point of leadership. Handsome, affable, and well liked in Chongqing and neighboring Sichuan, Bo was a formidable threat to Xi. When Xi came to power, Bo almost immediately became embroiled in a bribery, embezzlement, and abuse-of-power scandal. It represented a display of the Communist Party's teeth and ended with a British businessman found dead in a French villa and Bo's wife convicted of the Brit's murder and sentenced to death.

"We all liked him [Bo]," Old Wang asserted, nodding and fanning himself. "He got things done for us." Sichuan Province and Chongqing had lagged behind the coastal cities economically but had experienced tremendous growth since 2007. In 1997, Chongqing was made one of the four municipalities in China (the others are Beijing, Shanghai, and Tianjin) that are controlled directly by the central government. Chongqing and surrounding Sichuan Province were prospering, and many attributed the change to Bo's "Chongqing model" of governance, his ability to attract business and government stimulus to the area, and his emphasis on rooting out corruption.

"What happened to Mr. Bo?" I asked.

"He lost," Old Wang replied. He rummaged through the wellspring of Chinese dynastic idioms and reminded me, "A change of sovereign brings a change of ministers."*

Months before Xi became president, Bo was removed from his position as the Party chief for the city. Many Chinese regard Bo's downfall as politically motivated, with Xi consolidating his power by implicating, or simply bringing to light, the involvement of his political adversaries in vast networks of bribery and scandal. Although Bo was removed from office before Xi began his anticorruption campaign, many consider Bo the first big political tiger (senior official) caught by it. However, that does not mean Bo had clean hands. *The New York Times*, reporting on the life sentence handed to a Bo associate in 2016, noted that, in 2012, before Bo was dismissed from the Party and his position, "the police chief of Chongqing had told American diplomats that Mr. Bo's wife, Gu Kailai, had murdered a British businessman by poisoning him, and the police chief later turned himself in to senior party officials. Evidence provided by the police chief, Wang Lijun, was then used to bring down Mr. Bo, who had many enemies in the party."[7] "It is government," Old Wang countered. "Show me one official with clean hands!" By 2016, 185 tigers had been "caught" and prosecuted for corruption said to amount to nearly three billion RMB,

---

*一朝天子一朝臣: *Yī cháo tiān zǐ yī cháo chén.*

or US$430 million, combined.[8] Most Western media outlets, a significant number of Chinese forum sites, and the casual street gossips were skeptical of these moves; the new sovereign was merely changing his ministers and consolidating his power, they said.[9]

The media and pundits focused on political tigers because they are big news. But how many people actually see a tiger? For the average person, the flap about corruption was nothing more than fodder for the tabloids.

But flies? Flies—low-level officials—pester everyone.

"When my parents wanted to open a restaurant in Guangzhou, they spent half of their start-up money sending gifts—bottles of Maotai baijiu, cartons of expensive cigarettes. In a word, palm greasing," a friend had explained as we walked along a fish market in China's third-most-productive city, Guangzhou. "Now you couldn't beg a permit official to accept a bottle of Maotai," he said chuckling. "They're all scared shitless they'll get swept up in the anticorruption campaign."

Xi's catching tigers and flies campaign had a very real effect at the local level, significantly slowing the prohibitively expensive palm greasing typically demanded by local township officials. In China the tools of business had more often been extravagant dinners and cartons of cigarettes than sound business models and precise timing. Currying favor with local officials often had determined whether one sank or swam. Now local entrepreneurs believed this was changing. Alongside the anticorruption campaign, the Party led a media campaign trumpeting the success of the catching tigers and swatting flies program. A major part of the anticorruption campaign was being seen by the public as taking down corrupt officials. Whether Xi's anticorruption campaign was merely a power play or not, catching tigers and swatting flies was having a major impact on the way people viewed the Party.

Tom's mother was not impressed by the government's efforts to change. Tom had tried to help his family start an online version of their bakery on Alibaba's Taobao. They had passed all the health and safety tests that would authorize them to ship their goods within the province, but a local official had held up their plans.

"He's a low-level official trying to assert himself, to exercise power over somebody. He wants a small gift or something like that," she said. Still, the family's online shop could not open because of this bureaucrat's demand.

Over the years I met many Party officials, both low level and high ranking. At a conference on the aging of the population of Shenyang, the fastest-aging city in China, the mayor gave a speech to open the proceedings. Without saying a word, her two closest lieutenants were immediately identifiable through their demeanor and the style of their business suits. "Chinese value 城府—*chéngfǔ*," Tom had explained. It means "subtle, shrewd"—a mind hard to fathom. One of its secondary definitions is "sophisticated." When we argued about the details of what happened in Tiananmen Square in 1989, he chided me for allowing my face to reveal what I was thinking. "You can't show your emotions on your face in China, for business," Tom had told me, "and especially if you're going to work in government." Other Chinese friends also often chided me for being too easy to read. "Like a child," Tom said. At the aging conference I attended, the Party officials' faces were like masks, rarely moving or betraying any emotion, and their suits were meticulously tailored to appear totally unremarkable.

One of Tom's mentors, a professor, had arranged for us to meet with the regional head of development for the Chinese Communist Party in Chengdu. It was a big deal. This man was responsible for much of the government's investment in industry in what Milken ranked as the best performing city economy in China in 2015,

Chengdu.[10] Tom was nervous; this man could make or break his career.

We met in a Starbucks. The regional head of industrial development lived in a new development in the southern part of Chengdu, just south of the New Century Global Center, the largest single building in the world, in an area not yet served by the subway system. But Chengdu was building toward the south, away from Pengzhou to the north and toward the regional head's apartment complex. Among real estate professionals his area was known as the best investment in Chengdu. The shopping district where we met was so busy that we had to leave Starbucks and meet in a private room in a nearby Japanese teahouse.

The head of industrial development had a doctoral degree. He was intelligent and relaxed, almost informal. Tom, normally forthcoming with his ideas, clammed up as soon as we entered the teahouse. He took on the role of underling, pouring tea for the cadre and me. In turn, the regional head of industrial development was cold to Tom. When the government official spoke, he rarely looked at Tom. Sometimes the man interrupted Tom, as if he did not realize Tom was speaking. The man also did not acknowledge Tom for pouring the tea. The power dynamic was clear. The functionary knew Tom wanted to work in government, and therefore Tom was at the bottom of the food chain.

I asked the official to name the most important characteristic for a cadre who aspires to leadership positions in the Party. "Relationships," he said without hesitation. "The ability to work well with other people and within the Party." He went on to say that government is not the cushy place to work that people generally imagine—a man reading the paper with a big mug of tea at his desk while he accrues wealth and influence. Relationships (*guanxi*), and the ability to navigate the internal politics of the Party, not just the politics of a city or even national politics, rank highest among key skills for young leadership candidates. I followed up and asked about the place of merit and hard work. He shrugged. "In my experience, emotional intelligence and the ability to manage relationships is the most important part." He thanked me as I placed another biscuit on his plate.

Tom was frustrated when we left the meeting. "He means ass kissing. It is the same old bureaucracy." Despite all the noise about catching tigers and flies, Tom believed that the government had not changed enough, and he wanted to help put that change in motion.

To Cindy, government had changed, and that made Tom less appealing. Eliminating corruption meant government positions had become nothing more than bureaucratic jobs with low-wage ceilings and minimal perks. In 2015, President Xi Jinping received a 62 percent pay raise to about US$22,000 a year.[11] If that was the president's salary, how much could a middling official earn? Cindy's interest in government was minimal, unless she was talking about the Party's highly publicized encouragement of entrepreneurs. Then her eyes began to shine.

In appearing to shut China's back doors, eliminating corruption had opened the front door to entrepreneurship. To young Chinese, the anticorruption campaign was a signal that if you worked hard, you could reap the rewards of your effort, an enormous shift that encouraged Chinese innovators and entrepreneurs to strive, strive, strive.

The Party was also filling the news with word of its new policy, which it dubbed "A Multitude of Entrepreneurs, a Thousand Innovations."* The idea was to cut the red tape and make starting a company easier financially, perhaps by having to pay little to no rent. In tandem with massive new nationwide policies to encourage innovation and entrepreneurship, especially among young people, the Chi-

---

*大众创业，万众创新: *Dàzhòng chuàngyè, wànzhòng chuàngxīn.*

nese government was attempting to give Chinese young people the freedom they desired.

The combination of eliminating corruption and encouraging entrepreneurship may very well be the secret sauce for China's transition from a manufacturing economy to an innovation and entrepreneurial economy. China's entrepreneurial spirit and desire to get ahead were bubbling within the country. Xi and the Party wanted to simply open the floodgates and get out of the way.

Perhaps most important to the Party is that Xi's anticorruption campaign, accompanied by a voluble propaganda campaign, has been an unmistakable signal to Chinese citizens that the government is going to be less prominent in their lives. The government was not going to meddle in a young person's ability to control their own future. Add to that the policies promoting entrepreneurialism, and the Chinese government was delivering a version of freedom that Cindy and her cohort found increasingly easy to accept.

Xia Xia's Chinese high school history textbooks were spread out on the coffee table. An open high school history book from Taiwan rested next to a mainland history book. Both were open to their respective sections on Tiananmen Square, 1989.

China has invested a large amount of time in crafting and telling its story. The psychoanalyst Carl Jung believed that we all have a personal myth, the story of our life and personal history we tell ourselves and are emotionally invested in. The stories are just that, stories, not entirely true—more our interpretation of our life's specific events within a larger narrative, be it a hero's journey, a romantic tragedy, or a comedic adventure. Our version of our story shapes our identity.

Countries also have their own myths, the stories told in history classes as we are growing up that shape the way we see our place in the world. They have their own truthiness. British and American history books have different accounts of the Boston Tea Party. American history books and Native American history books tell the Thanksgiving story very differently; and, as Tom and I knew, mainland Chinese history books and Taiwanese history books have different accounts of Tiananmen Square. Omission can be one of the storyteller's most efficient tools. Taiwan, interested in distinguishing its own government from that of mainland China, spent three pages on the protests and violent repression at Tiananmen Square. Xia Xia's history books spent a paragraph.

China's post-90s generation grew up on a much different story than the previous generation. In the wake of the events at Tiananmen Square in 1989 (the Tiananmen Square Massacre, Event, or Incident, depending on which history you're reading), Deng Xiaoping gave a speech to members of the Chinese military elite, during which he stated, "During the last ten years our biggest mistake was made in the field of education, primarily in ideological and political education—not just of students but of the people in general. We didn't tell them enough about the need for hard struggle, about what China was like in the old days and what kind of a country it was to become."[12]

The Patriotic Education Campaign began in China in 1991, two years after Tiananmen, and two years before Tom was born. China was going through an identity crisis. Actually, in the parlance of the Communist Party, China was going through three: "A crisis of faith in socialism, crisis of belief in Marxism, and crisis of trust in the Party."* The Patriotic Education Campaign fundamentally changed

---

*信心危机, 信仰危机, 信任危机: *Xìnxīn wéijī, xìnyǎng wéijī, xìnrèn wéijī.*

the way Chinese history and culture were taught in schools. China's teachers stopped lionizing Mao and started emphasizing China's long history as a wealthy, powerful nation-state.

The Patriotic Education Campaign also emphasized China's decline in the early 1800s and the Opium Wars (1839–60). In retrospect, Chinese blame themselves for allowing their country to be so insular, falling behind the international community technologically, and allowing themselves to be taken advantage of. They also blamed the international community for taking advantage of the Chinese but acknowledged their role in allowing themselves to be taken advantage of by commemorating China's Century of Humiliation. It was a mix of pride and shame: "Look at how great we were," followed by "look how far we've fallen." According to Zhao Suisheng, author of *A Nation State by Construction*, the Patriotic Education Campaign "elevated nationalism to the status of a spiritual pillar of the communist state."[13]

Tom noted that the American Dream and the Chinese Dream are practically identical except ours focused on the individual. Tom said, "Our rags-to-riches story is about our whole country. When I was young, my country was in rags—our shabby clothing, our poor houses, our meager income and little food. Twenty-three years later we've cast off the rags and are now working toward riches. And it is probably our government system that has enabled us to do so."

Another key difference is that China's dream is not a rise; it is a return. A return is more a vindication. It signals that a fall had taken place.

China's fall into the Century of Humiliation begins with the Opium War. China had demanded that the British pay cash for Chinese goods because the Chinese had no interest in trading for British goods. To balance this trade deficit, the British smuggled opium into China and sold it to Chinese. The Chinese government then destroyed a shipment of opium; the British brought a military force to Canton and marched it up the coastline, and China was forced, as it views the proceedings, into a peace treaty expanding trade ports and extraterritoriality for British subjects in China. The Chinese regard what happened as a weakness on their part and abuse by the British and French (a British-French alliance squared off against the Chinese in the Second Opium War), a trend of foreign aggression that would continue with other Western powers and then the Japanese. Recasting China's narrative focusing on the country's historic success, which saw its end at the hands of foreign aggression, instead of primarily emphasizing the glories of Mao Zedong and post-WWII and civil war China, was not only more factually correct but also created a unifying narrative of China against the world. Since the Tiananmen Square protests, Chinese "party leaders have made a priority of inoculating them against liberal values," coaching them to see that "the Communist Party has been the sole engine of progress in modern Chinese history, rescuing the country from humiliating subjugation to foreigners and restoring their nation to a position of respect and power on the global stage."[14] This patriotic education campaign and a refocusing of history away from Mao is why, when the United States sends ships to intervene in the South China Sea, members of China's youngest generation are likely to say, "It's just foreign powers trying to restrict China's return to power again."

"Our system is country-focused. The success of the country will bring the success of individuals," Tom explained. "Yours is the opposite: the success of individuals will bring about the success of the country."

I asked Tom, "So any threat to the Party is a threat to the success of the people? That's why journalists and lawyers who undermine the Party become 'enemies of the people'?"

"Right," Tom said. "We remember rags. Now, as a country, it feels we are returning to riches. We're doing it faster and on a larger scale than any other country or empire in the history of the world as we know it. For that, you have to sacrifice."

Back in the early 1980s, when China was laying plans for its new economy, Deng Xiaoping became known for explaining China's path into modernity through almost classically poetic terms: China will "cross the river by feeling the stones." It's gorgeous imagery, vivid and evocative. What he was saying, though, was that China had no real idea what it was doing, that it was standing in the rushing river of time and politics, reaching out with one leg, groping around with its foot, and if the rock beneath felt sturdy enough, shifting its weight forward. Missteps in Deng's vision were inevitable. The risk of being swept downstream was high.

Deng also meant that China was charting a new path. To its political left was Western democracy, a solid bridge with a sturdy hold on the banks of modernity. To its political right was the narrower path of Soviet communism. China looked at both and chose to wade into an uncharted stretch of river.

To think of China as communist or capitalist is not particularly useful. The Chinese government confounds the categories I learned in school to describe government systems; to jam the Chinese into any one box results in more confusion than clarification. In reality the Chinese government is creating something new.

七

One summer night, Tom and I walked along one of Chengdu's canals after dinner. We had been cooped up all day in the apartment—he was translating a sixty-page philosophy treatise from English to Chinese for a professor. Although he can barely speak English, Tom, like many young Chinese people, can read and write it at a decent level. The process, though, was extremely taxing. To blow off some steam, we'd gotten into the habit of walking along the stone canal after dinner, when Sichuan's muggy heat eases into a warm breeze.

Chinese neighborhoods come alive at dusk in summer, and the waterway offered an especially lively stretch. Just before the sun dipped below the high-rises, a tinny portable stereo would blast bouncy Chinese pop as mothers, aunts, grandmothers, neighbors, a smattering of kids still in their school uniforms, and the odd uncle or two began their choreographed evening aerobics routines.

As Tom and I spoke, we weaved through the plastic stools and tables set up alongside the canal where families were having their supper or adults smoked or played cards while the children ran and played. Tree branches hung lazily over the walkway. The sound of dance pop faded out; ballroom music faded in. To our left dozens of older Chinese men and women were practicing the waltz. The woman who received packages in our apartment building—one of a small platoon of aunts and uncles in the building who do it in shifts—told me that's where older men and women go to spark new romances. Sellers of noodles or cakes set up their wares with stools alongside their stalls. Young couples ordered barbecue or bowls of thick-cut noodles in sweet sauce, a Sichuanese specialty. Everywhere we heard the *click-clack-click-clack* of mahjong tiles mixed with the *slap-slap-slap* of sandals against the stone pathway.

But that evening, Tom was clearly distracted again by thoughts of Cindy. He pulled out his phone and powered it off.

"Big Brother?" I asked. Tom didn't laugh. He said he didn't want to be thinking about her texts anymore.

Cindy's ambivalence about Tom's government ambitions felt to him like an insult to all of society. She and his peers didn't see the value in his dream. He declared that, in a pinch, if he had to choose a classic science fiction dystopia for comparison with China, he would have to say his country was becoming more like *Brave New World* than *1984*. Aldous Huxley's classic, written eighteen years before Orwell's, describes a population numbed by material pursuits, discouragement of individual thought, and the drug soma. Money, materialism, lavishness, extravagance—they distracted people from the pursuit of truth and decency.

Tom had said he wanted to join government to make a difference, because he believed in the cause and wanted to help make people's lives better. Cindy wasn't interested in his goal because he wouldn't make any money. She saw him as sacrificing his own freedom, giving up social mobility and accepting the shackles of a set wage with little hope of earning much more. Tom couldn't see why she was unable to understand the virtue in his pursuit.

During one year I asked a hundred people if Chinese people had a belief system. The majority answered, "Money." Second choice was simply no. It's crass, but money was actually not a bad answer. Just as parents elsewhere bestow their religion on their children, parents in China bestow on theirs a faith in money, a practical, survival-based faith the parents had inherited from their own mothers and fathers.

We walked until we arrived at an apartment complex where a friend of Tom's lived. We took a few bottles of beer to the roof. Tom sat on the ledge of the thirty-four-story building. A stiff wind might have blown him off. From there we could see about a square mile of

Chengdu before an opaque gray fuzz of smog sealed off the rest of the city. Apartment buildings in China are put up in clusters, eight at a time in a tight grouping. Some tall, some short, some new and gleaming, others squat and concrete.

Tom then told me that he was still resolved to join the government. I asked Tom what his greatest fear was. As he looked out at the city, beer in hand, Tom was contemplative. He did not seem to be afraid of heights. He chewed on the question. "My greatest fear is having to make my kids ride the subway," he said. He then sat silently watching the churn of traffic. From our perch the city looked like an ant farm. "I'm afraid I'm going to be so average that I'm going to not be able to provide or create something of myself and actualize my potential. That's the pitfall of my future, not an extreme failure or even success with large failure, just fading into the middle, into mediocrity." He took another swig of beer and said, "And then my kid will have to ride the subway."

It was hard not to feel alone in a Chinese city. For China's Me Generation, everything around them—throngs of cars lined up for miles, hundreds of efficient, sterile apartment complexes as far as the eye can see, swarms getting on the subway—was telling them they weren't unique. From the rooftop Tom could take in the whole scene with a glance. From up there, the individuality that China's urban young people insist on made sense: if they weren't absolutely sure of their uniqueness, their surroundings would swallow them up.

"That is the risk of the path I'm taking. It is a slow climb, and it is easy to get stuck living a mediocre life," Tom said. He gestured at all the bright lights of the city. "Maybe next time you come back, I'll be the mayor of all that. Who knows, right? We'll just have to wait and see."

Acknowledgments

I owe deep gratitude to a number of people who supported me throughout the process of writing this book, which began long before the idea for a book was conceived at all. First and foremost, thank you to my family. I know I've not always made it easy for the three of you ("can you obsess over something closer to home?"), and I truly appreciate your finding it in your hearts to encourage my dreams, as inconveniently located as they may be. Also, thank you to my mom for your editor's eye, patience, and deep, nourishing love. Thank you to my dad for being an eager and challenging student and a wise and loving soul. Thank you to my sister for your playfulness and generosity of spirit and for trying to keep me tethered to reality.

A special thank you to Grandpa Seymour, Grandma Pearl, and Grandma Sally. Your unconditional love propelled me, and I wish I were able to share this with you now. Thank you as well to Uncle Alan, Grandpa Ray, and the Kent family for your unremitting love and support. A big loving thank you to the whole Katz family for the love and support. Justin, thank you for talking to me about the Warriors all four years while I was away.

I would in particular like to acknowledge the people who welcomed me into their lives. Xiao Ye and Lao Li, you two have given me a home many times over. The whole Liu family, especially Wei Wei and Xia Xia, you have been great friends and supportive family. Thank you to Huan Huan for early brotherhood.

Of course, I owe a tremendous debt of gratitude to everyone who allowed me to write about them. I especially want to acknowledge Bella, William, Tom, Debbie, Joy, and Ju Chao. I am lucky to have you as friends.

Beyond these few, there were countless others who invited me into their homes, sat and talked with me, ate, drank, tolerated the occasional awkwardness of having a conspicuous outsider hanging around, and willingly showed me their world. I would not have been so driven to write this book were it not for those kindnesses. I really can't stress that part enough.

On the writing side of things, this book would not have been possible without Gerald Sindell, who helped me be a real writer. From ideation to character development to cultural translation, your eyes and ideas helped get me to the end. Thank you to Elizabeth Kaplan, who took a chance on an enthusiastic twenty-four-year-old with some ideas and no experience. Thank you to Elisabeth Dyssegaard and the kind folks at St. Martin's Press for taking that chance as well, and for being both patient and critical. Thank you to Laura Apperson as well for your consistent support.

Thank you to my surrogate Chinese family: Chungliang Al Huang, for giving me a name and a start in mainland China, and Godfather Phillip, for giving me the feeling of home and a start in

Hong Kong. Thank you to my godfather Jayme for the love and challenging visions of the future.

I also want to thank Eli, Jon, Daria, and Ile for your consistent support and friendship. I know I don't always make it easy. Thank you as well to the team at Chengdu Living as well as Koko and the team at SinoStage. Milly, Neri, Paddy, Riley, Sam, Steve, Jonny, Rox, Davey, and Ariel, thank you for your friendship and curiosity in Hong Kong. Conor, I hope this book honors your spirit of exploration and bridge-building.

There were people who visited at different points to offer me guidance: a very special thank-you to Chip Baird, John Zweig, Jim Elms, Amory Lovins, Robert Dilenschneider, and Joan Avagliano. A special thank you to Robert Dilenschneider for seeing potential in me and giving me both a landing pad and a platform back in the States to begin to bridge the gap between the U.S. and China.

Thank you to Matthew, Jessica, and the Upchurch family for your generous spirits and exciting visions of what could be.

I was very lucky to have excellent teachers and professors who introduced me to China, books, and writing. Thank you to Professor Montas and Professor Awn for your guidance and support far beyond the call of a normal Columbia professor. Professor Lydia Liu, thank you for introducing me to the wonders of modern Chinese literature. Thank you to Mrs. Maguire, Mrs. Long, Mrs. Kilmartin, Mr. Simmons, and other teachers who taught me to love communicating and books. Thank you to Anne Randolph for encouraging me to write, write, write.

Jackson and Bill, thank you for being proof that foreigners can learn ice cold Chinese, and for being role models, even if you weren't aware.

I need to also extend a large thank you and hug to the whole Smith family: Nick and Aaron for tolerating and encouraging me; June, Brian Bene, Jake, Lexie, Andy, Sean, Scotty, and Charlie. You've all offered support, encouragement, and invaluable friendship when writing a book felt too big.

Thank you to that one Visa agent, Agent Guo, who chose not to throw me out of the country that one time. You didn't have to do that.

Notes

1. Organ-Stealing Prostitutes

1. *Hurun Report—Global Rich List 2017*, Hurun Report, Inc., March 7, 2017, up.hurun.net/Hufiles/201701/201703/20170327091656648.docx; Central Intelligence Agency, "Country Comparison: Distribution of Family Income—Gini Index," The World Factbook, https://www.cia.gov/library/publications/the-world-factbook/rankorder/2172rank.html.
2. Min Ding and Jie Xu, "The Generations," chap. 2 in *The Chinese Way* (New York: Routledge, 2015), https://books.google.com/books?id=qI09BAAAQBAJ&pg=PA133&lpg=PA133&dq=chinese+generation+born+after+%2750&source=bl&ots=OA5H7vxRYt&sig=qf5eUixSEQIByukx2fvd4tMbDnY&hl=en&sa=X&ved=0ahUKEwjDouD7iPXUAhXDYVAKHQwzChAQ6AEINzAD#v=onepage&q=chinese%20generation%20born%20after%20%2750&f=false.
3. Peter Simpson, "China's Urban Population Exceeds Rural for First Time Ever," *The Telegraph* (UK). January 17, 2012, http://www.telegraph.co.uk/news/worldnews/asia/china/9020486/Chinas-urban

-population-exceeds-rural-for-first-time-ever.html; "Services, etc., Value Added (% of GDP), 1960–2016," The World Bank: Data, http://data.worldbank.org/indicator/NV.SRV.TETC.ZS?locations=CN.

4. "Transformation of the Refrigerator Market in China," United Nations report, Case Studies of Market Transformation: Energy Efficiency and Renewable Energy, http://www.un.org/esa/sustdev/publications/energy_casestudies/section1.pdf.
5. "Urban Population (% of Total), 1960–2016," The World Bank: Data, http://data.worldbank.org/indicator/SP.URB.TOTL.IN.ZS?locations=CN.
6. Roderic Broadhurst et al., *Business and the Risk of Crime in China*, Asian Studies Monograph Series 3 (Canberra: Australian National University E Press, 2011).
7. Farhad Manjoo, "The Unrecognizable Internet of 1996," *Slate*, February 24, 2009, http://www.slate.com/articles/technology/technology/2009/02/jurassic_web.html.
8. Nicholas D. Kristof, "Unmasking Horror—A Special Report," *The New York Times*, March 17, 1995, http://www.nytimes.com/1995/03/17/world/unmasking-horror-a-special-report-japan-confronting-gruesome-war-atrocity.html?pagewanted=all.
9. "What the World Eats," *National Geographic*, http://www.nationalgeographic.com/what-the-world-eats/.
10. Xiang Li, *Chinese Outbound Tourism 2.0* (Oakville, ON: Apple Academic Press, 2016), 366.
11. Eric Olander and Cobus Von Staden, "South Africa Tourism in Crisis as Chinese Reject New Visa Regulations," *China in Africa Podcast* (podcast), June 20, 2015, http://chinaafrica-podcast.com/south-africa-tourism-in-crisis-as-chinese-reject-new-visa-regulations.
12. Rajeshni Naidu-Ghelani, "World's 10 Largest Auto Markets," *CNBC.com*, February 03, 2012, http://www.cnbc.com/2011/09/12/Worlds-10-Largest-Auto-Markets.html?slide=11.
13. Po Hou and Roger Chung, *New Era of China's Film Industry*, Deloitte Perspective, https://www2.deloitte.com/content/dam

/Deloitte/cn/Documents/about-deloitte/dttp/deloitte-cn-dttp-vol5-chapter5-en.pdf.

14. David Moser, *A Billion Voices: China's Search for a Common Language* (ebook, Penguin Books China, 2016).
15. Jeffrey Hayes, "Trains in China: History, Train Life, New Lines, and Great Leap Culture," *Facts and Details*, April 2012, http://factsanddetails.com/china/cat13/sub86/item315.html; "China Has Built the World's Largest Bullet-Train Network," *The Economist*, January 13, 2017, https://www.economist.com/news/china/21714383-and-theres-lot-more-come-it-waste-money-china-has-built-worlds-largest.
16. "Chinese Writing," Asia Society, http://asiasociety.org/china-learning-initiatives/chinese-writing.
17. Alberto Lucas Lopez, "INFOGRAPHIC: A World of Languages—and How Many Speak Them," *South China Morning Post*, November 25, 2015, http://www.scmp.com/infographics/article/1810040/infographic-world-languages.

2. Bella and the Books

1. Yojana Sharma, "What Do You Do With Millions of Extra Graduates?" BBC News, July 1, 2014, http://www.bbc.com/news/business-28062071; Li Lixu, "China's Higher Education Reform 1998–2003: A Summary," *Asia Pacific Educ. Rev.* (2004) 5: 14.
2. George W. Bush, *Decision Points* (New York: Broadway, 2011).

3. Uneasy Lies the Head That Wears the Crown

1. Wang Feng, Baochang Gu, and Yong Cai, "The End of China's One-Child Policy," *Studies in Family Planning* 47, no. 1 (2016): 83–86. doi:10.1111/j.1728-4465.2016.00052.x.
2. Y. Xu, W. Zhang, R. Yang, C. Zou, and Z. Zhao, "Infant Mortality and Life Expectancy in China," *Medical Science Monitor: International*

Medical Journal of Experimental and Clinical Research 20 (2014): 379–385.

3. "China Infant Mortality Rate," China Infant Mortality Rate—Demographics, http://www.indexmundi.com/china/infant_mortality_rate.html.
4. Claire Groden, "New Study Blames Chinese Grandparents for Obese Kids," *Fortune.com*, July 30, 2015, http://fortune.com/2015/07/30/study-chinese-obese-youth/.
5. Laurie Burkitt, "As Obesity Rises, Chinese Kids Are Almost as Fat as Americans," *The Wall Street Journal*, May 30, 2014, http://blogs.wsj.com/chinarealtime/2014/05/29/as-obesity-rises-chinese-kids-are-almost-as-fat-as-americans/.
6. K. S. Babiarz, K. Eggleston, G. Miller, and Q. Zhang, "An Exploration of China's Mortality Decline Under Mao: A Provincial Analysis, 1950–80," *Population Studies* 69, no. 1 (2015): 39–56; "China Life Expectancy at Birth," China Life Expectancy at Birth—Demographics, http://www.indexmundi.com/china/life_expectancy_at_birth.html.
7. Pew Research Center, "Aging in the U.S. and Other Countries, 2010 to 2050," chap. 2 in *Attitudes About Aging: A Global Perspective*, January 30, 2014, http://www.pewglobal.org/2014/01/30/chapter-2-aging-in-the-u-s-and-other-countries-2010-to-2050/.
8. Rahul Jacob, "Drop in China's Local Land Sales Poses Threat to Growth," *Financial Times*, December 7, 2011, https://www.ft.com/content/710ea3da-1f14-11e1-ab49-00144feabdc0; Simon Rabinovitch, "Worries Grow as China's Land Sales Slump," *Financial Times*, January 5, 2012, https://www.ft.com/content/ef4fa68c-3773-11e1-a5e0-00144feabdc0.
9. Barry Naughton, *The Chinese Economy: Transitions and Growth* (Cambridge, MA: MIT Press, 2007), 170.
10. T. Falbo and D. L. Poston, "The Academic, Personality, and Physical Outcomes of Only Children in China," *Child Development* 64 (1993): 18–35.

4. How to Eat Your Parents

1. Ben Wolford, "All That Schooling May Have Made You Nearsighted," *Medical Daily*, June 29, 2014, http://www.medicaldaily.com/education-linked-nearsightedness-researchers-find-more-schooling-means-more-myopia-290574.
2. Hui Chen, 《从中西比较看"啃老"现象》["Comparing the Parent Eater Phenomenon in the East and West"], *RenMin Wang*, April 23, 2012, http://theory.people.com.cn/GB/49154/49156/17720834.html.
3. Adam Davidson, "It's Official: The Boomerang Kids Won't Leave," *The New York Times*, June 20, 2014, https://www.nytimes.com/2014/06/22/magazine/its-official-the-boomerang-kids-wont-leave.html.
4. Chen, "Comparing the Parent Eater Phenomenon in the East and West."
5. Jordan Weissmann, "Why Do So Many Millennials Live with Their Parents? Two Theories: Marriage and Debt," *Slate*, February 10, 2015, http://www.slate.com/blogs/moneybox/2015/02/10/millennials_living_with_parents_it_s_harder_to_explain_why_young_adults.html; Emily Dugan, "The Neet Generation: Why Young Britons Have Been Hardest Hit by the Economic Downturn," *Independent* (UK), February 27, 2014, http://www.independent.co.uk/news/uk/politics/the-neet-generation-why-young-britons-have-been-hardest-hit-by-the-economic-downturn-9155640.html; Adam Davidson, "The Boomerang Kids Won't Leave," *The New York Times Magazine*, June 20, 2014, https://www.nytimes.com/2014/06/22/magazine/its-official-the-boomerang-kids-wont-leave.html?_r=0; Maria Arias and Yi Wen, "Recovery from the Great Recession Has Varied Around the World," Federal Reserve Bank of St. Louis, October 2015, https://www.stlouisfed.org/publications/regional-economist/october-2015/recovery-from-the-great-recession-has-varied-around-the-world.
6. Xiaotong Fei, "家庭结构变动中的老年赡养问题：再论中国家庭结构的变动" [Problems Arising from Changing Family Structure:

Re-examining Chinese Family Structure Changes], *Peking University Paper*, 1983, vol. 3. Summary can be found at http://www.aisixiang.com/data/43595.html.

7. Qihui Gao, "Average Marriage Age for Shanghai Women Over 30," *Chinadaily.com.cn*, February 28, 2013, http://www.chinadaily.com.cn/china/2013-02/28/content_16265274.htm.
8. Nielsen, "Nielsen: Innovative Marketing Needed to Connect with Post-90s Consumers," press release, March 20, 2014, http://www.nielsen.com/cn/en/press-room/2014/nielsen-innovative-marketing-needed-to-connect-with-post-90s-consumers.html.
9. Ana Swanson, "How China Used More Cement in 3 Years Than the U.S. Did in the Entire 20th Century," *The Washington Post*, March 24, 2015, https://www.washingtonpost.com/news/wonk/wp/2015/03/24/how-china-used-more-cement-in-3-years-than-the-u-s-did-in-the-entire-20th-century/?utm_term=.149b3ef56a74.
10. "Population, China," World Bank, http://data.worldbank.org/indicator/SP.POP.TOTL?locations=CN.
11. Ian Johnson, "China's Great Uprooting: Moving 250 Million Into Cities," *The New York Times*, June 15, 2013, http://www.nytimes.com/2013/06/16/world/asia/chinas-great-uprooting-moving-250-million-into-cities.html?pagewanted=all.
12. Wade Shepard, "How People in China Afford Their Outrageously Expensive Homes," *Forbes*, April 04, 2016, https://www.forbes.com/sites/wadeshepard/2016/03/30/how-people-in-china-afford-their-outrageously-expensive-homes/#7b5f37eea3ce.
13. Tianzhi Hu, "为什么中国人如此热衷买房子？" ["Why Are Chinese So Obsessed with Buying Apartments?"] *Sohu*, March 9, 2016, http://cul.sohu.com/20160309/n439876566.shtml.
14. Qin Shuo, "The Chinese Economy Is Being Held Hostage by Real Estate," *Sina Finance*, trans. by author, March 7, 2016, http://finance.sina.com.cn/zl/china/2016-03-07/zl-ifxqaffy3682965.shtml.
15. Wade Shepard, "How People in China Afford Their Outrageously

Expensive Homes," *Forbes*, April 4, 2016, https://www.forbes.com/sites/wadeshepard/2016/03/30/how-people-in-china-afford-their-outrageously-expensive-homes/#3835a7bea3ce.

16. "Gross savings (% of GDP)," World Bank—Data, http://data.worldbank.org/indicator/NY.GNS.ICTR.ZS?locations=CN.

5. Sex for Fun

1. Yongbin Wang, Original text: 百善孝为先， 万恶淫为源 [*Fireside Chats*].
2. A. Taylor, "China's Sexual Revolution Has Reached the Point of No Return," *Business Insider*, August 31, 2012, http://www.businessinsider.com/the-incredible-story-of-chinas-sexual-revolution-2012-8 (accessed July 30, 2017).
3. Yinhe Li, 《中国女性的性与爱》 [*Sexuality and Love of Chinese Women*] (Hong Kong: Oxford University Press, 1996).
4. "2015 Marriage Research Has Come Out, Female Doctoral Students Are Surprisingly Master Daters," trans. by author, http://news.163.com/16/0114/07/BD99SFUU00014Q4P.html.
5. Richard Burger, *Behind the Red Door: Sex in China* (Hong Kong: Earnshaw Books, 2012), 17.
6. Lily Kuo, "China's Latest Crackdown on Porn Has Little to Do with Porn," *Quartz Media*, April 14, 2014, http://qz.com/198932/china-latest-crackdown-on-porn-has-little-to-do-with-porn/.
7. Dan Levin, "With Glut of Lonely Men, China Has an Approved Outlet for Unrequited Lust," *The New York Times*, November 26, 2013, http://www.nytimes.com/2013/11/27/world/asia/with-glut-of-lonely-men-china-has-an-approved-outlet-for-unrequited-lust.html; Quanlin Qiu, "Sales of Adult Toys Soar on Hot Demand," *Chinadaily.com.cn*, February 16, 2016, http://europe.chinadaily.com.cn/business/2016-02/16/content_23498213.htm (accessed July 29, 2017); Jie Jiang, "Sex Toy Industry Lacks Govt Oversight, Unsafe Products Infiltrate Market," *Global Times*, November 26, 2015,

http://www.globaltimes.cn/content/955132.shtml (accessed July 29, 2017).

8. Jing Liu, "30 Million Chinese Men to Be Wifeless Over the Next 30 Years," *Chinadaily.com.cn*, February 13, 2017, http://www.chinadaily.com.cn/china/2017-02/13/content_28183839.htm.
9. Richard Burger, Kaiser Kuo, Jeremy Goldkorn, and Graham Earnshaw, "Sex in China," *Sinica Podcast* (audio blog), May 8, 2013, http://popupchinese.com/lessons/sinica/sex-in-china.

6. A Leftover Woman

1. Leta Hong Fincher, *Leftover Women* (Zed Books, 2014), 3.
2. Josh Horwitz, "China Is Home to Two-thirds of the World's Self-made Female Billionaires," *Quartz Media*, October 20, 2015, http://qz.com/529508/china-is-home-to-two-thirds-of-the-worlds-self-made-female-billionaires/.
3. "Proportion of Seats Held by Women in National Parliaments (%)," World Bank—Data, http://data.worldbank.org/indicator/SG.GEN.PARL.ZS (accessed July 29, 2017).
4. Cheng Li, "Status of China's Women Leaders on the Eve of 19th Party Congress," Brookings Institution, April 27, 2017, https://www.brookings.edu/opinions/status-of-chinas-women-leaders-on-the-eve-of-19th-party-congress/.
5. Leta Hong Fincher, "Leftover Women—Gender Inequality in Contemporary China and Japan," Lecture, University of San Francisco, San Francisco, October 2015.
6. "Males Outnumber Females by 34 Million in China," *Xinhua | English.news.cn*, January 30, 2015, http://news.xinhuanet.com/english/video/2015-01/30/c_133958783.htm (accessed July 30, 2017).
7. Fincher, *Leftover Women*, 15; original Chinese article found here: Xinhua News Agency, "For Late Marrying Women, Sooner Is Better Than Later," November 18, 2008, trans. by author, http://news.xinhuanet.com/lady/2008-11/18/content_10375694.htm.

7. Double Eyelids for Double 11

1. Jacob Poushter, "Smartphone Ownership and Internet Usage Continues to Climb in Emerging Economies," Global Attitudes Project, Pew Research Center, February 22, 2016, http://www.pewglobal.org/2016/02/22/smartphone-ownership-and-internet-usage-continues-to-climb-in-emerging-economies/.
2. "Nielsen: Chinese Smartphone Market Now Driven by Upgrading," press release, June 16, 2015, http://www.nielsen.com/cn/en/press-room/2015/Nielsen-Chinese-Smartphone-Market-Now-Driven-by-Upgrading-EN.html.
3. "Chinese Singles Now Closing in on 200 Million; Unmarried Women Giving Birth Charged with Fine," December 4, 2015, trans. by author, http://health.people.com.cn/n/2015/1204/c398004-27888743.html.
4. Amanda Lee, "How Alibaba Turned China's Singles' Day Into The World's Biggest Shopping Bonanza," *Forbes*, November 7, 2016, https://www.forbes.com/sites/ahylee/2016/11/07/how-alibaba-turned-chinas-singles-day-into-the-worlds-biggest-shopping-bonanza/#137b1e9776c0 (accessed July 29, 2017).
5. Steven Millward, "China's Singles Day vs America's Black Friday and Cyber Monday," *Tech in Asia*, November 2, 2016, https://www.techinasia.com/china-singles-day-versus-black-friday-cyber-monday-sales.
6. Ibid.
7. Liyan Chen, "China's Singles Day Is Already Bigger Than Black Friday, Now It's Going Global," *Forbes*, November 11, 2015, https://www.forbes.com/sites/liyanchen/2015/11/10/chinas-singles-day-is-already-bigger-than-black-friday-now-its-going-global/#7196947f71aa (accessed July 29, 2017).
8. Frank Lavin, "Singles' Day Sales Scorecard: A Day In China Now Bigger Than A Year In Brazil," *Forbes*, November 16, 2016, https://www.forbes.com/sites/franklavin/2016/11/15/singles-day-scorecard-a-day-in-china-now-bigger-than-a-year-in-brazil/#4a710df51076

(accessed July 29, 2017). The article notes "projected e-commerce sales" from Brazil and the number was later verified through "Annual Online Shopping Turnover in Brazil from 2011 to 2017 (in Billion Brazilian Reals)," Statista, https://www.statista.com/statistics/222115/online-retail-revenue-in-brazil-projection/.

9. "Singles' Day Obliterates Cyber Monday's Sales in 2 Hours," *Fortune.com*, November 11, 2016, http://fortune.com/2016/11/10/alibaba-singles-day-sale-total/.
10. Haiguang Xin, "双十一电商疯狂之夜，马云说了什么?" ["On Double 11, E-Commerce's Night of Craziness, What Did Jack Ma Say?"], *Sina.com.cn*, November 12, 2014, trans. by author, http://blog.sina.com.cn/s/blog_49bc1a2d0102vbj8.html?tj=tech.
11. "Growing Upper Middle Class Creates Attractive Market: Report," *China.org.cn*, March 20, 2014, http://www.china.org.cn/business/2014-03/20/content_31858451.htm.
12. Sherisse Pham, "Singles Day: Alibaba Posts Jaw-Dropping Numbers," CNNMoney, November 11, 2016, http://money.cnn.com/2016/11/11/technology/alibaba-by-the-numbers/index.html.
13. Ibid; "Singles' Day: China Splurges $9.3Bn in 12 Hours on World's Biggest Online Shopping Day," *The Guardian*, November 11, 2015, https://www.theguardian.com/business/2015/nov/11/china-singles-day-new-record-online-shopping-alibaba.
14. "Taobao Cries Foul Over Study's Claim That It Sells Fake, Substandard Goods," *South China Morning Post*, April 17, 2015, http://www.scmp.com/news/china/article/1693396/taobao-cries-foul-over-studys-claim-it-sells-fake-substandard-goods (accessed July 29, 2017).
15. "Internet Trends: Post-90's Become Online Market's Cutting Edge," October 1, 2016, trans. by author, https://kknews.cc/zh-my/tech/vn3va4.html.
16. Paul Liu, Xuemei Bennink Bai, Jason Jia, and Eva Wang, "The Accelerating Disruption of China's Economy," *Fortune.com*, June 26, 2017, http://fortune.com/2017/06/26/china-alibaba-jack-ma-retail-ecommerce-e-commerce-new/ (accessed July 29, 2017).
17. "Chinese New Year Travel Underway: Estimates Predict 3.6 Billion

One-Way Journeys," January 16, 2014, trans. by author, http://www.bbc.com/zhongwen/trad/china/2014/01/140116_china_chunyun; "How Is Chinese New Year Travel's 3.6 Billion Calculated?" February 8, 2014, trans. by author, http://politics.people.com.cn/n/2014/0208/c70731-24296732.html.

18. Frank Lavin, "Singles' Day Sales Scorecard: A Day in China Now Bigger Than a Year in Brazil," *Forbes*, November 16, 2016, https://www.forbes.com/sites/franklavin/2016/11/15/singles-day-scorecard-a-day-in-china-now-bigger-than-a-year-in-brazil/#4a710df51076 (accessed July 29, 2017); Julia Zhu, "China's E-Commerce Goes Mobile in 2014," *Tech in Asia*, December 30, 2013, https://www.techinasia.com/china-ecommerce-goes-mobile-2014.
19. Phil Wahba, "Cyber Monday 2016 Tops All Time Sales Record," *Fortune.com*, November 29, 2016, http://fortune.com/2016/11/29/cyber-monday-2016-sales/.
20. Catherine Cadell, "Alibaba's Singles" Day Sales Race Past $5 Billion in First Hour," *Business Insider*, November 11, 2016, http://www.businessinsider.com/r-alibaba-singles-day-sales-race-past-5-billion-in-first-hour-2016-11.

8. Test Monsters Dream of Innovation

1. Richard Wike and Bridget Parker, "Corruption, Pollution, Inequality Are Top Concerns in China," Global Attitudes Project, Pew Research Center, September 24, 2015, http://www.pewglobal.org/2015/09/24/corruption-pollution-inequality-are-top-concerns-in-china/.
2. "International Student Totals by Place of Origin, 2008/09—2009/10," All Places of Origin, Institute of International Education, https://www.iie.org/Research-and-Insights/Open-Doors/Data/International-Students/All-Places-of-Origin/2009-10 (accessed July 29, 2017).
3. "Chinese Students Return from Study Abroad Job Market Official Report," Ministry of Education of the People's Republic of China,

March 25, 2016, trans. by author, http://www.moe.edu.cn/jyb_xwfb/xw_fbh/moe_2069/xwfbh_2016n/xwfb_160325_01/160325_sfcl01/201603/t20160325_235214.html.

4. Zoe Baird and Emily Parker, "New American Jobs, Made in China," *The Wall Street Journal*, May 30–31, 2015.
5. Sharon Yin, "The Economic Impact of Chinese International Students in the United States," *Yale Economic Review*, August 3, 2013, http://www.yaleeconomicreview.org/archives/294.
6. "Peking University Report: China's One Percent Own One Third of Household Wealth," January 1, 2016, trans. by author, http://phtv.ifeng.com/a/20160116/41540417_0.shtml.
7. Zheping Huang, "Chinese Students Are Studying Abroad in Record Numbers—Then Coming Home in Droves," *Quartz*, March 29, 2016, https://qz.com/650511/chinese-students-are-studying-abroad-in-record-numbers-then-coming-home-to-xx/ (accessed July 29, 2017). Original report in Chinese: http://www.moe.edu.cn/jyb_xwfb/xw_fbh/moe_2069/xwfbh_2016n/xwfb_160325_01/160325_sfcl01/201603/t20160325_235214.html.
8. "Put Off by Trump? Baidu's Li Urges Silicon Valley Talent to Call China Home," *South China Morning Post*, November 18, 2016, http://www.scmp.com/business/article/2047324/put-trump-baidus-li-urges-silicon-valley-talent-call-china-home (accessed July 29, 2017).
9. Stuart Clark, "China: The New Space Superpower," *The Observer*, August 28, 2016, https://www.theguardian.com/science/2016/aug/28/china-new-space-superpower-lunar-mars-missions (accessed July 29, 2017).

9. The Good Comrade

1. Jianfen Wang, "Report Identifies LGBT Preferences in Capital," *Chinadaily.com.cn*, http://www.chinadaily.com.cn/china/2016-06/29/content_25896418.htm (accessed July 29, 2017).
2. "2015 China LGBT Spending Habits Report," Danlan, Novem-

ber 11, 2015, trans. by author, http://www.danlan.org/disparticle_52160.htm.

3. Ibid.
4. Yinhe L., "Regarding Gay Wives," *Sina Weibo*, trans. by author, http://blog.sina.com.cn/s/blog_473d53360100dkiv.html.
5. "Collateral Damage," *The Economist*, March 20, 2010, http://www.economist.com/node/15731324 (accessed July 29, 2017).
6. "Chinese Gay Wives: Millions of Heterosexual Women Marrying Closeted Men," *Sohu*, February 2, 2017, http://www.sohu.com/a/126266833_349547.
7. "China Officially Connected to the Internet in 1994," CCTV, April 20, 2014, http://english.cntv.cn/2014/04/20/VIDE1397997720861267.shtml (accessed July 29, 2017).
8. "Michael Jackson: Your Number One Music Icon," CNN, August 27, 2010, http://edition.cnn.com/2010/SHOWBIZ/Music/08/24/music.icon.gallery/ (accessed July 29, 2017).
9. "China's 'Pink Market' Value Estimated at US$470B Annually," *Ecns.com.cn*, July 18, 2014. http://www.ecns.cn/business/2014/07-18/125007.shtml.
10. Victoria Ho, "Grindr Sells 60% Stake to Chinese Investor, Faces Growing Competition," Mashable, January 12, 2016, http://mashable.com/2016/01/12/grindr-china-blued/#LNIrCsW8fuqj (accessed July 29, 2017).
11. Zhu Wenqian, "China's Gay App Blued Taps into Pink Economy," *Chinadaily.com.cn*, June 2, 2016, http://www.chinadaily.com.cn/business/tech/2016-06/02/content_25584439.htm.

10. Learning to Play

1. Gu Ban, *The History of the Former Han Dynasty*. Full text and specific scroll can be accessed for free online through Chinese Text Project: http://ctext.org/wiki.pl?if=en&chapter=684848&remap=gb#p36.
2. "Empire of the Pig," *The Economist*, December 17, 2014, http://www.economist.com/news/christmas-specials/21636507-chinas-insatiable

-appetite-pork-symbol-countrys-rise-it-also; Lexin Cai et al., "China's Astounding Appetite for Pork: Recent Trends and Implications for International Trade," Penn Wharton Public Policy Initiative, April 2, 2015, http://publicpolicy.wharton.upenn.edu/live/news/644-chinas-astounding-appetite-for-pork-recent-trends; Kelsey Nowakowski, "Why Corn—Not Rice—Is King in China," *The Plate* (blog), *National Geographic*, May 18, 2015, http://theplate.nationalgeographic.com/2015/05/18/why-corn-not-rice-is-king-in-china/.

3. Xuetai Wang, "中华饮食文化精神" ["The Essence of Chinese Culinary Culture"], trans. by author, *Guang Ming Daily*, November 30, 2006, http://www.gmw.cn/01gmrb/2006-11/30/content_514905.htm.
4. *The Works of Mencius.* Full text and specific portion can be accessed in English and Chinese for free online through Chinese Text Project, however alternate translation used: http://ctext.org/mengzi/gaozi-i.
5. Wang, "The Essence of Chinese Culinary Culture."
6. "Conversation with Yu Jiawen at Super Schedule HQ," interview by author, February 1, 2015. One of the first clips of Yu Jiawen to go viral where he is participating in a TV gameshow can be seen here: https://v.qq.com/x/page/p0320uvdlc0.html.
7. Jon Russell, "Tencent Takes Full Control Of 'League Of Legends' Creator Riot Games," *TechCrunch*, December 17, 2015, https://techcrunch.com/2015/12/17/tencent-takes-full-control-of-league-of-legends-creator-riot-games/ (accessed July 30, 2017).
8. Don Monroe, "Speaking Tonal Languages Promotes Perfect Pitch," *Scientific American*, November 9, 2004, https://www.scientificamerican.com/article/speaking-tonal-languages/.

11. Be There Now

1. "Harbin, China," *Encyclopaedia Britannica*, https://www.britannica.com/place/Harbin; "St. Sophia Cathedral," Travel China Guide,

https://www.travelchinaguide.com/attraction/heilongjiang/harbin/st-sophia-church.htm.

2. Alan Taylor, "The 2015 Harbin Ice and Snow Festival," *The Atlantic*, January 6, 2015, https://www.theatlantic.com/photo/2015/01/the-2015-harbin-ice-and-snow-festival/384265/.
3. "China Becomes World's Largest Outbound Tourism Market," *Chinadaily.com.cn*, December 28, 2016, http://www.chinadaily.com.cn/business/2016-12/28/content_27798009.htm.
4. Ibid.
5. 《中国语言生活状况报告 (2016) 》["The State of the Chinese Language (2016)"] The Ministry of Education of the People's Republic of China. May 31, 2016. http://www.moe.edu.cn/s78/A19/moe_814/201605/t20160531_247149.html
6. Sho Kawano, Joshua Lu, Ricky Tsang, and Jingyuan Liu, "The Chinese Tourist Boom," *Goldman Sachs Investor Insight*, November 20, 2015, http://www.goldmansachs.com/our-thinking/pages/macroeconomic-insights-folder/chinese-tourist-boom/report.pdf.
7. Jung-pang Lo, "Zheng He: Chinese Explorer," *Encyclopaedia Britannica*, https://www.britannica.com/biography/Zheng-He; Frank Viviano, "China's Great Armada," *National Geographic*, July 2005, http://ngm.nationalgeographic.com/ngm/0507/feature2/; Ishaan Faroor, "Voyages of Mariner Zheng He: Symbolism for Modern China, *Time*, March 8, 2010, http://content.time.com/time/world/article/0,8599,1969939,00.html.
8. Li Keqiang, draft of "Li Keqiang's Speech at the Opening Ceremony of the First World Conference on Tourism for Development," May 19, 2016, http://www.cnta.com/English_Column/201605/t20160520_771546.shtml; see also Li Keqiang, "Report on the Work of the Government," March 5, 2017, http://english.gov.cn/premier/news/2017/03/16/content_281475597911192.htm.
9. "未来三年: 中国旅游'515战略' (组图)" ["China Tourism 'Strategy 515' in the Three Years to Come"], trans. by author, *Wang Yi News*, January 21, 2015, http://news.163.com/15/0121/08/AGFHN53S00014Q4P.html.

10. “Mass Tourism Era Can Be Expected as Premier Li Encourages Paid Vacations,” *China Daily USA*, March 8, 2016, http://usa.chinadaily.com.cn/travel/2016-03/08/content_23781932_2.htm; “Li Keqiang’s Speech at the Opening Ceremony of the First World Conference on Tourism for Development,” China National Tourism Association, May 20, 2016, http://www.cnta.com/English_Column/201605/t20160520_771546.shtml (accessed July 30, 2017).

12. A Young Man and His Party

1. Hans Tung and Jixun Foo, “200 Million Trendsetters: China’s Millennials are Shaping the Global Economy,” *Medium*, January 14, 2016, https://medium.com/ggv-capital/200-million-trendsetters-china-s-millennials-are-shaping-the-global-economy-f52c392d54bb (accessed July 30, 2017).
2. Perry Link, “China: The Anaconda in the Chandelier,” *The New York Review of Books*, April 11, 2002, http://www.chinafile.com/library/nyrb-china-archive/china-anaconda-chandelier.
3. John Lee, “Pitfalls of an Aging China,” Hudson Institute, January 2, 2013, https://www.hudson.org/research/9443-pitfalls-of-an-aging-china (accessed July 30, 2017).
4. Richard Wike and Bridget Parker, “Corruption, Pollution, Inequality Are Top Concerns in China,” Pew Research Center’s Global Attitudes Project, September 24, 2015, http://www.pewglobal.org/2015/09/24/corruption-pollution-inequality-are-top-concerns-in-china/ (accessed July 30, 2017).
5. “Four Years On, Xi’s War on Corruption Is More Than Hunting Tigers, Flies,” *Chinadaily.com.cn*, December 9, 2016, http://usa.chinadaily.com.cn/china/2016-12/09/content_27627002.htm.
6. Tania Branigan, “Xi Jinping Vows to Fight ‘Tigers’ and ‘Flies’ in Anti-Corruption Drive,” *The Guardian*, January 22, 2013, https://www.theguardian.com/world/2013/jan/22/xi-jinping-tigers-flies-corruption (accessed July 30, 2017).
7. Edward Wong, “Chinese Court Upholds Life Sentence for Top Aide

to Bo Xilai," *The New York Times*, March 1, 2016, https://www.nytimes.com/2016/03/02/world/asia/china-bo-xilai-aide-wu-wenkang.html.

8. "Visualizing China's Anti-Corruption Campaign" *ChinaFile*, January 21, 2016, http://www.chinafile.com/infographics/visualizing-chinas-anti-corruption-campaign.
9. See, for example, Javier C. Hernández, "China Corruption Fight Extends to Top Officials in Beijing and Shanghai," *The New York Times*, November 11, 2015, https://www.nytimes.com/2015/11/12/world/asia/china-crackdown-corruption-beijing-shanghai-ai-baojun-lu-xiwen.html.
10. Perry Wong and Michael C. Y. Lin, "Best Performing Cities, CHINA 2015: The Nation's Most Successful Economies," The Milken Institute, September 2015, http://www.best-cities-china.org/best-performing-cities-china-2015.pdf.
11. "Chinese President Xi Jinping 'Given 62% Pay Rise'," BBC News, January 20, 2015, http://www.bbc.com/news/business-30896205 (accessed July 30, 2017).
12. William A. Callahan, *China: The Pessoptimist Nation* (New York: Oxford University Press, 2010), 32.
13. Suisheng Zhao, *A Nation-State by Construction: Dynamics of Modern Chinese Nationalism* (Stanford, CA: Stanford University Press, 2004), 214.
14. Chris Buckley, "China Says Its Students, Even Those Abroad, Need More 'Patriotic Education,'" *The New York Times*, February 10, 2016, https://www.nytimes.com/2016/02/11/world/asia/china-patriotic-education.html.